John Wolinski
Gwen Coates

AQA A-level Business

For A-level Year 1 and AS

1

Answer Guide

Acknowledgement

AQA examination questions are reproduced by permission of AQA. AQA have not seen or approved the suggested answers included in this volume.

Every effort has been made to trace all copyright holders, but if any have been inadvertently overlooked the Publishers will be pleased to make the necessary arrangements at the first opportunity.

Although every effort has been made to ensure that website addresses are correct at time of going to press, Hodder Education cannot be held responsible for the content of any website mentioned in this book. It is sometimes possible to find a relocated web page by typing in the address of the home page for a website in the URL window of your browser.

Hachette UK's policy is to use papers that are natural, renewable and recyclable products and made from wood grown in sustainable forests. The logging and manufacturing processes are expected to conform to the environmental regulations of the country of origin.

Orders: please contact Bookpoint Ltd, 130 Milton Park, Abingdon, Oxon OX14 4SE. Telephone: +44 (0)1235 827720. Fax: +44 (0)1235 400454. Lines are open 9.00a.m.–5.00p.m., Monday to Saturday, with a 24-hour message answering service. Visit our website at www.hoddereducation.co.uk

First published in 2015 by
Hodder Education,
An Hachette UK Company
Carmelite House, 50 Victoria Embankment
London, EC4Y 0DZ

Impression number   10 9 8 7 6 5 4 3 2 1

Year   2019 2018 2017 2016 2015

Cover photo © Rawpixel - Fotolia

Typeset in DIN Light 11/13 by Integra Software Services Pvt. Ltd., Pondicherry, India

Printed in the UK by Hobbs the Printers Ltd, Brunel Road, Totton, Hampshire, SO40 3WX

A catalogue record for this title is available from the British Library

ISBN 978 1471 83610 7

Contents

Introduction

This teacher guide is written to accompany the AQA AS/ Year 1 A-level Business (third edition) textbook written by John Wolinski and Gwen Coates, and published by Hodder Education. Pages from this guide can be photocopied for use with students.

The chapters of this book contain two main sets of questions: practice exercises and case studies. Both of these sets of questions are intended to achieve two main aims:

1 to allow students to test their understanding of the content, on completion of a chapter or during the examination revision period

2 to enable students to practise answering exam-style questions within the time constraints they will face during the final examinations.

The primary aim of the **practice exercises** is to test your understanding, and so most questions are focused on straightforward tests of knowledge and understanding, alongside general questions testing application and analysis. Paper 1 of the AS level includes multiple-choice questions and short-answer questions, while Paper 1 of the A-level consists entirely of multiple-choice questions, short-answer questions and essays. Therefore, the practice exercises provide practice for some of the types of questions students may face in the examinations.

Most AQA questions require two (or possibly three) lines of argument. The exercises in the book may ask for more arguments or factors because, for revision purposes, it is felt that students need to be able to understand a wider range of ideas for a full understanding of a particular topic.

In the AS level, Paper 1 includes two data response articles while Paper 2 is based on a case study. For A-level, Paper 2 is based on three data response articles and Paper 3 is based on a case study. The **case studies** in the textbook are a blend of data response articles and case studies, so that questions on these case studies will provide good practice for these examination papers.

Marking the practice exercises and case studies

Multiple-choice questions: One mark is awarded for a correct answer – no explanation is required.

Calculations: A correct answer earns full marks. Elements of the calculation are awarded a mark, so that a student can earn part marks for their working, even if the final answer is incorrect.

Short-answer questions: In most cases these questions are marked by levels of response, using the three levels of response grid included in this introduction. For questions of 6 marks, 2 marks are awarded for each level. For 5 mark questions, level 1 would have only 1 mark; for 4 mark questions level 2 would be the only level with 2 marks (i.e. 2–3 marks for level 2).

The questions linked to each case study in the AS textbook are based on the format of the AQA AS and/or A-level Business examinations. Please note, however, that the case studies as individual entities do not match the format of the AQA examinations. The content of each chapter has a limited focus and so, with a few exceptions, it has not been appropriate to exactly match the overall AQA format.

The marking scheme for each case study question consists of two sections:

1 a summary of the potential relevant ideas that candidates might include in their answer

2 a marking template showing how the marks are allocated to each skill.

The summaries of the potential relevant ideas that candidates might include are presented in each chapter of this guide. In order to show the skill requirements of each question, a set of templates is provided on pages 5–8 for use with the summaries.

The templates show the AQA 'levels of response' approach to marking, indicating what is expected from a candidate in order to reach a given level. It should be noted that these templates are only a guide. Depending on the structure of individual examination papers, it is possible that there are minor differences in the marks allocated for each level, especially for low mark questions.

Levels of response for a 6 mark question

(This can be adapted for 3–5 mark questions)

Level	The student will typically demonstrate:	Marks
3	**A good response overall that focuses on many of the demands of the question.** Provides an answer to the question set that: ● demonstrates a good knowledge and understanding of issues in the question ● demonstrates analysis which is well developed and is applied effectively to the context.	5–6 marks
2	**A reasonable response overall that focuses on some of the demands of the question.** Provides an answer to the question set that: ● demonstrates a reasonable knowledge and understanding of issues in the question ● demonstrates analysis which is developed and is applied to the context.	3–4 marks
1	**A limited response overall with little focus on the demands of the question.** Provides an answer to the question set that: ● demonstrates a limited knowledge and understanding of issues in the question ● demonstrates analysis with little development and with mainly descriptive application to the context.	1–2 marks

Levels of response for a 9 mark question

Level	The student will typically demonstrate:	Marks
3	**A good response overall that focuses on many of the demands of the question.** Provides an answer to the question set that: ● demonstrates a depth and range of knowledge and understanding of issues in the question ● demonstrates analysis which is well developed and is applied effectively to the context.	7–9 marks
2	**A reasonable response overall that focuses on some of the demands of the question.** Provides an answer to the question set that: ● demonstrates a limited knowledge and understanding of a range of issues in the question or a good knowledge and understanding of relatively few issues in the question ● demonstrates analysis which is developed and is applied to the context.	4–6 marks
1	**A limited response overall with little focus on the demands of the question.** Provides an answer to the question set that: ● demonstrates a limited range and depth of knowledge and understanding of issues in the question ● demonstrates analysis with little development and with mainly descriptive application to the context.	1–3 marks

Levels of response for a 12 mark question

Level	The student will typically demonstrate:	Marks
3	**A good response overall that focuses on many of the demands of the question.** Provides an answer to the question set that: ● demonstrates a depth and range of knowledge and understanding of issues in the question ● demonstrates analysis which is well developed and is applied effectively to the context.	9–12 marks
2	**A reasonable response overall that focuses on some of the demands of the question.** Provides an answer to the question set that: ● demonstrates a limited knowledge and understanding of a range of issues in the question or a good knowledge and understanding of relatively few issues in the question ● demonstrates analysis which is developed and is applied to the context.	5–8 marks
1	**A limited response overall with little focus on the demands of the question.** Provides an answer to the question set that: ● demonstrates a limited range and depth of knowledge and understanding of issues in the question ● demonstrates analysis with little development and with mainly descriptive application to the context.	1–4 marks

Levels of response for a 16 mark question:

Level	The student will typically demonstrate:	Marks
4	**An excellent response overall that is fully focused on the key demands of the question.** Provides an answer to the question set that: • demonstrates a depth and range of knowledge and understanding that is precise and well selected in relation to issues in the question • demonstrates analysis throughout which is well developed, is applied effectively to the context and considers a balanced range of the issues in the question • makes judgements or provides solutions which are built effectively on analysis, show balance and have a clear focus on the question as a whole throughout.	13–16 marks
3	**A good response overall that focuses on many of the demands of the question.** Provides an answer to the question set that: • demonstrates a depth and range of knowledge and understanding of issues in the question • demonstrates analysis that is well developed, applied effectively to the context and considers a range of issues in the question • makes judgements or provides solutions which are built on analysis, show balance and address the question as a whole.	9–12 marks
2	**A reasonable response overall that focuses on some of the demands of the question.** Provides an answer to the question set that: • demonstrates a limited knowledge and understanding of a range of issues in the question or a good knowledge and understanding of relatively few issues in the question • demonstrates analysis which is developed, applied to the context and considers some of the issues in the question • makes judgements or provides solutions which are built on analysis, but lack balance and are not fully focused on the question as a whole.	5–8 marks
1	**A limited response overall with little focus on the demands of the question.** Provides an answer to the question set that: • demonstrates a limited range and depth of knowledge and understanding of issues in the question • demonstrates analysis with little development, mainly descriptive application to the context and considers a limited number of issues in the question • makes judgements or proposes solutions which have limited links to analysis or limited focus on the question as a whole.	1–4 marks

Levels of response for a 20 mark question:

(Please note that the descriptors for these 5 levels also apply to the 5 levels described in 24 and 25 mark questions)

Level	The student will typically demonstrate:	Marks
5	**An excellent response overall that is fully focused on the key demands of the question.** Provides an answer to the question set that: • demonstrates a depth and range of knowledge and understanding that is precise and well selected in relation to issues in the question • demonstrates analysis throughout which is well developed, is applied effectively to the context and considers a balanced range of the issues in the question • makes judgements or provides solutions which are built effectively on analysis, show balance and have a clear focus on the question as a whole throughout.	17–20 marks
4	**A good response overall that focuses on many of the demands of the question.** Provides an answer to the question set that: • demonstrates a depth and range of knowledge and understanding of issues in the question. • demonstrates analysis which is well developed, applied effectively to the context and considers a range of issues in the question • makes judgements or provides solutions which are built on analysis, show balance and address the question as a whole.	13–16 marks

3	**A reasonable response overall that focuses on some of the demands of the question.** Provides an answer to the question set that: • demonstrates a limited knowledge and understanding of a range of issues in the question or a good knowledge and understanding of relatively few issues in the question • demonstrates analysis which is developed, applied to the context and considers some of the issues in the question • makes judgements or provides solutions which are built on analysis, but lack balance and are not fully focused on the question as a whole.	9–12 marks
2	**A limited response overall with little focus on the demands of the question.** Provides an answer to the question set that: • demonstrates a limited range and depth of knowledge and understanding of issues in the question • demonstrates analysis with little development, mainly descriptive application to the context and considers a limited number of issues in the question • makes judgements or proposes solutions which have limited links to analysis or limited focus on the question as a whole.	5–8 marks
1	**A weak response overall lacking focus on the demands of the question.** Provides an answer to the question set that: • demonstrates isolated or imprecise knowledge and understanding • demonstrates undeveloped analysis with descriptive application to the context and lacking focus on the question • makes judgements or proposes solutions based on assertions.	1–4 marks

Levels of response for a 24 mark question

Level	The student will typically demonstrate:	Marks
5	**An excellent response overall that is fully focused on the key demands of the question.** Provides an answer to the question set that: • demonstrates a depth and range of knowledge and understanding that is precise and well selected in relation to issues in the question • demonstrates analysis throughout which is well developed, is applied effectively to the context and considers a balanced range of the issues in the question • makes judgements or provides solutions which are built effectively on analysis, show balance and have a clear focus on the question as a whole throughout.	21–24 marks
4	**A good response overall that focuses on many of the demands of the question.** Provides an answer to the question set that: • demonstrates a depth and range of knowledge and understanding of issues in the question • demonstrates analysis which is well developed, applied effectively to the context and considers a range of issues in the question • makes judgements or provides solutions which are built on analysis, show balance and address the question as a whole.	16–20 marks
3	**A reasonable response overall that focuses on some of the demands of the question.** Provides an answer to the question set that: • demonstrates a limited knowledge and understanding of a range of issues in the question or a good knowledge and understanding of relatively few issues in the question • demonstrates analysis which is developed, applied to the context and considers some of the issues in the question • makes judgements or provides solutions which are built on analysis, but lack balance and are not fully focused on the question as a whole.	10–15 marks
2	**A reasonable response overall that focuses on some of the demands of the question.** Provides an answer to the question set that: • demonstrates a limited range and depth of knowledge and understanding of issues in the question • demonstrates analysis with little development, mainly descriptive application to the context and considers a limited number of issues in the question • makes judgements or proposes solutions which have limited links to analysis or limited focus on the question as a whole.	5–9 marks
1	**A weak response overall lacking focus on the demands of the question.** Provides an answer to the question set that: • demonstrates isolated or imprecise knowledge and understanding • demonstrates undeveloped analysis with descriptive application to the context and lacking focus on the question • makes judgements or proposes solutions based on assertions.	1–4 marks

Levels of response for a 25 mark question

Level	The student will typically demonstrate:	Marks
5	**An excellent response overall that is fully focused on the key demands of the question.** Provides an answer to the question set that: • demonstrates a depth and range of knowledge and understanding that is precise and well selected in relation to issues in the question. • demonstrates analysis throughout which is well developed, is applied effectively to the context and considers a balanced range of the issues in the question. • makes judgements or provides solutions which are built effectively on analysis, show balance and have a clear focus on the question as a whole throughout.	21–25 marks
4	**A good response overall that focuses on many of the demands of the question.** Provides an answer to the question set that: • demonstrates a depth and range of knowledge and understanding of issues in the question. • demonstrates analysis which is well developed, applied effectively to the context and considers a range of issues in the question. • makes judgements or provides solutions which are built on analysis, show balance and address the question as a whole.	16–20 marks
3	**A reasonable response overall that focuses on some of the demands of the question.** Provides an answer to the question set that: • demonstrates a limited knowledge and understanding of a range of issues in the question or a good knowledge and understanding of relatively few issues in the question. • demonstrates analysis which is developed, applied to the context and considers some of the issues in the question. • makes judgements or provides solutions which are built on analysis, but lack balance and are not fully focused on the question as a whole.	11–15 marks
2	**A reasonable response overall that focuses on some of the demands of the question.** Provides an answer to the question set that: • demonstrates a limited range and depth of knowledge and understanding of issues in the question. • demonstrates analysis with little development, mainly descriptive application to the context and considers a limited number of issues in the question. • makes judgements or proposes solutions which have limited links to analysis or limited focus on the question as a whole.	6–10 marks
1	**A weak response overall lacking focus on the demands of the question.** Provides an answer to the question set that: • demonstrates isolated or imprecise knowledge and understanding. • demonstrates undeveloped analysis with descriptive application to the context and lacking focus on the question. • makes judgements or proposes solutions based on assertions.	1–5 marks

Higher mark questions (16 to 25 marks) also include a requirement to show evaluation.

1 Understanding the nature and purpose of business

Practice exercise 1 (45 marks), page 8

1 Explain one reason for businesses to exist. (4)

Businesses exist essentially to provide goods and services for customers, but also to contribute to the local community, to make use of a talent or skill of the founder, or to fill a gap in the market.

2 What does the term 'mission' mean for a business? (3)

'Mission' is an organisation's aims or long-term intentions and its ultimate purpose; a business mission is sometimes the same as its corporate aims.

3 What are business objectives? (4)

Business objectives are the goals that must be achieved in order to realise the stated aims of an organisation, department or individual team. Business objectives tend to be medium to long term, and can be corporate or functional.

4 Explain the relationship between mission and objectives. (4)

Business objectives are designed to enable a business to achieve its mission.

5 When might survival be an important business objective? (4)

Survival is likely to be an important business objective when:

- a business is small or new, especially if it is operating in a highly competitive market;
- economic conditions are difficult and uncertain, for example during a recession when incomes are falling and demand is weak.

6 Analyse the reasons why growth is an important objective for a newly established estate agency operating in a competitive market. (8)

Growth will be an important objective because by expanding the number of offices in different areas, the business will be able to compete more effectively, gain more clients, make more sales and gradually improve its position in the market.

7 Analyse why social and ethical objectives might contribute to the achievement of profit and growth-related objectives for a fashion retailer. (8)

Social and ethical objectives are likely to enhance brand image and reputation, and therefore contribute to increasing sales and profits.

8 What does the mnemonic SMART stand for in relation to objectives? (5)

SMART objectives are: specific, measurable, agreed, realistic and timed.

9 Which of the following objectives is more likely to be a SMART objective? (1)
  a 'To increase sales by 3% over the next 18 months.'
  b 'To improve market share in the near future.'
  c 'To expand the business to cover more areas of the UK.'

The answer is a.

10 Explain why there is a hierarchy of objectives in most organisations. (4)

A hierarchy of objectives encourages a logical and coordinated approach to achieving goals. The hierarchy is usually: mission → corporate aims → corporate objectives → functional or departmental objectives; mission and broad corporate aims are translated into more specific but still company-wide objectives, which are in turn translated into specific functional or departmental objectives.

Case study: Sainsbury plc (45 marks), pages 9–10

1 Analyse why a business such as Sainsbury's might set social and ethical objectives. (9)

Social and ethical objectives:

- demonstrate that the business has a real commitment to improve community/environment/living standards and work conditions;
- can improve brand image and reputation, and thus lead to increased sales and profits.

2 Evaluate the benefits to a company of having detailed business objectives. (16)

Answers might include the following.

The benefits include:

- providing a collective view that helps to build team spirit and encourage commitment;
- acting as a focus for decision making and effort;
- ensuring that activities are coordinated;
- acting as a yardstick against which success or failure can be measured.

Evaluation: These factors are particularly important for large organisations like Sainsbury's because they help employees across the country/at different levels/with different roles to understand how their role/particular department contributes to the company achieving its overall aims. Without objectives there is likely to be less coordination of activities, for example between different functional areas. Without SMART objectives, the measurement of performance is likely to be less effective and the business is less likely to be able to judge whether it is being successful in achieving its goals.

3 To what extent does the case study illustrate the importance to a business of ensuring a clear relationship between mission and objectives? (20)

Answers might include the following.

The hierarchy of objectives (mission → corporate aims → corporate objectives → divisional or departmental objectives) ensures that the mission is translated into more specific but still company-wide objectives, which are in turn translated into specific functional or departmental objectives – all of which allow for a logical and coordinated approach to achieving the overall aims and mission.

Sainsbury's mission is to be 'the most trusted retailer where people love to work and shop'. Its business objectives are set to enable it to achieve its mission. The case study indicates the progress being made to achieve these objectives. The ethical and environmental objectives also contribute to its mission of being 'the most trusted retailer'.

Evaluation: Without a clear relationship between mission and objectives, business activities are likely to be less coherent, employees at all levels are likely to have less of an understanding of the link between what they do and what the company is aiming to achieve, and there is likely to be less effective monitoring of progress in achieving the overall mission.

Practice exercise 2 (20 marks), page 16

1 Calculate the profit made from selling 400 shirts. (4)
Total revenue = 400 × £15 = £6,000
Total costs = £1,600 + £120 + £80 + £60 + £400 + £2,220 = £4,480
Profit = £6,000 – £4,480 = £1,520

2 The retailers that buy the shirts have said that they will buy 600 shirts if the price is reduced to £13. Calculate the profit made if the textile manufacturer increases output and sales to 600 shirts, with the selling price at £13 per unit. (6)

(1 mark for total revenue, 1 mark for fixed costs, 2 marks for variable costs, 1 mark for total costs and 1 mark for final profit. Use the 'own figure rule' to reward correct working if an error in working leads to a subsequent incorrect answer.)
Total revenue = 600 × £13 = £7,800

Fixed costs stay the same (marketing + heating/lighting + property rent): £120 + £60 + £400 = £580

Variable costs rise by 50% as output rises from 400 to 600: 200/400 × 100 = 50%

Therefore, variable costs increase as follows:

Raw materials increase from £1,600 to £2,400.

Power increases from £80 to £120.

Wages increase from £2,220 to £3,330.

Total variable costs rise from £3,900 to £5,850.
New profit = total revenue – total costs:
£7,800 – (£580 + £5,850) = £7,800 – £6,430 = £1,370.

3 Using quantitative and qualitative factors, advise the manufacturer on whether it should charge a price of £13 or £15. (10)

Quantitative factors:
- Profit falls from £1,520 to £1,370, which obviously is not good for the manufacturer.
- With a significantly increased output (50%), there may be a rise in fixed costs, damaging profitability further.
- However, there may be some savings in variable costs per unit through bulk buying or other efficiencies.

Qualitative factors:
- Goodwill may be received from the retailer if the price is cut to £13, or the retailer may choose an alternative supplier if the price is not cut.
- Other retailers may now become interested if they believe £13 is a more reasonable price.
- The lower price and consequently higher output will put more pressure on resources such as machinery and workers.

- The £13 price may not represent an effective use of company resources. There could be a more profitable use for the extra resources needed to increase output by 50%.
- The firm may want to maintain a reputation of high quality. This is more likely to be achieved by refusing the new order.
- Does the company have sufficient spare capacity (unused resources) to increase output by 200 shirts?
- Agreeing to cut the price may make it more difficult to increase the price in the future.

Evaluation: Unless there is a high probability that cutting the price to £13 is the only way of keeping the contract with the retailer, both the quantitative and qualitative factors suggest that it should keep its price at £15. Furthermore, even if it does lose the contract, there may be other retailers who will be prepared to pay more than £13.

Practice exercise 3 (14 marks), page 16

1 Which of the following is a variable cost? (1)
  a Advertising expenditure
  b Office equipment
  c Stationery supplies
  d Wages.

  The answer is d.

2 Which of the following is a fixed cost? (1)
  a Direct labour
  b Power
  c Property rent
  d Raw materials.

  The answer is c.

3 The table shows some costs and revenue data at different levels of output.
  a What are the total fixed costs? (2)

  The fixed cost of producing four units is £20. Therefore, the fixed cost of producing any level of output is £20.

  b What is the selling price of the product? (2)
  Sales revenue from selling three units is £75. Therefore, the selling price is: £75/3 = £25.

c What are the variable costs per unit? (2)
  The variable cost of making six units is £90. Therefore, the variable cost is: £90/6 = £15.

  d Using the information, complete the table by filling in the gaps. (6)

  (1 mark each for correct columns: sales revenue, fixed costs, variable costs and total costs. 2 marks for correct profit column.)

  (Figures in bold are those provided in the question.)

Output level	Sales revenue	Fixed costs	Variable costs	Total costs	Profit
0	**0**	20	0	20	(20)
1	25	20	15	35	(10)
2	50	20	30	50	0
3	**75**	20	45	65	10
4	100	**20**	60	80	20
5	125	20	75	95	30
6	150	20	**90**	110	40

Case study: Gnomes United (35 marks), page 17

1 Name two other terms that also mean 'revenue'. (2)

  Possible answers are: income, total revenue, sales revenue, sales turnover.

2 Jim is wondering whether to expand the restaurant at the garden centre. This will lead to 8,000 more customers a year and increase his revenue by

£60,000 per annum. However, his variable costs are £2.20 per customer and he will incur extra fixed costs of £15,000. He estimates that the space needed will cut his profit on plant sales by £20,000 per annum. Use calculations to show whether expanding his restaurant will improve his overall level of profit. (6)

Extra revenue per annum = £60,000
Extra costs/lost profit from plant sales:

variable costs = £2.20 x 8,000	£17,600
increase in fixed costs	£15,000
lost profit from plant sales	£20,000
Total extra costs / lost profit from plant sales:	£52,600
Extra profit:	£7,400

3 Based on the figures in the case study, calculate the extra profit that Jim hopes to make from the Christmas tree lights. (6)

Extra revenue = price × quantity

= £24.99 × 200	= £4,998

Extra costs:

variable costs = £16.50 per box × 200 boxes	= £3,300
additional part-time hours needed: 4 × £7.25	= £29
Additional costs	£3,329

Extra profit = extra revenue – extra costs = £1,669

4 Analyse one reason why it would be difficult to estimate the effect of stocking Christmas tree lights on the number of part-time hours needed. (5)

Possible reasons are:

- In a business selling so many different products it would be very difficult to link the time spent by an individual employee to any one product.
- Most people buy Christmas lights alongside other products, making estimates of time spent more difficult.
- There is unlikely to be any reliable benchmark or standard for this. Gnomes United appears to be estimating four hours (240 minutes) for 200 boxes, which is 1.2 minutes (72 seconds) for each box.
- The time taken will depend on how much care is taken or needed to display the lights properly.

- The time spent may be irrelevant. If the centre is not busy there may not be any need to employ extra part-time staff, and the job will be done by existing staff.

5 Evaluate the other factors that Jim should consider before deciding whether to stock the Christmas tree lights. (16)

In addition to the contribution of £1,669, other factors to consider include:

- Will there be increases in fixed costs or other variable costs that have not been included in the calculations?
- What is the opportunity cost? Could the space have been used more profitably for other items? There may be storage problems too.
- How accurate is Jim's market research? The sample is small and the other information is based on competitors' situations.
- What are the expectations of customers? They may not visit a garden centre to buy Christmas lights.
- How will Christmas lights affect other sales? The case study indicates that 20% of Jim's customers first came to his garden centre in order to buy Christmas products. The lights may help to build customer loyalty and encourage shoppers to buy garden products from the store.
- What is the likely impact of the superstore? Does Jim need to diversify away from plants and garden tools?
- Recent experience suggests that increases in the range of products have helped Jim's business.

Evaluation: The final three factors strongly suggest that Jim should sell the lights as part of a diversification strategy. With the expected profit too, there is overwhelming evidence to suggest that he should sell the lights. The major factor suggesting caution is the poor quality of his market research.

2 Understanding different business forms

Practice exercise 1 (60 marks), page 32

1 Explain the implications for someone starting a business without having limited liability. (4)
- There is no distinction in law between the owners and the business.
- The owners of a business are liable for all the debts that the business may incur.
- If the debts of the business are greater than the personal assets of the owners, they may be forced into bankruptcy.

The main types of business with unlimited liability are sole traders and partnerships.

2 Explain one advantage and one disadvantage of a sole trader as compared with a partnership. (6)

Advantages of a sole trader compared with a partnership might include:
- easy to set up – no need for a partnership agreement;
- able to respond quickly to changes in circumstances – no need to consult anyone else;
- the owner takes all of the profit and hence there is good motivation;
- independence – the owner makes all the decisions.

Disadvantages of a sole trader compared with a partnership might include:
- collateral to support loans is limited to that provided by the single owner;
- capital for investment and expansion is limited to that provided by the single owner;
- more difficult for the owner to take holidays or have time off due to illness.

3 Distinguish between a private limited company and a public limited company. (6)
- A private limited company is a small- to medium-sized business that is usually run by a family or a small group of individuals who own it. It can keep its affairs reasonably private. It is funded by shares that cannot be sold without the agreement of the other shareholders. The share capital of private limited companies may be less then £50,000. It must have 'ltd' after the company name to warn people that its owners (shareholders) have limited liability.
- A public limited company is a business with limited liability and a share capital of over £50,000. It must have two directors, a qualified company secretary and at least two shareholders. Its shares are traded on the Stock Exchange and its performance and financial affairs are available for public scrutiny. Public limited companies must have 'plc' after the company name.

4 Explain one advantage and one disadvantage of a private limited company over a public limited company. (6)

Advantages of a private limited company over a public limited company may include:
- more privacy than a plc, as it is only required to divulge a limited amount of financial information;
- less pressure from outside investors and greater ability to focus on long-term strategy;
- more flexible than a plc;
- avoids the high cost of meeting the regulatory requirements for public limited companies.

Disadvantages of a private limited company over a public limited company may include:
- shares are less attractive, as they cannot be traded on the Stock Exchange and hence could be difficult to sell;
- less flexible if expansion needs finance, which is more difficult to raise than for a plc;
- less likely to gain positive publicity because its shares are not traded on the Stock Exchange.

5 Which one of the following business forms is likely to be most suitable for a non-profit organisation? (1)
a sole trader
b public limited company
c private company limited by guarantee.
The answer is c.

6 Company A has 5 million ordinary shares that were issued at a price of £5 each. The current market price of each share is £50.

   a Calculate Company A's market capitalisation and explain why this differs from its ordinary share capital. (7)

Company A's market capitalisation is £250 million (5 million shares x market price of £50 each). It differs from the ordinary share capital because market capitalisation is based on the current market price of shares, not the price at which they were first issued, which is what ordinary share capital is based upon. Ordinary share capital is £25 million (5 million shares x issue price of £5 each).

   b Explain two reasons why people might decide to invest in shares. (6)

Reasons might include:

* to provide financial support for a business and to be involved in running it (more relevant to a private limited company);
* to gain control of a business by buying up 51% of shares;
* for the dividends that may be paid;
* to make a capital gain by selling shares at a higher price than they were bought for;
* to build a larger investment fund as share prices rise over time.

   c Identify and explain two factors that might influence the price of shares. (6)

Factors include: state of the economy; performance of the company; competition in the market; proposed takeovers; investors' expectations and their response to rumours.

7 Identify and explain three factors that are likely to influence the choice of a company's legal structure. (9)

* The need for finance in order to expand. A business that intends to become large and have multiple sites or expand abroad is more likely to start as a private limited company and may eventually choose to become a plc.
* The size of the business, and the level and type of investment required. A small business trading from a single small shop is likely to begin as a sole trader.
* The need for limited liability. A manufacturing business requiring heavy investment in plant and equipment before anything can be sold may need limited liability in order to raise sufficient funds; in other cases, image might be vitally important and the word 'ltd' after a name may add status, and 'plc' even more so.
* The degree of control desired by the original owners. Where a family wishes to retain control of a business, a private limited company is likely to be the most appropriate structure.
* The nature of the business and the level of risk involved. Where risk is high, a business with limited liability is likely to be the only way of encouraging investors.

8 Identify and explain three effects of different business ownership on a company's mission and its objectives. (9)

* Public sector organisations generally focus on meeting social needs and providing essential services.
* Non-profit organisations often focus on generating sufficient profit or surpluses to reinvest in their particular field of interest.
* Private sector for-profit organisations mostly aim to maximise profit for their owners as well as having other objectives related to growth, quality, environmental protection, etc.
* As private sector businesses grow – from sole trader, to partnership to private limited company and then plc, their mission and objectives will change as their size and legal structure changes.

Case study: Staying private (60 marks), pages 32–3

1 At various times in its history, Timpson has been a sole trader, a private limited company and a public limited company. Evaluate how appropriate the sole trader and public limited company business forms might have been as the business grew and developed. (20)

Answers might include the following.

* Advantages of sole trader status: easy and cheap to set up; few legal formalities; able to respond quickly to changes in circumstances; owner takes all profit so good motivation; independence; more privacy than other legal structures.
* Disadvantages of sole trader status: unlimited liability; limited collateral to support applications for loans; limited capital for investment and expansion; difficulties when owner wishes to have time off or is ill.
* Advantages of public limited company status: limited liability and separate legal identity; easier to raise finance; greater scope for new investment; can gain positive publicity from

trading on the Stock Exchange; suppliers more willing to offer credit.

- Disadvantages of public limited company status: must publish a lot of financial information about its performance; greater public scrutiny of its activities; significant administrative costs; founders of firm may lose control if shareholdings fall below 51%; pressure from investors for short-term financial performance.

Evaluation: It is likely that sole trader status was the most appropriate form when the business was first set up. As it grew this business form would not have been suitable for the reasons identified as disadvantages above. As the business grew much larger and more successful, the plc form might have been advantageous, particularly in raising finance and providing scope for greater investment. However, as indicated in the disadvantages noted above, there are dangers in this business form. For Timpson, these disadvantages are likely to have outweighed the advantages.

2 For some of its history, Timpson was a public limited company. Analyse the factors that might influence the share price of a public limited company in a similar market to Timpson and evaluate the factors that would persuade an investor to buy shares in a company like Timpson. [20]

Answers might include the following.

Factors influencing share price:

- state of the economy – when incomes rise, investors feel more confident and are likely to buy shares and push up share prices
- performance of the company – if the company is performing well, demand for its shares will rise and share prices will rise; competition in the market is linked to this point
- proposed takeovers – can influence share prices and will reflect whether shareholders think the proposal is likely to be successful
- investors' expectations and their response to rumours – the 'bandwagon' effect on share prices.

Factors influencing investors to buy shares:

- to provide financial support for a business and to be involved in running it (more relevant to a private limited company);
- to gain control of a business by buying up 51% of shares;
- for the dividends that may be paid;
- to make a capital gain by selling shares at a higher price than they were bought for;

- to build a larger investment fund as share prices rise over time.

Evaluation: Timpson is in the shoe repair, photo store and dry cleaning businesses. Shoe repair and dry cleaning could be business sectors that do well when economic conditions are difficult and uncertain because people have less to spend on new shoes and clothes. There is relatively little competition from rival firms in the sectors that Timpson operates in. These factors may mean that a company like Timpson is able to perform well in most economic conditions. This is likely to encourage investors to buy shares and retain them in order to benefit as share prices rise steadily. It could also mean that a large investor, such as another company, might want to try to buy enough shares to gain control of the company and develop it further.

3 Discuss the factors that John Timpson might have taken into account in judging that 'staying private is the best way to run the business'. [20]

Answers might include the following.

- The need for finance in order to expand. Timpson would have considered whether there was a need to raise additional finance by becoming a plc and issuing shares. The firm clearly decided that the way to expand was by buying up other businesses and remaining as a private limited company.
- The degree of control desired by the original owners. Where a family, like Timpson, wishes to retain control of a business, a private limited company will be the most appropriate structure.
- The degree of privacy the business wishes to retain. A business like Timpson does not want to have its performance constantly open to media scrutiny.
- Media scrutiny of plcs can lead to too much emphasis on short-term policies to bolster share prices, which may detract from long-term decision making. By remaining as a private limited company, Timpson clearly wishes to avoid any unnecessary influence on its decisions about strategic development.

Evaluation: This decision is probably influenced by the wish to remain in control and not to have the business constantly scrutinised by the media. Timpson is not alone in making such a decision; a number of high-profile companies, such as Virgin, have reverted to private limited company status. The decision must also be based on the fact that the company is sufficiently successful to raise whatever finance it needs from private sources rather than offering shares to the public.

3 Understanding that businesses operate within an external environment

Practice exercise 1 (20 marks), page 49

1 What was the % change in GDP between 2004 and 2005? (2)

% change in GDP between 2004 and 2005 = increase of 2.8% (whether calculated on basis of change in index numbers or change in actual GDP figures).

2 What was the % change in GDP between 2007 and 2008? (2)

% change in GDP between 2007 and 2008 = fall of 0.28% (if calculated on the basis of change in index numbers) or fall of 0.33% (if calculated on the basis of change in actual GDP figures). (Note: difference is due to rounding up in official index number figures.)

3 What is meant by the term 'index number'? (3)

An 'index number' is a means of showing comparisons of data over time using a base year of 100.

4 Based on this data, has the UK economy recovered from the recession? (4)

Based on the data in the table, it appears that the UK economy has recovered from the recession. GDP fell in 2008 and in 2009 but since then it has been increasing, and in 2013 was above the 2007 level.

5 Analyse the implications of this data for UK retailers of household goods, such as electrical appliances and furniture. (9)

- Between 2007 and 2009, demand for electrical appliances and furniture is likely to have fallen – as a result of falling levels of income, less discretionary income, people delaying purchasing new products, fewer new homes being built.
- From 2010, demand is likely to have started to rise again – as a result of incomes increasing, discretionary income rising, people being able to afford to replace old products, more new homes being built.

Practice exercise 2 (70 marks), page 56

1 Explain each of the following terms:

a interest rates (3)

Interest rates mean the cost of borrowing money and the return for lending money.

b demographic factors (3)

Demographic factors are related to changes in the characteristics of the population of a country.

c environmental issues (3)

Environmental issues are related to protecting the natural world and preserving the capability of the environment to support all forms of life.

2 Explain one example of how competition might affect business costs, and one example of how competition might affect the demand for goods and services. (8)

- Competition might affect business costs in the following ways: to be competitive, firms need to be efficient, which may lead to reduced costs; marketing costs are likely to increase as firms try to compete; to be competitive firms may have to adopt new technology which may increase costs in the short term, even if it reduces costs in the long term; to be competitive may involve attracting well qualified staff, training them, retaining them and motivating them, all of which might increase costs.
- Competition might affect the demand for goods and services: if a competitor's strategies are more successful (lower prices, better product, etc.) this may reduce demand; to be

competitive may mean reducing costs so much that product quality declines and demand falls; to be competitive may mean producing in an unethical manner that reduces demand. (In each case above, the opposite might occur and demand may rise.)

3 Explain one example of how a change in income levels might affect business costs, and one example of how a change in income levels might affect the demand for goods and services. (6)

- A change in income levels might affect business costs: if the minimum wage increases or the general level of wages increases, costs will rise – and vice versa.

- A change in income levels might affect the demand for goods and services: as incomes increase, overall demand increases – and vice versa; the pattern of demand for different products will vary depending on whether they are essential or non-essential goods, or whether they are normal or inferior goods.

4 Identify and explain three different ways in which a fall in interest rates is likely to affect the demand for goods and services. (9)

- Demand for goods people buy on credit (e.g. cars, furniture) will increase as the lower cost of interest payments will make the purchase more attractive.

- Mortgage and other loan and credit payments will fall, meaning people will have more discretionary income to spend. This will increase demand for goods and services.

- Lower interest rates will make savings less attractive because they will grow in value at a slower rate. This may lead to some individuals deciding to spend rather than save money, so there will be more spending on consumer goods.

- It will be cheaper to purchase expensive capital equipment on credit, meaning firms may bring forward planned future investment or increase the level of capital investment.

5 Explain two ways in which a rise in interest rates might affect business costs. (6)

- Fixed costs for highly geared firms will rise.

- Other costs of production may increase if prices generally begin to rise.

- These changes may cause a firm to consider increasing the price of its products or reducing its profit margins.

6 Identify three examples of demographic changes and explain how these might affect the demand for goods and services or business costs. (9)

- Ageing population – older people in the workforce may lead to reduced business costs

because they have lower labour turnover and absence rates; increased demand for goods and services from this age group.

- More women in the workforce – more protective employment legislation in relation to maternity and childcare, which adds to business costs; more demand for certain types of services, such as nurseries and crèche facilities.

- Ethnically diverse population – may allow businesses to cut costs if certain groups of immigrants are prepared to work at rates below those acceptable to UK citizens; an ethnically diverse population leads to the growth in demand for a huge range of different types of products.

- Geographical shifts – more people in the South East leads to increased demand for housing, goods and services in these areas.

- Size of households – leads to demand for smaller pack sizes for food and household goods and for more flats rather than family houses.

7 Why might a business be able to respond to demographic change more effectively than it might to changes in competition, income and interest rates? (4)

Demographic change happens slowly and can be anticipated, analysed and understood. The other factors tend to happen much more quickly and cannot always be predicted and prepared for in the same way.

8 Explain two examples of how a business that adopts an environmentally friendly approach to its operations might incur additional costs. (6)

Examples of additional costs include: high costs of using renewable resources; high cost of disposing of harmful waste; high cost of alternative methods of production in order to reduce waste.

9 Why might adopting an environmentally friendly approach have a positive effect on the demand for a firm's products? (5)

A good reputation in relation to environmental issues can act as a positive marketing tool that encourages consumers to choose one brand over another.

10 What is meant by the term 'fair trade'? (3)

'Fair trade' is a means of benefiting small-scale famers and workers in developing countries through trade rather than aid. It enables them to maintain their livelihoods by continuing to grow their traditional produce and trading it at fair prices.

11 Why might an individual firm decide to include fair trade products in its business? (5)

This demonstrates ethical and environmentally sustainable credentials, which might improve reputation and thus sales; it might differentiate a business from its competitors, thus improving sales; it may improve recruitment and retention of staff because more and more people are concerned about these issues.

Case study: HMV's failure to keep pace with competition (30 marks), page 57

1 To what extent does the case study suggest that the effects of competition on HMV's costs and the demand for its products led to its eventual closure? (15)

Answers might include the following.

Competition came from: cut-price offers from supermarkets such as Tesco and Sainsbury's; online retailers such as Amazon; internet downloads. In comparison with these competitors, HMV incurred high rents and other costs for its high street stores. Customers are likely to be influenced by price, and thus demand for products from the competitors mentioned above would increase at the expense of HMV.

Evaluation: The effects of competition on HMV's costs and demand for its products led to the demise of the business. HMV failed to keep up with competitors in terms of price, because it incurred additional costs compared with its rivals. Probably more importantly, it failed to take account of the way people were beginning to buy music and related products – browsing online rather than in a shop.

2 Identify and explain the possible changes HMV could have introduced, in order to remain competitive, and what impact these might have had on its costs and the demand for its products. (15)

Answers might include the following.

The threats identified in 2002 included: online retailers, downloadable music, supermarket discounting. The MD at the time dismissed the seriousness of these threats. HMV could have built on its strong brand and the success it had in the 1980s and 1990s by exploiting the internet and the developing technology as effectively as its competitors were doing. It could have taken more seriously the changing nature of how people were beginning to buy the type of products it sold. It could have reviewed its cost structures to see if high street shopping was likely to remain cost effective. Leadership that is more open to considering the impact of changes in the external environment on business strategy would have enabled HMV to keep up with developments in its market.

Evaluation: If it moved more of its business online and reduced the number of shops, this might have reduced costs. This would have allowed it to compete on price more effectively. A stronger online presence would have enabled it to take advantage of the way customers want to buy products and thus maintained demand.

Practice exercise 3 (15 marks), page 58

1 Evaluate the extent to which factors, other than competition, in the external environment of these businesses had an impact on their costs and the demand for their goods and services. (15)

Answers might include the following.

- Changing technology linked to new products and new ways of purchasing online, including new ways of getting advice online, reduces business costs and increases demand. The opposite – high street shops while footfall declines, in – store advice and products such as cameras that people no longer want – means higher costs, less flexibility and reduced demand.
- Changing social and economic factors – people are unable to pay high prices, more people want foreign holidays, flying is no longer considered a luxury and people are happy to accept a 'no-frills' approach if the price is low enough – reduces business costs and increases demand. The opposite – national carriers that maintained the traditional level of service – had much higher costs and prices and much lower demand.
- Demonstrating ethical and environmentally sustainable credentials improves customer loyalty, attracts new customers and may attract and help retain better quality employees – this may lead to some increase in costs but the increase in demand is likely to compensate for this. The opposite is clear in the case of Nike – in aiming to reduce its costs it ignored the condition of workers abroad; as a result, demand for its products fell and its reputation was severely damaged.

Evaluation: A variety of external factors had an effect on the costs of these firms and the demand for their products. Other than the issue of competition, the factors mainly relate to social changes – in terms of people's expectations about what they require for their money (e.g. 'no frills' airlines) and how to shop (e.g. online or on the high street); technological factors – in terms of online availability of products and advice and the changing nature of products (e.g. cameras and smartphones); environmental – in terms of demonstrating ethical and environmental credentials (e.g. working conditions in developing countries where products are being made). No single factor is more important than the others, and some factors have more of an impact on demand than on costs, and vice versa. The important issue for business is to constantly review the external environment, taking account of and responding to changes.

4 Understanding management, leadership and decision making

Practice exercise 1 (65 marks), page 73

1 Which of the following activities is not included in the main role of a manager? (1)
   a Setting objectives
   b Analysing data
   c Promoting products
   d Making decisions
   e Reviewing.

   The answer is c.

2 Distinguish between leadership and management. (6)

   Leadership is deciding on a direction in relation to a firm's objectives and inspiring staff to achieve these objectives. Management is getting things done by organising other people to do it.

3 Outline the main characteristics of:
   a an authoritarian management and leadership style (4)

   Communication is one-way and top-down; rewards and punishments are used; strict control and close supervision are employed, with clear lines of authority.

   b a paternalistic management and leadership style (4)

   Communication is two-way – decisions are taken by the manager, but workers' views are heard; rewards are used rather than punishment; close supervision is employed, but there is a desire to look after the interests of the workers.

   c a democratic management and leadership style (4)

   Decisions result from consultation and agreement; decision making is slower because of the need to gather opinions; workers' morale should improve and better, more informed, decisions should be taken.

   d a laissez-faire leadership style (4)

   Responsibility is abdicated and a 'hands-off' approach is used; the leader has minimal input in the decision-making process and essentially leaves the running of the business to the staff.

4 Contrast the management and leadership characteristics of McGregor's Theory X and Theory Y managers. (6)
   • Theory X managers assume that workers are lazy and need to be supervised closely. Managers believe that workers are not interested in the needs of the organisation and do not wish to take responsibility. Consequently, managers will try to coerce workers and give them clear directions.
   • Theory Y managers assume that workers enjoy work and seek satisfaction from it. Workers will take responsibility and do not need close supervision. Theory Y managers believe that workers are interested in the needs of the organisation and wish to contribute to its success. Consequently, managers will want employees to exercise responsibility and creativity in finding solutions to organisational problems.

5 Contrast the management and leadership styles indicated in the two extremes (level 1 and level 7) of the Tannenbaum Schmidt continuum. (6)
   • Level 1: the manager makes the decision and 'tells' the team the decision.
   • Level 7: the manager allows the team to identify the problem, develop the options and make the decision within set limits; the manager 'shares the problem' with the team.

6 Which of the following leadership styles is not on the Mouton Blake grid? (1)
   a Country club leader
   b Team leader
   c Produce or perish leader
   d Laissez-faire leader.

   The answer is d.

7 In the Blake Mouton grid, why is the 'middle of the road' leader not judged to be the best management and leadership style for an organisation? (4)

The 'middle of the road' leader means medium concern for production and for people. By compromising, neither production nor people needs are fully met. There may be harmony in the team but team members are unlikely to be particularly happy or particularly dissatisfied. Leaders who use this style settle for average performance.

8 Use two different examples to explain 'the particular situation' as an influence on management and leadership style. (6)

Examples could include:

- A crisis situation (such as a natural disaster or dangerous faults found in a product) may require authoritarian leadership that is very task-orientated so that urgent action is coordinated and tightly focused.

- A stable situation, with skilled and experienced staff, may need democratic leadership in order to maintain/enhance the motivation and goodwill of employees, and encourage them to maximise their performance.

- Other examples include changes in any of the factors in the external business and competitive environment for which management and leadership styles might be most appropriate.

9 Apart from 'the particular situation', identify four other influences on the type of management and leadership style adopted in any organisation. (4)

Company structure; organisational culture and traditions; nature of tasks involved; employees and their skills and abilities; group size; personalities and skills of managers and leaders; time frame.

10 Is it possible to say that one leadership style is more effective than another? Justify your view. (15)

Answers might include the following.

- An explanation of the term 'leadership style'.
- Identification and explanation of the main styles of leadership – authoritarian, paternalistic, democratic and laissez-faire.
- Analysis of the crucial role which leadership style plays in determining the success of a business and the key influences on leadership styles.

Evaluation: One leadership style may be more effective than another in a particular context. For example, in a crisis situation, an authoritarian leadership approach might be most appropriate. Equally, authoritarian leadership might be most appropriate where the size of the group is large and group members are unskilled and inexperienced. However, a key factor in most situations is that employees trust their leaders because this will make them more willing to contribute effectively. This is more likely to be the case with a democratic or participatory style of leadership – although a paternalistic leadership style, where workers trust the leader to remain focused on their interests, could be equally appropriate.

Practice exercise 2 (30 marks), page 74

1 Refer to the fact files on Steve Jobs and Warren Buffett. Evidence indicates that the leadership styles of both men have been highly effective in bringing about success for their companies. Does this mean that their particular styles are the ones all managers and leaders should copy in order to ensure the success of their organisations? Justify your view. (15)

Answers might include the following:

An analysis of the crucial role the particular leadership styles of Steve Jobs and Warren Buffett played in determining the success of their businesses. For example:

- Steve Jobs – said to be an inspirational leader who had a clear vision and ensured employees bought into that vision; said to have a passion for the company (Apple) and its products; his own skills at product design and his passion inspired trust; he used his intuition, foresight and single-mindedness to focus on key products.

- Warren Buffett – said to have a 'hands off' or laissez-faire approach to the management and leadership of Berkshire Hathaway Inc, a large multinational conglomerate holding company with a diverse range of businesses. This style allows managers of companies acquired to retain full autonomy, so they feel confident and motivated by their independence.

An analysis of the influences on management and leadership style: company structure; 'the particular situation'; organisational culture and traditions; nature of tasks involved; employees and their skills and abilities; group size; personalities and skills of managers and leaders; time frame.

Evaluation: Although Steve Jobs and Warren Buffett have been highly effective in bringing about success for their companies, this does not mean that their particular styles are the ones all managers and leaders should copy in order to ensure the success of their organisations. A range of factors influence which style of leadership is best in which situation. Although Steve Jobs is said to have been inspirational, his lack of good people management skills may have had a negative effect in a different context. Similarly, Warren Buffett's laissez-faire approach is unlikely to be effective if staff do not have the skills or motivation to operate effectively. Thus the most appropriate style of management and leadership will vary depending on the particular context. Despite this, most companies are likely to benefit from leaders with characteristics of Blake Mouton's 'team leader' or 'sound leader'.

2 Business A is a medium-sized manufacturing business with a relatively inexperienced and low-skilled workforce. It is losing sales because of strong competition and may have to make job cuts unless significant changes are made to its operations and procedures. Business B is a small and relatively new IT business. The owner employs a team of young, highly skilled, very motivated graduates who pride themselves on their creativity and commitment to the business. The business is doing very well and the owner wants it to grow steadily while retaining its innovative approaches. For each business, explain the leadership style you would recommend should be used and evaluate why the two businesses should use different leadership styles. (15)

Answers might include the following.

- Business A: likely to require an authoritarian leader with strong top-down communication, tight control, close supervision and clear lines of authority. This is because the workforce is inexperienced and low-skilled, and because the business must improve its performance if it is not to make job cuts. A paternalistic style might also be helpful if this keeps the workforce more motivated. The required style is more likely to match level 1 of the Tannenbaum Schmidt continuum.

- Business B: likely to require a democratic leader who makes decisions as a result of consultation and agreement. This is because the workforce is highly skilled and very motivated. If the workforce is sufficiently committed and focused, a laissez-faire approach could be employed to give them more responsibility. The required style is more likely to match level 7 of the Tannenbaum Schmidt continuum.

Evaluation: The leadership style in Business A should differ from that in Business B because the businesses themselves are so different. The most appropriate leadership style in any business will vary depending on the particular context. Context includes issues such as company structure; 'the particular situation'; organisational culture and traditions; nature of tasks involved; employees and their skills and abilities; group size; personalities and skills of managers and leaders; time frame. Despite the above, leadership style in both companies might benefit from characteristics of Blake Mouton's 'team leader' or 'sound leader'.

5 Understanding management decision making

Practice exercise 1 (30 marks), page 81

1 Distinguish between scientific decision making and decision making based on intuition and hunches.   (6)

- Scientific decision making is a logical and research-based approach to decision making.
- Decisions based on intuition or hunches are those based upon a gut feeling held by a manager and influenced by their personal views.

2 Which of the following are not key stages in the decision-making process?   (1)

a Setting objectives

b Gathering data

c Analysing data

d Recording data.

The answer is d.

3 Explain two benefits of using scientific decision making.   (6)

- It is a systematic process that allows decisions to be made in an objective manner.
- Use of well-researched factual evidence removes bias and subjectivity.
- Easier to defend decisions made on the basis of good planning and data analysis.

4 Explain one reason for basing decisions on intuition.   (4)

- Much quicker and cheaper than using a scientific decision-making approach.

- Can be more creative and more innovative than a systems-based approach.
- May be based on up-to-date data and a more 'qualitative' understanding of issues.

5 Briefly explain how risks, rewards and uncertainty are likely to be a feature of any decision.   (6)

Most business decisions involve an element of risk. They are taken in the expectation of some form of reward or benefit. Just because a particular project is risky does not mean a decision to pursue it should not be made. Uncertainty about future risks and rewards following a decision cannot be removed but can be reduced, for example by test marketing a new product or doing a test run or pilot of a new strategy.

6 Define the term 'opportunity cost'.   (2)

'Opportunity cost' is the 'real cost' of taking a particular action. It is the next best alternative foregone, i.e. the next best thing that you could have chosen but did not.

7 Why is opportunity cost an important element of any decision?   (5)

Opportunity cost is the real cost of a decision in terms of the next best alternative. Every decision has an opportunity cost because resources, including time and money, are scarce. Therefore choosing one thing inevitably results in foregoing something else.

Practice exercise 2 (50 marks), page 91

1 What is a decision tree?   (3)

A decision tree is a tool to assist decision making. A decision tree diagram resembles the branches of a tree and maps out the different options available, the possible outcomes of these options and the points where decisions have to be made. Calculations based on decision trees can be used to determine the best option to select.

2 Explain three advantages of using decision trees in a business context.   (9)

- They allow problems to be set out clearly, therefore encouraging a logical approach to decision making.
- They enable a quantitative approach to be taken that may improve the results and mean that the process can be computerised.
- They take into account uncertainty, risk and reward.
- They encourage consideration of all alternatives, making the process more objective.

3 Explain two disadvantages of using decision trees in a business context. (6)
- They ignore the constantly changing nature of the business environment.
- It can be difficult to get accurate and realistic data in order to estimate probabilities.
- They may lead to managers taking less account of important qualitative issues.
- They are less useful in relation to completely new decisions or where there is no previous reliable data for probabilities.

4 If the probability of success is 0.6, what is the probability of failure and why? (2)

The probability of failure is 0.4 because the total probability of any outcome adds to 1.0 (100%).

5 A particular outcome has a 40% chance of earning £40,000 and a 60% chance of earning £100,000. What is its expected value? (4)

The expected value is £76,000. It is calculated as follows:
0.4 × £40,000 =   £16,000
0.6 × £100,000 =   £60,000
                   £76,000

6 Outline two situations where decision trees are likely to be a valuable tool. (6)
- When choosing between several options, where it is also useful to form a balanced picture of the risks and rewards associated with each option.
- When quantitative data are available on risks and rewards, and similar scenarios have occurred before so that realistic estimates of probabilities and financial returns can be made.

- When the decision is about choosing the option that gives the highest financial reward.

7 Outline one situation where decision trees are unlikely to be useful. (4)
- Completely new or one-off situations exist and thus realistic or reliable data on the probability of particular outcomes occurring do not exist.
- When decisions do not involve clear-cut alternatives.
- When circumstances are very uncertain or changing rapidly.

8 Analyse two ways in which each of the following factors is likely to influence a firm's corporate decision making:
a ethics (8)
- A decision made on ethical grounds might reject the most profitable solution in favour of one that provides greater benefit to society as a whole, or to particular groups of stakeholders.
- A business may make a decision based on a seemingly ethical position when in fact the decision is made because it is popular with customers and may lead to increased sales.
b resource constraints (8)
- If a company is unable to generate sufficient financial resources, this will affect its corporate decision making; e.g. decisions about expansion or diversification will depend on a business having sufficient funds to support these developments.
- The availability of human resources will influence decisions; e.g. whether sufficient trained employees are available may influence decisions about whether to undertake a new project.

Case study: Lynne Lilley crafts (20 marks), pages 91–2

1 Draw the decision tree and calculate the expected value and net gain of each option. (9)

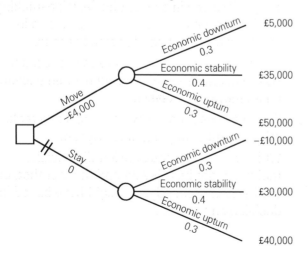

Move to cheaper premises
0.3 × £5,000 =	1,500
0.4 × £35,000 =	£14,000
0.3 × £50,000 =	£15,000
Expected value	£30,500
less costs	–£4,000
Net gain	£26,500

Continue as at present
0.3 × –£10,000 =	£3,000
0.4 × £30,000 =	£12,000
0.3 × £40,000 =	£12,000
Expected value and net gain*	£21,000

(* Expected value is the same as net gain because no costs were deducted)

2 On the basis of your calculations, which option should Lynne choose and why? (2)

Lynne should move to cheaper premises because the net gain is greater than continuing where she is at present.

3 Consider how useful decision tree analysis is in helping Lynne to make her decision. (9)

- The advantages of using decision trees are: setting out problems clearly; encouraging a logical approach to decision making; taking a quantitative approach that may improve the results and means that the process can be computerised; and taking risk and uncertainty into account when making decisions.

- The disadvantages of using decision trees are: ignoring the constantly changing nature of the business environment; the difficulty in getting accurate and realistic data in order to estimate probabilities; and causing managers to take less account of important qualitative issues.

Evaluation: There is not a great deal of difference between the two outcomes of the decision tree. Lynne may wish to consider seriously other factors before making a decision. These factors might include the extent to which advertising is effective in attracting customers to a new location, the proportion of sales that are made to large stores and the proportion of sales that go to passing tourist trade.

Case study: Decision making at Dyson (30 marks), page 92

1 How might factors in the external environment have influenced Dyson in its decisions about how to price and market its products and to locate its manufacturing processes in Malaysia? (15)

Answers might include the following.

Factors in the external environment to consider include:

- Changes in economic policy such as interest rates, which might influence decisions about expansion in the UK – high interest rates mean higher costs and thus higher prices.

- Environmental factors might influence decisions about methods of waste disposal and costs of waste disposal, which might influence price.

- Demographic trends as well as trends in incomes and in the types of products people aspire to buy might influence decisions about how to market the product to different groups of people.

- Actions of competitors might influence decisions about pricing – the case study says that the market had previously been focused exclusively on price.

Features of Dyson products – prices are much higher than competitors' products; products are best-sellers; marketing campaigns are low key; superior technology sells the products; the fact that Dyson products have become 'aspirational purchases' means people are prepared to pay high prices to own one.

Reason for moving to Malaysia – production costs were 30% cheaper overseas; component suppliers were based in the region; some of its biggest markets were based in the region so transport costs would be much lower.

Evaluation: External factors, particularly in relation to costs of production, clearly influenced the move to Malaysia; marketing is low key and prices are high, suggesting that Dyson has clearly targeted the market and established itself as a 'must-have' product for people in the UK and around the world (Asia and US) as they become more affluent and want 'aspirational purchases'. Increased profits and market leadership in the USA suggest Dyson's strategies were appropriate.

2 Assess the extent to which a scientific decision-making model might have benefited Dyson in deciding on its production move from England to Malaysia. (15)

Answers might include the following.

- An explanation of what a scientific decision-making model is, compared to decisions based on intuition and hunch.

- Identification and explanation of the main stages involved in a scientific decision-making model and the importance of each stage in ensuring that the best decision is made.

- Use of the stages to illustrate the process that Dyson might have gone through when deciding on its move to Malaysia.

- Which advantages of scientific decision making might be most important for Dyson.

- Which disadvantages of scientific decision making might be relevant and the fact that, on the basis of these, Dyson might have based its decision on a hunch.

Evaluation: Conclude that some form of the scientific decision-making model is likely to have been used in deciding to move production to Malaysia. Without such an approach, it is unlikely that Dyson would have contemplated the move in the first place, or that it would have achieved the success it did.

Case study: Decision making at JCPenny (50 marks), page 93

1 Under what circumstances might decision making based on intuition benefit a business? (9)

- When speed and timing are important – decision making based on intuition is much quicker and cheaper than using a scientific decision-making approach.
- When a business needs a more creative and innovative approach than a systems-based one.
- When it needs to be based on up-to-the minute data and a more 'qualitative' understanding of issues.

2 Assess how Ron Johnson's strategy of introducing new approaches at JCPenny might have benefited from a more scientific decision-making approach. (16)

Answers might include the following.

- Explain what a scientific decision-making model is and distinguish this from decisions based on hunch.
- Identify and explain the main stages involved in a scientific decision-making model and assess the importance of each stage in ensuring that the best decision is made.
- Use the stages to illustrate the process that JCPenny might have gone through when deciding on whether to change its strategies.
- Outline the advantages of scientific decision making that would have been the most important for JCPenny.
- Outline the disadvantages of scientific decision making that might have applied to JCPenny and might have meant decisions were better if based on intuition and hunch.

Key issues re JCPenny and Ron Johnson – he used his intuition and gut instinct to make decisions. He ignored data presented to him, for example the results of focus groups, and was not interested in test-marketing changes before rolling them out across America.

Evaluation: Ron Johnson was at JCPenny for under two years. In that time costs rose and cash balances fell significantly; sales revenue fell by 25%; share prices fell and as a result market capitalisation fell by 50%. This suggests that his approach of using his intuition rather than scientific decision making was a bad one and had serious consequences for the company. His strategy of introducing new approaches would have benefited significantly from a more scientific decision-making approach.

3 Discuss the value of different approaches to decision making that are available to an organisation. (25)

Answers might include the following.

- Explain the importance of decision making to an organisation and identify the different types of decision making: short term/long term, tactical/strategic, functional/corporate.
- Explain the scientific approach to decision making and outline the advantages and disadvantages associated with it.
- Outline the process involved in using decision trees as an approach to decision making and assess their value.
- Explain the more intuitive approach to decision making, based on hunch, and outline the advantages and disadvantages associated with it.
- Assess how an organisation might choose between scientific and hunch-based decision making.
- Illustrate the answer with business examples where possible.

Evaluation: Conclude with the fact that whatever approach to decision making is used must suit the organisation and the nature of the decision being made. Note that there are many influences on the decision-making process and the decisions that will be made, including: whether decisions are tactical or strategic; mission and objectives; ethics; the external environment an organisation faces; resource constraints; the relative power of an organisation's stakeholders; and organisational culture.

6 Understanding the role and importance of stakeholders

Practice exercise 1 (70 marks), page 107

1 Distinguish between the terms 'shareholder' and 'stakeholder'. (4)
- A shareholder is a person or organisation that owns a part (share) of a business.
- A stakeholder is an individual or group with a direct interest in the activities and performance of an organisation. Stakeholders include shareholders as well as employees, consumers, the local community and suppliers.

2 Which of the following is not an internal stakeholder? (1)
a Shareholders
b Employees
c Managers
d Customers.

The answer is d.

3 Which of the following is not an external stakeholder? (1)
a Customers
b Suppliers
c Banks and investors
d Shareholders.

The answer is d.

4 Using the examples of two different stakeholder groups, explain why a business should consider stakeholders' needs when making decisions. (6)
- Meeting shareholders' needs will be important in a small family-owned business where each individual shareholder may have a great deal of influence.
- Meeting the needs of the local community or environmental pressure groups may be important where a business has a significant impact on the environment where it is located.
- Meeting customers' needs will be important for firms operating in highly competitive markets.

- Meeting the needs of employees may be important in sectors that need highly skilled employees who are hard to find.

5 Which of the following is least likely to be one of the employees' needs or objectives in relation to a business? (1)
a Low prices
b Job security
c High wages
d Good working conditions
e Opportunities to be consulted about decisions.

The answer is a.

6 'Stakeholder groups often have needs in common or that overlap.' Use two examples to explain this statement. (6)
- All stakeholders in an organisation, except its direct competitors, have much to gain from it being profitable and successful.
- A new factory or store might benefit the local community by providing more jobs, wealth and choice for consumers. It might also contribute positively to the local community if it has a pleasant external environment, e.g. landscaping and car parking. At the same time it will increase the demand for its suppliers' products.

7 Identify and explain two examples of stakeholder needs that conflict. (6)
- Lowering prices in order to please customers may result in lower profits and thus affect shareholders' dividends.
- Expansion of a business may help job security for employees and give consumers better access to products, but the developments may be at the expense of local residents through higher noise levels or damage to the environment.

- Closing a factory may be an efficient financial decision and benefit profitability and therefore shareholders in the long term, but will cause unemployment and hardship for the local community.

8 Distinguish between the traditional shareholder approach and the alternative stakeholder approach in relation to the objectives of a business. (8)

- The traditional shareholder approach is based on the view that firms were established to meet the needs of their owners (i.e. shareholders). Business aims and objectives should therefore be about meeting their needs, which means aiming to make profits for the owners (shareholders).
- The alternative stakeholder approach is taken when an organisation gives prominence to the views of other stakeholders. Objectives may therefore target the needs of different groups of stakeholders, such as the workforce, customers, the local community or suppliers, etc.

9 Distinguish between the 'win–lose' approach and the 'win–win' approach to meeting stakeholder needs. (6)

- The 'win–lose' approach to meeting stakeholder needs occurs when attempts to satisfy the needs of one group of stakeholders lead to adverse effects on another group of stakeholders. For example, reduced prices may satisfy customers but may lead to lower profits for shareholders.
- The 'win–win' approach to meeting stakeholder needs occurs when attempts to satisfy the needs of one group of stakeholders also lead to favourable effects on another group of stakeholders. For example, improving product quality benefits customers and may lead to increased sales and profits, thus benefiting shareholders.

10 Explain one purpose of stakeholder mapping. (4)

- It analyses different levels of stakeholder power and interest.
- It helps manage stakeholders' conflicting needs and objectives.

11 Which two of the following elements form the two axes of Mendelow's stakeholder mapping matrix? (2)

a Influence

b Power

c Impact

d Interest

e Control.

The answer is b and d.

12 Identify the key approach to stakeholders in each of the four quadrants of Mendelow's stakeholder mapping matrix. (4)

- High power/low interest – keep satisfied
- High power/high interest – key players
- Low power/low interest – minimal effort
- Low power/high interest – keep informed.

13 Explain two key influences on the relationship of a business with its stakeholders. (6)

Key influences on the relationship of a business with its stakeholders might include whether particular groups of stakeholders:

- have status and power within or outside the business
- have control of relevant resources or have relevant skills and knowledge
- are involved in the decision-making process
- have needs and objectives in common with, or in conflict with, other groups.

14 Explain two ways in which a business might attempt to manage the relationship between different stakeholders. (6)

- Any of Cyert and March's approaches – satisficing, sequential attention, side payments, exercise of power.
- Shareholder mapping such as Mendelow's power–interest matrix.
- Clear communication of the business mission.
- A focus on corporate social responsibility and ethics as a means of addressing stakeholder conflicts.

15 Why might communication and consultation be important in this process? (6)

- Taking into account stakeholder views and keeping them informed can reduce conflict and improve the chances of success of a project.
- Gaining support from powerful stakeholders can influence the supply of resources and the success of a project.

16 Give three examples of channels to use for communicating and consulting with stakeholders about a project. (3)

Formal consultations; formal and informal meetings; public forums; newsletters; website information; media releases; advertisements; information displays; tours and demonstrations.

Case study: Tesco plc (70 marks), pages 108–9

1 Analyse how stakeholder mapping might assist Tesco in achieving success in relation to its operations and their impact on its stakeholders. (9)

- Stakeholder mapping can assist Tesco to analyse different levels of stakeholder power and interest and help to manage stakeholders' conflicting needs and objectives.
- Mendelow's power–interest matrix can be used to analyse different stakeholder groups and determine the most appropriate level of involvement to allow the business to achieve success while ensuring stakeholder needs are taken into account.
- The case study indicates that Tesco is already identifying the needs of different groups of stakeholders and introducing different ways of engaging with these different groups.

2 Analyse the different ways Tesco attempts to manage the relationship with its stakeholders. (9)

- Tesco manages the relationship with its stakeholders by engaging with different groups of stakeholders in a range of different ways. These include customer focus groups, employee feedback, work with community groups, information leaflets and supplier surveys.
- As a result of the different ways it engages with its stakeholders, Tesco has identified the needs and objectives of different groups of stakeholders, including customers, employees, communities, suppliers and government.
- The case study suggests that Tesco acknowledges that it cannot meet the needs of each group of stakeholders at all times, but by listening to them Tesco aims to take their views into account in its strategies.

3 Assess the extent to which different stakeholder groups have needs and objectives in common or that overlap, and how this could benefit Tesco. (16)

Answers might include the following.

- All of Tesco's stakeholder groups have much to gain from the business being profitable and successful. The case study notes the needs of different groups – a profitable and successful company is likely to satisfy many of the needs identified.
- Different groups of stakeholders can also benefit from particular initiatives, such as a new store opening. For example, this might benefit the local community by providing more jobs and thus more local spending, more choice for consumers; it might also contribute positively to the local community

if it has a pleasant external environment, e.g. landscaping and car parking; it will increase the demand for suppliers' products; it may increase profits and thus benefit shareholders in terms of share price and dividend payments, and government via taxation.

Evaluation: Although different stakeholder groups may have different needs and objectives, many of these needs and objectives can be satisfied simultaneously if a business is successful and profitable. The fact that Tesco's recent performance has not been as strong as in the past might make this more difficult. The ability to satisfy most groups of stakeholders is likely to benefit Tesco because it will mean, for example, satisfied customers, motivated workers and a supportive local community. This is like a 'win–win' approach to meeting stakeholder needs because strategies that satisfy the needs of one group of stakeholders also have favourable effects on other groups of stakeholders.

4 Assess the potential conflict of needs and objectives among Tesco's stakeholders and the possible impact on Tesco and its stakeholders of such conflict. (16)

Answers might include the following.

Examples of potential conflict of needs and objectives include:

- shareholders who want Tesco to achieve high profit levels either by keeping costs low or by charging high prices – conflict with customers wanting low prices and employees wanting high wages
- employees who want job security, good working conditions, high levels of pay, promotional opportunities and job enrichment – conflict with customers wanting low prices and shareholders wanting high profits
- customers who want Tesco to provide high-quality products at low prices, and to offer a good service and a wide choice – conflict with shareholders wanting high profits.

Evaluation: Tesco acknowledges that it cannot meet the needs of all stakeholders all the time – but it gives assurance that it listens and takes views into account when balancing different considerations. All stakeholder groups will benefit if Tesco is a successful, efficient and well-run business. The case study suggests that Tesco's performance is deteriorating, which is more likely to increase any conflict between stakeholders.

5 Tesco's core purpose and values suggest it takes a stakeholder rather than a shareholder approach. Discuss the relative benefits of such an approach to the company and to its various stakeholders compared with a more traditional shareholder approach. (20)

Answers might include the following.

- The case study indicates that Tesco feels it must demonstrate a purpose that is 'more than just profit' and that it wants to 'always do the right thing, to inspire and to earn trust and loyalty' from all of its stakeholders.
- An explanation of a stakeholder approach. The case study indicates that Tesco has identified the needs and objectives of different groups of stakeholders and uses different methods to engage with them.
- An explanation of a shareholder approach.

The benefits of a stakeholder approach:

- Satisfying the needs of employees may result in a loyal and more motivated workforce, which may in turn lead to reduced costs (due to lower labour turnover and absenteeism) and improved productivity.
- Satisfying customers' needs may lead to increased sales.
- Serving the needs of both employees and customers may enable a business to grow and achieve high profits.

Evaluation: Although shareholders and other stakeholders may have needs and objectives that conflict, by focusing on a stakeholder approach rather than a traditional shareholder approach, Tesco is more likely to be able to satisfy them all in the long term. Its current weaker performance is only likely to improve if it ensures the needs of stakeholders, such as customers and employees, are met. This may mean some sacrifice by shareholders in the short term, but they, and all other stakeholders, are more likely to benefit in the longer term.

7 Setting marketing objectives

Practice exercise 1 (50 marks), pages 121–2

1 How large was the market for new cars in the UK in 2013? (1)

2,264,737 cars.

2 What was the percentage change in market growth between 2012 and in 2013? (2)

10.8% or +10.8%
(2,264,737 – 2,044,609 = 220,128)
220,128/2,044,609 x 100 = 10.8%

3 Which company was the market leader? (1)

Ford.

4 Between 2012 and 2013, Ford had the largest increase in the number (volume) of cars sold. Calculate their increase in sales volume. (2)

310,865 – 281,917 = 28,948 cars

5 Between 2012 and 2013, which firm had the largest percentage increase in its sale of cars? (1)

Mercedes-Benz: +19.2%.

6 Hyundai fell from tenth to eleventh place in the UK market in 2013, despite recording a sales increase of 3.5% between 2012 and 2013. If Hyundai sold 76,918 cars in 2013, how many cars did it sell in 2012? (3)

Hyundai sales in 2012 were 76,918 / 1.035 = 74,317 cars (accept 74,316)

7 Why might the use of volume (the number of cars sold) give a misleading impression of the market share of a car manufacturer? (4)

Volume might give a misleading impression of market share because cars vary in price – a car manufacturer such as Rolls-Royce will find it difficult to sell the same volume as Citroën because the price of a Rolls-Royce may be more than ten times that of a Citroën.

Sales value, which measures revenue, is a better indicator because it takes into account both the number of cars sold and the price charged. It is therefore a 'fairer' measure and is a more accurate assessment of how well a firm has performed. A company might increase its volume of sales by cutting the price and selling the cars at a very low price; but this may not be a successful move in terms of profit.

8 How was it possible for Ford to have the largest increase in sales volume and yet experience a decrease in its market share? (7)

Volume is the quantity of items (cars) sold. Ford is the market leader because it sells more cars than any other company. However, market share is based on the percentage of a company's sales compared with other companies. Ford's growth of 28,948 was high but other companies, such as Mercedes Benz and Audi, grew more quickly. In total the car market grew by 10.8% between 2012 and 2013. A company would need its individual sales to grow by 10.8% to keep the same market share. Ford's sales grew by 10.3% (slightly below 10.8% growth for the market) and so its market share fell slightly (from 13.8% to 13.7%). Car manufacturers whose sales grew faster than the market (such as Mercedes-Benz and Audi) gained market share. Car manufacturers whose sales grew more slowly than the market (such as Volkswagen and Peugeot) lost market share.

9 Volkswagen occupies third place in terms of UK market share. However, Volkswagen is part of a business that also owns Audi, Skoda and Seat (fourth, thirteenth and nineteenth in the market). Explain why a firm might make a decision to use different brand names for different cars in this way. (8)

Reasons might include:

● Brand loyalty – some car buyers are very loyal to certain brands and so, by keeping the old brand names when it takes over other companies, Volkswagen can satisfy those customers who only want to buy a specific brand, such as Audi.

● Some cars are associated with certain countries. People living in the Czech Republic may prefer to buy a car that they associate with their country (such as a Skoda) rather than a 'German' Volkswagen.

- Different brands appeal to different market segments. Customers wanting a luxury car might choose Audi. Those wanting a reliable, high-quality car may choose a Volkswagen. Skoda is associated more with consumers wanting value for money. By using different brand names, Volkswagen can appeal to a broader cross-section of consumers.

- Multi-branding (the approach used by Volkswagen) protects the various parts of the company from bad publicity caused by individual products. If a Seat car gets a bad image, this may not affect the other brands within Volkswagen. In contrast, if a Ford model creates a negative image, it may affect sales across the whole range of Ford cars.

10 Analyse three factors that might influence the market size of the new car market in the UK. (9)

Five factors are noted and analysed but many other factors are relevant:

- Incomes of consumers. The richer the country, the more people can afford to buy cars. There is also a shift towards the more luxurious brands such as BMW, which means that the size of the market (measured by sales value) will be higher if incomes in a country are higher.

- Prices. If the car industry is able to keep costs of production low and thus charge lower prices, this will enable more people to buy new cars rather than relying on the second-hand car market. This will lead to a larger market size if sales volume is the measure used. However, it may not mean a larger value.

- Social changes. In the UK, lifestyles tend to encourage the use of cars. Businesses are not always located in places that are easily accessed by public transport or within walking distance of employees. Leisure activities are easier and quicker to reach by car than alternative methods of transport.

- Prices and convenience of alternatives. The cost, reliability and frequency of public transport will all influence the attractiveness of cars as a form of transport. In many places the perceived weaknesses of these alternatives will encourage the purchase of cars. However, places well served by public transport, such as London, may have fewer car users.

- Features of cars. High prices of complementary products, such as petrol and car insurance, may reduce the demand for cars. The flexibility of car transport will also affect its market size.

11 Evaluate the usefulness of the information in Table 7.2 to a Chinese car manufacturer that wishes to establish itself in the UK market for new cars. (12)

Reasons why the information in Table 7.2 is useful:

- The table shows what the main brands are. The business can use this to undertake market research into the reasons why the British public prefers these particular brands. The Chinese manufacturer can use this information to plan and design cars that are suited to the UK market.

- It shows the overall size of the market. With some additional market research into population data, this information will help the manufacturer to calculate the potential sales it can achieve in its area, in order to see if it is viable to try to sell cars in the UK.

- Data over time might show levels of brand loyalty. Since the demise of UK car manufacturers under British ownership there appears to be less brand loyalty in the UK, compared to countries such as France and Germany. This would suggest that the UK might be an easier market to enter than markets such as France. Cars manufactured in the UK represent less than 10% of total sales in the UK market (although many cars are exported to other countries).

- Specific details, such as the relatively large growth of luxury cars like Audi and Mercedes-Benz, will help the Chinese manufacturer to identify the areas of growth in the market that it can target. It might also investigate details such as the geographical locations in which certain cars are sold most, in order to decide where it needs to base its garages.

Reasons why the information in Table 7.2 is not useful:

- The data are from past performance (in 2012–2013) and may not be a reliable indicator for the future.

- The table provides no information to explain why the cars were sold; without this information the sales force will not understand the nature of the market for new cars.

- The data in the table gives no indication of price or sales value. As indicated earlier, sales volume alone is not the best measure of success in the car market.

- The data apply to large-scale makers of cars; the new manufacturer is likely to be a small-scale seller of cars, at least when it first enters the UK market. Therefore we are not really studying the same markets.

Evaluation: Overall the data are helpful because they show the potential for car sales in the UK.

However, more detailed local investigation needs to be done to assess the chances of success for a new manufacturer. The data are of limited use because they are based on the past and the information gives no guarantee of future tastes in cars. The franchisee would need to look at sales trends over a number of years and forecasts for the future. The firm would also need to carry out research based on its brand of cars. Detailed information is also needed on costs and revenue – the volume of sales is only a limited indicator of success.

Practice exercise 2 (60 marks), page 126

1 Which of the following is an internal factor that might influence a firm's marketing objectives? (1)
   a Changes in suppliers
   b Growth of the economy
   c Level of skills of its employees
   d New legislation.

   The answer is c.

2 What does the formula below measure? (1)

$$\frac{\text{Market size in year} - \text{Market size in previous year}}{\text{Market size in previous year}} \times 100$$

   a Market size
   b Market growth
   c Market share.

   The answer is b.

3 Analyse two advantages that a restaurant might gain from setting marketing objectives. (9)

   (This question is very broad. The advantages given below are just examples of a possible approach to this question.)

   SMART objectives should give a restaurant advantages in comparison with other businesses. For example:
   - Specific objectives give a clear sense of direction to all staff and help to ensure that everyone is working towards the same goals, thus improving efficiency.
   - Measurable objectives enable a business to ensure that employees and managers can assess whether the objective has been achieved.
   - Agreed objectives can prove to be a motivator, as staff will recognise that they have been given a share of the responsibility for setting the objectives. This process is also likely to provide realistic objectives which will provide a genuine but achievable target.
   - Timed objectives give employees clarity on how long they have to reach the target outlined in the marketing objective.

4 Analyse two possible problems involved in using marketing objectives to assess the performance of the marketing department. (9)
   - External factors may change. A new competitor may take away market share and force down a business's prices. Both of these consequences may make it much harder to achieve a marketing objective that was originally realistic. Similarly, a competitor going into liquidation may make an objective much easier to achieve and disguise weaknesses within the business.
   - Internal factors may change. Problems with staff recruitment or operational problems in the factory might lead to faulty products. These issues may lead to lower sales and a reputation for poor quality.
   - Unrealistic objectives may have been set, perhaps because a manager wanted to show ambition or because of a lack of awareness of the market itself. As a result, the department may not be able to reach its objectives.

5 Explain one advantage and one disadvantage of using market share as a marketing objective. (8)
   - Advantage: market share is a good objective because it considers a business's performance in comparison to its competitors. A business that is gaining market share would seem to be outperforming competitors. In effect, factors outside the business's control, such as a recession, are not used to judge performance.
   - Disadvantage: a weakness is that the achievements of a marketing department should be related to actual outcomes. If the market itself is declining, should the marketing department have identified this issue and encouraged movement into other markets? It may be gaining market share because more astute competitors have decided to leave the market.

6 In Chapter 1 the concept of SMART objectives was introduced. Give four examples of SMART marketing objectives. (4)

   Possible SMART marketing objectives are:
   - Increase market share by 2%.
   - Achieve sales revenue of £2 million within two years.
   - Introduce three new products by 2020.
   - Increase consumer recognition of the corporate logo by 10% in 2016.
   - Improve overall added value on a specific product by £2 per unit this year.
   - Record 'repeat purchases' from 60% of customers within three years.

7 What problem might arise if a firm's marketing department ignored its corporate objectives? (4)

This situation is likely to lead to a lack of coordination within the business as a whole. The marketing department's targets may not be clear to the other departments, which would be working towards the corporate aims. Consequently, the marketing strategies are likely to fail.

8 Analyse two reasons why a printing company would set marketing objectives. (6)

- To allow the printing company to assess whether it has succeeded. By comparing the actual outcome with the target (e.g. a certain market share), success or failure can be ascertained.
- To motivate members of the marketing department, who can be rewarded for their ability to achieve their targets. These rewards do not necessarily have to be financial.

9 Identify and explain two internal factors that might influence a fashion retailer's marketing objectives. (9)

- **Corporate objectives**. If these emphasise the quality of the fashion garments, then the marketing objectives cannot be focused on a target that is inconsistent with this aim, such as a marketing objective to achieve low pricing.

- **Human resources**. Marketing objectives must be achievable and therefore will be influenced by the capabilities of the workforce, particularly where additional training might be needed to achieve the objective.
- **Finances**. It is vital that any marketing objective is realistic in terms of the marketing budget available to support marketing activities. This will limit the ambition of some marketing objectives.

10 Identify and explain two external factors that might influence a fashion retailer's marketing objectives. (9)

- **Fashion**. If tastes change suddenly, the business may find it easier to achieve its objectives if it successfully anticipated the change, but more difficult if it did not foresee the latest fashion changes.
- **Economic changes**. A recession or decline in economic activity will lead to a fall in sales of most products, particularly fashion products, which are often deemed to be luxury items and not essential purchases.
- **Competition**. The actions of competitors can have a major impact on the sales of business and therefore its ability to hit its marketing objectives. For example, a price war initiated by a competitor is likely to undermine the achievement of marketing objectives.

Case study: Vodafone's marketing objectives (60 marks), pages 127–8

1 Based on its marketing objectives and achievements between 2011 and 2013, some analysts believe that Vodafone's marketing decision making was at its best in 2012. Do you agree? Justify your view. (20)

Reasons why 2012 was the year in which Vodafone's marketing achieved its best performance:

- Table 7.3 shows that 2012 was a year in which sales revenue continued to grow and in which the marketing objective for sales revenue growth was achieved. In contrast, 2013 was a year in which sales revenue growth fell by 1.9%, leading to a failure to achieve the sales revenue growth marketing objective.
- The target for integrated contracts was met in all three years and shows steady growth, implying that all three years were successful.
- The target for the percentage of customers using smartphones increased each year. The comment on performance implies that the objective has been achieved in each year and is on track for future years.
- In all three years, market share was gained or held in the majority of its markets. However, this was only 53% in 2011 and 2013 whereas

in 2012 it was 65%. This suggests that performance in this aspect of the business in 2012 was significantly better than it was in the other two years under consideration.

- Vodafone successfully increased the number of markets in which it had the highest brand loyalty (NPS) from eight markets to eleven markets in 2012. However, in 2012 this figure fell back to eight markets. These data suggest that 2012 represented a significantly better performance than the other two years.

Reasons why 2012 was NOT the year in which Vodafone's marketing function achieved its best performance:

- Although the marketing objective was hit in both 2011 in 2012, sales revenue growth was higher in 2011 (+2.1% compared to +1.5% in 2012). These data suggest that performance was better in 2011 than 2012.
- Closer scrutiny of the data for integrated contracts indicates a 17% increase in 2012 but a 23% increase in 2013. This suggests that performance in 2013 may have been superior to that in 2012.
- Closer scrutiny of the data for smartphone use indicates an 8% increase in 2012 but

a 9% increase in 2013. This suggests that performance was almost equal in both years, but performance in 2013 was marginally better than performance in 2012.

- The data in the table give no indication of whether performance in 2011 was higher than in 2010, although it does allow the absolute performance to be compared with the other two years.

Evaluation: Overall the data indicate that 2012 was the year in which market share and brand loyalty were at their highest levels and that the differences were of some significance. However, the data also show that integrated contracts and smartphone use grew most quickly in 2013. However, the differences between 2012 and 2013 were minor. 2011 showed the best sales revenue growth, but did not show any other apparent strengths.

The conclusion that performance was best in 2012 would depend on the relative importance of each marketing objective. It could be argued that sales growth is the primary aim – this would eliminate 2013 from the reckoning but imply that 2011 was perhaps the best year. However, future sales revenue will depend on the other four objectives and so it could be argued that 2012 was the year in which the best foundations for future growth were being established (as well as a reasonable growth being achieved in that year).

2 To what extent do you think that the achievements of Vodafone's marketing department indicate that the company's marketing objectives have been chosen well? (20)

Well-chosen marketing objectives should enable a business to satisfy the needs of its stakeholders.

- Sales revenue growth is fundamental to the success of the business and would therefore be an objective that is very important to most, if not all, stakeholders.

- Integrated contracts are seen by Vodafone as the best way of attracting customers and also achieving greater revenue from each customer. This would suggest that the objective is helping Vodafone to meet its customers' needs, but also the needs of other stakeholders, such as shareholders and employees whose dividends and employment will be more secure.

- Smartphones also provide a better service to customers and a greater revenue stream, and therefore will be important in meeting broader stakeholder needs.

- Market share is an excellent measure of how effective a business is in comparison to its competitors. The market for mobile phones has proved to be quite volatile, with profits fluctuating considerably according to market circumstances. However, using market share eliminates those external factors because they should have a similar effect on all competitors.

- Brand loyalty is often seen as the key to future growth and the ability to earn high added value. Therefore it is also a well-chosen objective.

Well-chosen marketing objectives should also meet the SMART criteria. They should be specific, measurable, agreed, realistic and time bound.

- Each objective applies to a specific aspect of the business and one which is relevant to its overall success.

- Although there is no actual mention of the measurement of some of these objectives, the comments and the data in Table 7.3 suggest that there are specific measurable targets for each marketing objective.

- It is not possible to assess whether these marketing objectives have been agreed.

- Overall, the objectives appear to be reasonably challenging, and the fact that some target have been missed, but most targets have been reached, suggests that realistic targets have been set.

- There appear to be targets for each year, and in some cases a target to be reached in the future, such as the smartphone target for 2015.

Evaluation: The specific marketing objectives that Vodafone has set would appear to be a good way of assessing the performance of a marketing department. Some, such as revenue growth and market share, are arguably the key measures of success of the marketing function. Other objectives, such as brand loyalty and integrated contracts, would appear to be measures that are likely to indicate future success. It might be possible to improve on some of these targets, such as giving targets that specify a particular market share percentage and perhaps setting a more ambitious sales growth target. However, reaching these targets would indicate a successful company. Finally, with the information provided, Vodafone appears to be using SMART objectives, although further details on the particular nature of each objective would be necessary to confirm this conclusion.

3 Do you believe that external factors are more likely to influence Vodafone's marketing objectives than internal factors? Justify your view. (20)

External influences vs internal influences:

Vodafone's review of the mobile phone market from 2013 provides an indication of the factors that it believes will implement its performance.

Internal factors:

- High levels of brand loyalty are expected to provide future growth for Vodafone.
- A well-developed infrastructure to support mobile networks around the world is essential to success – these networks are internal factors as they have been built up by the mobile phone companies.
- Vodafone perceives itself as a market leader in a wide range of large countries; this factor should support its future growth.
- Recent internal developments have enabled it to develop 3G and 4G capabilities, to serve the needs of its customers.
- Vodafone's economies of scale make it very competitive in comparison with many of its competitors.

External factors:

- Recent growth has tended to depend on emerging markets, with 90% of the population possessing mobile phones.
- Economic difficulties in Europe and North America have led to problems for Vodafone and other mobile providers.
- Emerging markets tend to be much more price-conscious than developed markets. Vodafone's economies of scale should therefore be a particular benefit in these growing markets.
- Large firms compete fiercely for market share in most markets.
- The mobile phone market is very heavily regulated by national government and restrictive legislation.
- External factors are changing the revenue stream for this market, with a move away from traditional phone calls providing 75% of current income towards internet browsing and email.
- Rapid technological change is a feature of this market.

Evaluation: Vodafone's marketing objectives must reflect the reality of the situation in which they find themselves. There are many significant changes in external factors that will impact upon Vodafone's performance and therefore the objectives it should set for its marketing activities. For example, Vodafone is already setting higher growth targets for emerging markets than for Europe and North America. Similarly, its revenue targets are more ambitious for internet browsing and email revenue than for traditional phone calls. However, internal factors are also vital as marketing objectives must consider factors such as Vodafone's infrastructure, its brand loyalty and its scope for economies of scale. Overall, the marketing objectives must take into consideration both sets of factors, although the pressure for change in the near future would appear to be coming from external factors to a greater extent than internal factors.

8 Understanding markets and customers

Practice exercise 1 (50 marks), page 138

1   What is the difference between market research that has been collected for 'explanatory' reasons and market research that has been gathered for 'predictive' reasons? (6)

- 'Explanatory' research is to help understand why things happen – this type of market research will try to recognise causes, such as the main factors that influence demand.
- 'Predictive' research is used to help forecast future trends, or to discover links between data: for example, to help understand how many additional sales may be created from an advertising campaign.

2   Distinguish between primary market research and secondary market research. (4)

- Primary market research is the collection of information firsthand for a specific purpose.
- Secondary market research is the use of data that have already been collected for a different purpose.

3   Why might secondary market research be carried out before primary market research? (4)

Secondary data are cheaper to collect, so a firm will use secondary research to find out what data are already available before it plans any primary research. Primary market research will then be used to fill the gaps and/or ensure that research is up to date.

4   A music shop analyses the sales figures of a competitor to improve its understanding of its market. This is an example of: (1)

a   qualitative primary market research
b   quantitative primary market research
c   qualitative secondary market research
d   quantitative secondary market research.

The answer is d.

5   Explain one benefit of using personal interviews. (4)

- Consumers may be more likely to answer a questionnaire if asked personally, rather than by telephone or post.

- The interviewer can adapt the questions according to the respondent or the answers given to specific questions, thus increasing the relevance of the answers.
- The interviewer can explain uncertainties to the interviewee, so that all questions are fully understood.
- Personal interviews can provide quick responses if speed of reply is important.
- The location of a personal interview can be linked to the subject of the questionnaire: for example, asking questions outside a shop.

6   Explain one problem of using postal surveys. (4)

- Response rates are usually low (often below 2%), reducing the reliability of the answers.
- People replying are not a random sample – in fact, there is usually a bias as the answers will represent people with strong views or plenty of time to complete a survey.
- For each completed survey received it can be expensive to collect the data, especially if there is a low response rate.
- If a question is ambiguous, the respondent has nobody to help clarify its meaning.

7   State three different sources of secondary market research. (3)

Some of the more significant sources are: government sources (especially the Office for National Statistics in the UK), newspapers, company records, market research organisations, loyalty card records, magazines, publications by competitors, the internet.

8   What is the difference between 'quantitative' and 'qualitative' market research? (4)

- Quantitative market research involves the collection of information that can be expressed in numerical form, such as sales figures.
- Qualitative market research involves the collection of information about subjective factors, such as why people buy a product or their views on an issue.

9 A business operates in a market which includes many well-established competitors that regularly introduce new, innovative products. The business has suffered a significant decline in its sales levels. The marketing director believes that the business should focus on gathering secondary market research in order to improve its understanding of this situation. Do you agree? Justify your view. (20)

Advantages of secondary research are that:
- It is quick to access, helping firms to act rapidly.
- It is cheaper than collecting primary market research because it does not require time-consuming surveys.
- It can be used to show trends over time where the data are collected regularly.

Disadvantages are that:
- Secondary data may be out of date and therefore of limited accuracy.
- Secondary research has open access and so will probably not tell a firm more than its competitors know.
- There is no guarantee that relevant secondary data exist.
- A firm is unlikely to know the level of accuracy of the data.

Context: The business needs to find out why it has suffered a significant decline in its sales levels. Secondary market research should enable it to get a picture of what has been happening in the market, to see if it has been losing sales to competitors or whether the market has been declining. However, the data collected will be based on external sources and so its reliability will not be known. The business's competitors are large and innovative. It may be necessary to conduct primary market research to find out why people are buying products from competitors – is it because they have economies of scale and therefore cheaper prices, or is it because their products are more innovative? This business appears to be in a changing dynamic market and therefore secondary market research, even if it explains why their market has declined, is unlikely to help them to overcome this problem.

Evaluation: The business would need to conduct both primary and secondary research. The secondary research may explain the business's decline, but the primary market research is likely to be more useful in deciding what action to take. In changing markets, secondary market research is likely to date quickly, and successful businesses will be those that have current information on consumer tastes and opinions. On balance, it would appear that the marketing director's priority is mistaken, although it could be that the directive is emphasising secondary market research is the first step, and should be used as a way of helping the business to decide which primary research should then be conducted.

Practice exercise 2 (35 marks), page 139

1 What is meant by the term 'market mapping'? (2)

Market mapping is a technique that analyses markets by looking at the features that distinguish different products or firms.

2 Figure 8.2 (page 137) shows a market map that uses 'price' and 'fashion' to map different firms in the female clothing market.

a Suggest two different ways in which the car market could be mapped. (2)

Price: high–low

Family appeal: large family–single user

b Justify your choices. (6)

When purchasing cars, people are often working within a particular budget, only looking for cars within a certain price range. Therefore cars are often recognised as appealing to those with high or low budgets.

The use of the car can vary considerably, depending on whether it is for family use or just for a single person. A family car would need more capacity and factors such as a large boot space and more safety features. Cars for single users tend to be designed to provide better performance and are smaller in size.

3 Analyse the possible reasons why there is a cluster of firms in a similar place in the top right-hand quadrant of Figure 8.2. (9)

- This segment of the map may be the part that shows the factors that are most likely to appeal to customers in the market. As a consequence, many retailers will gear their product range to consumers in this sector.
- Females tend to place a higher value on fashion than male consumers, so the female clothing market needs more retailers that provide fashion items.
- Demographic change. Over time there has been a growth in single females in their 20s, as people tend to start their families at a later age. This is an important sector of the female

fashion market who can afford premium prices and are fashion conscious.

- The costs of production of the textile industry are likely to be closely related to the extent to which a garment is fashionable. Fashionable items may require more features, which will add costs. They may also require more individual, tailored manufacture which will increase unit costs.

- High-price, fashionable clothes are likely to be the most profitable area of the market, encouraging businesses to target that segment.

4 Information in Figure 8.2 suggests a gap in the market for functional clothing that is in the middle range of the price levels. Evaluate the advantages and disadvantages of setting up a business that fills this gap.   (16)

Arguments for:

- There is a clear gap in the market, so customers wanting functional clothing that is set in the middle range of the price levels are not having their needs met by existing retailers.

- The lack of firms on this part of the map suggests that a retailer might also attract a wider range of consumers – there are only two close competitors Marks & Spencer and BHS, and neither of these stores are in the mid-price range. The business may also appeal to consumers who also want functional clothes at budget

prices, but who do not wish to buy clothes that are as cheap as those sold at George at Asda.

- Functional clothing is less risky than fashion clothing and there should be reasonable scope for profit from a mid-range price.

Arguments against:

- The gap may show that there are few, if any, customers interested in this type of product. There are 19 companies identified on the map – why are there no shops targeting these consumers already?

- People buying functional clothing may have specific wants – either a high-quality, durable product or one that is very cheap and therefore easy to replace. These requirements are fully met by the existing retailers.

- The concentration of firms on the fashion side of the grid indicates that, despite the pressures of competition, there is a greater chance of success in the fashion side of the market.

Evaluation: The overall conclusion should be based on the strengths of the arguments presented. But also, firms such as Marks & Spencer and BHS are currently less successful than Next and Topshop. This implies that this sector should be ignored. The firms closest to this sector tend to target older customers. This probably confirms its lack of suitability to most consumers (but could suggest that there is a gap for a retailer which targets younger consumers).

Practice exercise 3 (65 marks), pages 149–50

1 State three possible sources for the data in Table 8.4.   (3)

Possible sources of data include: government statistics (ONS); surveys; newspaper articles; magazines related to tourism; internet surveys; government departments (e.g. Culture, Media and Sport). (There are many other possible sources.)

2 Explain one way in which technology might be used to analyse the data in Table 8.3.   (5)

- Data analysis software would enable this data to be analysed in order to estimate factors such as the likelihood of a certain percentage of people being influenced by a given factor, such as location, or quality.

- Comparison with the coffee shop's own database might enable it to analyse how the factors that affect its popularity compare to the national factors shown in Table 8.3. This analysis might enable it to detect its strengths and weaknesses.

3 Based on Table 8.3, are the following statements true or false:

a We can be 95% certain that between 30.43% and 31.57% of customers rate quality as the most important factor.   (1)

TRUE (if based on a survey of 25,000 people, but not if the sample was 2,500 people)

b We can be 95% certain that location is the most important factor influencing choice of coffee shop.   (1)

TRUE

c We can be 95% certain that fewer than 21% of coffee shop users value the atmosphere most when choosing a coffee shop.   (1)

FALSE

d If these figures had been acquired from a survey of 2,500 people, we could be 95% certain that more than 30% of coffee shop users believe that quality is the most important factor.   (1)

FALSE (it would be true if 25,000 had been surveyed).

4 Explain how a coffee shop might use the data in Table 8.3 to increase its market share. (6)

Regardless of whether 25,000 people or 2,500 people were surveyed, the statistics in the table clearly indicate that there is more than a 95% chance that location is the most important factor when choosing a coffee shop. It also indicates that quality is a very important factor, while atmosphere is the third most important factor. If a coffee shop can provide a good location, quality and atmosphere then it will meet the needs of 97% of coffee shop users. It also informs the coffee shop owner that price or loyalty cards have very little impact on customer choices.

5 Identify two factors that would reduce the confidence interval (margin of error) of a survey. (2)

A larger sample size; a smaller population size; the percentage of the sample choosing a particular answer being very high OR very low.

6 Select one of the factors you have chosen in question 5 and explain why that factor would reduce the confidence interval. (4)

A larger sample size is the most important factor. Any sample may contain individuals with responses that are not those normally given by the type of person being sampled. In a small sample these may distort the overall figures. In a large sample these individuals will have less of an impact on the 'average' opinions being expressed, and so the survey is more likely to give a true picture of the opinions being requested.

7 Study Table 8.4. Based on the data in columns 1 and 3, use extrapolation to calculate the annual increase in domestic holiday visits in the UK. Show your working. (3)

Annual increase is (44.9m – 40.4m)/ 7 years = 4.5m/7 = 0.64m per year.

Accept 0.6 million or 640,000 or 600,000.

8 Use your answer in question 7 to forecast the level of domestic holiday visits in the UK for:

a 2014 (2)
Domestic visits = 2013 figure + annual increase = 44.9 +0.64 = 45.54 million visitors (or 44.9 + 0.6 = 45.5 million)

b 2017 (2)
Domestic visits = 2013 figure + four annual increases = 44.9 + (4 x 0.64) = 44.9 + 2.56 = 47.46 or 47.5 million.
Accept 44.9 + (4 x 0.6) = 44.9 + 2.4 = 47.3 million
Also accept 45.54 million visitors (or 44.9 + 0.6 = 45.5 million)

9 Use your answer in question 7 to answer the following question: In which year are domestic holiday visits in the UK expected to exceed 49.0 million? Show your working. (4)

2013 = 44.9m
Annual increase = 0.64m
Target increase = 49– 44.9 = 4.1m
4.1m/0.64 m = 6.4 years

Therefore after seven years the target will be surpassed.
2013 + 7 = 2020

Based on 0.6m per year growth, calculation is 4.1m/0.6m = 6.8 years. Therefore after seven years the target to be surpassed (2020).

10 Using Figure 8.7, use extrapolation to forecast the level of domestic holiday visits in the UK for:

a 2014 (1)
b 2017 (1)

Extrapolation depends on the trend selected and how the eye interprets the trend in a diagram. There is usually a calculated line of best fit, which can be added to the diagram – Method (i). Alternatively, it can be based on the growth from the first year (40.4) to the last year (44.9) – Method (ii).It may also be based on the most recent trend, such as since numbers started to fall in 2011 – Method (iii) or the last year – Method (iv). Four possible answers are provided for this question, depending on which of the above methods was employed. However, future predictions must be consistent and so for Question 10b the only acceptable answer is the one based on the method chosen in response to Question 10a. The four possible pairs of responses are:

Method (i): 10a = 47.4 million   10b = 49.9 million

Method (ii): 10a = 45.5 million   10b = 47.4 million (approx.)

Method (iii): 10a = 44.5 million   10b = 42.3 million

Method (iv): 10a = 44.0 million   10b = 41.0 million

11 Use Figure 8.7 to answer the following question: In which year are domestic holiday visits in the UK expected to exceed 50.0 million? Explain your answer. (3)

This answer will depend on the answers to Question 10.

Method (i): 2018 (increase is 1.0m per annum)

Method (ii): 2020 (increase is 0.6m per annum)

12 Examine Figure 8.8.

    a Does it show positive or negative correlation?   (1)

Negative correlation.

    b Does it show high or low correlation?   (1)

Low correlation.

13 Use Figure 8.8 to forecast the number of domestic holiday visits in the UK, if the GDP index number reaches 250.   (1)

Reading from the line of best fit in Figure 8.8, the point vertically above a UK GDP index of 250 gives 43.6 million visitors.

14 Explain one reason why higher GDP appears to lead to a fall in domestic holiday visits in the UK.   (6)

One possible reason is the nature of UK holidays. People will tend to holiday in the UK because they cannot afford a holiday to a more exotic destination or one that can provide a better guarantee of sunshine than the UK. For this reason, UK holidays are often seen as an 'inferior good' by UK residents. For inferior goods, the quantity demanded will fall as GDP and thus people's incomes increase.

15 Having studied Figures 8.7 and 8.8, a market research manager believes that the business should use extrapolation rather than correlation in order to forecast future levels of domestic holiday visits in the UK. Based solely on the data in Figures 8.7 and 8.8, do you agree with his view? Justify your choice.   (16)

Relevant arguments:
- Extrapolation is ideal when there is a consistent trend over time. Figure 8.7 shows UK domestic tourism visits between 2006 and 2013. The line on the graph suggests that there is no clear trend. Although sales have increased over this time, sales peaked in 2009 and have actually fallen, then risen and then fallen since. Between 2006 and 2012, there was not a single instance in which the trend from the previous year was maintained. In both 2012 and 2013, there was a decline, but this is not sufficient evidence to suggest that the decline is likely to continue in the long-term.
- The magnitude of the changes also shows inconsistency. There was a big increase in demand in 2009 and then a fairly significant fall in 2010. However, in most of the other years the changes have been fairly small.
- The difficulty in achieving precise answers to questions 10 and 11 confirms the difficulty in using extrapolation with this data. The answer to Question 10a shows four valid approaches to

extrapolation for this data. For 2014 (the next year) the predictions vary from 44 million to 47.4 million. The predictions for 2017 vary from 41 million to 49.9 million.

- Correlation and regression analysis are ideal if there is a very strong correlation between a particular independent variable and the dependent variable. In Figure 8.8, UK GDP is the independent variable and domestic holidays is the dependent variable. The regression line (the red line in Figure 8.8) shows the predicted level of demand for domestic holidays based on different values of UK GDP.
- This method gives a clear prediction – for example, if the UK GDP index reaches 280 then domestic holiday visits will be just below 43 million. Similar predictions can be made for all other levels of GDP. In question 14 it was suggested that a domestic holiday is an inferior good and so this regression is based on sound logical reasoning.
- However, the blue dots on this scatter graph represent the actual data shown in Table 8.4. A close scrutiny of this data shows that the correlation between GDP and domestic holidays is very weak, because the points are scattered very widely around the diagram. Predictions would be much more reliable if the blue points were close to the red line. (Although it is not shown in the data, the correlation coefficient for this scatter graph is –0.15, suggesting that there is a very weak link between the two sets of data.)

Evaluation: In conclusion, both methods are providing unreliable forecasts. There is no clear pattern of sales over time and so extrapolation is not likely to provide an accurate figure. However, it could be used to provide a rough estimate so that the prediction is not based solely on hunch. The weak correlation between GDP and domestic holidays means that this should not be used either.

It would be advisable for the market research manager to investigate other factors that might influence tourism. The data may be of limited use to a specific company as the data apply to UK domestic tourism as a whole. The market research manager should search for specific factors that might have a strong correlation to the sales level of the company (visitors to the hotel or sales levels of the particular tourist attraction). Investigation of factors such as price and marketing spending may provide data which shows high correlation and can be used to predict sales.

Practice exercise 4 (50 marks), pages 158–9

1   An inferior good has a: (1)
    a   negative price elasticity of demand
    b   positive price elasticity of demand
    c   negative income elasticity of demand
    d   positive income elasticity of demand.

    The answer is c.

2   Which of these changes would lead to an increase
    in sales revenue for a product?   (1)
    a   An increase in price for a good that has price
        elastic demand.
    b   A decrease in price for a good that has price
        inelastic demand.
    c   An increase in consumer incomes for a product
        with negative income elasticity of demand.
    d   An increase in price for a good that has price
        inelastic demand.

    The answer is d.

3   In which two situations below will sales revenue
    stay the same? (You must choose two of the
    seven options.)   (2)
    a   Price rises by 10%; price elasticity of demand
        is −10
    b   Price rises by 2.5%; price elasticity of demand
        is −1.0
    c   Price rises by 5%; price elasticity of demand
        is −0.5
    d   Price rises by 7.5%; price elasticity of demand is 0
    e   Incomes rise by 10%; income elasticity of demand
        is −1.0
    f   Incomes rise by 5%; income elasticity of demand
        is +0.5
    g   Incomes rise by 2.5%; income elasticity of
        demand is 0.

    The answers are b and g.

4   What is meant by the term 'price elasticity
    of demand'?   (2)

    Price elasticity of demand is a measure of the
    responsiveness of the quantity demanded of a
    product to a change in price. It is calculated by
    the formula:
    price elasticity of demand = % change in quantity
    demanded/% change in price

5   State whether each of the following factors will
    make demand price elastic or price inelastic: (6)
    a   It is habit-forming.

    inelastic

    b   There are many substitutes.

    elastic

    c   It is aimed at a wealthy market segment.

    inelastic

    d   Advertising has created brand loyalty.

    inelastic

    e   The product is a necessity.

    inelastic

    f   It takes up a very small percentage of consumers'
        incomes.

    inelastic

6   Average incomes rise from £20,000 to £21,000 per
    annum. Sales of playing cards fall from 4 million
    to 3.9 million per annum. Calculate the income
    elasticity of demand.   (3)

    % change in quantity demanded = 3.9 − 4.0/4.0 × 100
    = −0.1/4.0 × 100 = −2.5%
    % change in price = 21 − 20/20 × 100 = 1/20 × 100 = 5%
    % change in quantity demanded/% change in
    income = −2.5/5.0% = (−)0.5
    NB It is quite usual to ignore the negative sign
    for price elasticity of demand.

7   Complete the sentence which follows. If demand
    changes by a greater percentage than the percentage
    change in price, the price elasticity of demand is
    said to be ....   (1)

    elastic

8   How should a business market a product that
    has price-inelastic demand and a high income
    elasticity of demand?   (9)

    Price-inelastic demand means that an increase
    in price will lead to a smaller percentage change
    in demand. Thus total revenue will increase if
    price rises. Therefore, a price skimming or high-
    price strategy should be used. With a slight fall
    in quantity demanded, the business may also
    benefit from a cut in its costs. (The price can be
    increased to the point at which demand stops
    being inelastic: in practice, a product would not
    have the same price elasticity at every price.)

    A high income elasticity of demand means that
    increases in consumers' incomes will lead to a
    larger percentage change in demand. Therefore,
    the product is likely to appeal to people on high
    incomes. It should be advertised as a luxury
    and sold at high prices in up-market stores to
    encourage consumers to perceive it as a luxury.

9   Analyse how a firm might increase the income
    elasticity of demand of one of its products.   (9)

    This question is best answered by examining the
    factors that influence income elasticity of demand
    and assessing how a business can influence them:
    •   Luxury. By focusing on production of a high
        quality good, a firm can help to make its
        demand more income elastic. Most mass

market products, such as clothing and food, have niche market elements which are focused on the wants of consumers on high incomes.

- Unique selling point. If a firm develops a unique selling point for its product, such as Apple's reputation for good design, it will create a USP. This will restrict customers' choices and should enable the business to sell at high prices to the consumers who place a high value on this feature.
- Brand loyalty. The marketing mix, especially product and promotion, can be used to influence income elasticity of demand. The more loyal consumers are to a brand, the more income elastic the demand will tend to be because it will appeal to consumers who can afford to buy it at any price.
- Income of consumers. By targeting affluent purchasers, who will generally be less worried about price rises, a firm can help to increase its sales revenue by adding features that appeal to people who want a status symbol.

Although some factors such as luxury can be hard to achieve, it is possible for firms to increase the income elasticity of demand of their products by making them more suited to the needs of the richer consumers, habit forming and by reducing the availability of close substitutes by adding unique features. However, the most realistic and manageable way of influencing elasticity is through marketing. In addition to trying to encourage consumers to buy more, a great deal of marketing is aimed at increasing brand loyalty in a way that makes consumers perceive the product to be more luxurious. Very often luxury branded products, such as perfumes, achieve their status through promotions rather than the product itself, although ideally a product with high income elasticity will be a high quality product supported by good advertising.

10 Discuss the reasons why it would be more difficult for a computer manufacturer to use elasticity of demand than it would for a company marketing pencils. (16)

Possible reasons are:

- Pencils are a fairly standard product with far fewer different features than computers, so evidence from past data or surveys about the elasticity of demand is more likely to be relevant to the pencil than to a specific computer, of which there are many kinds.
- A pencil is an easily understood product, but consumers may be thinking of different types of computer when questioned about that market. In surveys, consumers are therefore more likely to provide accurate and useful answers for the pencil manufacturer.
- The market for computers is much more dynamic. In any market that is constantly changing, it becomes more difficult to use information to predict elasticity of demand. New competitors, changes in consumer tastes and technological change (particularly the latter) will change perceptions of a product. Brand loyalty in the computer market will be lost if the product does not change rapidly with new technological developments.
- Price changes in the computer market are more likely to provoke a reaction from competitors than price changes in the pencil market, as price is probably a more significant factor in the computer market. Pencil prices are not a significant factor in overall expenditure for a consumer, so previous buying patterns tend to remain.

Evaluation: Fundamentally, change is the key difference between these two markets. The stability of the pencil market means that data on consumer buying (such as consumers' reactions to price changes) will be more constant and reliable. The continual evolution of the computer market creates uncertainty and makes any data on consumer reactions to price changes (and income changes) much harder to assess.

Case study: Non-store retailing (65 marks), pages 160–1

1 Using Figure 8.9, forecast the level of non-store sales for the following months:

a May 2015 (1)

Using the linear trend line, sales in May 2015 should be £500 million.

b January 2017 (1)

Using the linear trend line, sales in January 2017 should be £580 million.

(Answers to Questions 1 and 2 will be higher if a non-linear trend or trend based on the last two years is used.)

2 Explain why your forecasts in question 1 may be unreliable. (5)

The forecasts in question 1 may be unreliable because the trend may not be a linear trend, as shown by the black trend line. The figures tend to be curving upwards, suggesting a non-linear (curved) trend. Alternatively, the figures could be interpreted as a series of data in which the trend has shifted. The actual sales figures are fairly consistent in relation to the trend line until 2012, since when the rate of growth appears to have shifted upwards. Therefore, even if a linear trend line is used for forecasting it might be better to base it on the last few years, rather than a six-year time period.

3 Use Figure 8.10(a) to forecast the likely level of sales if the average monthly temperature is:

a 10° Celsius (1)

£440 million (accept 438 to 442)

b 20° Celsius (1)

£426 million (accept 422 to 430)

4 Is your prediction in question 3(a) likely to be more or less reliable than your prediction in question 3(b)? Justify your answer. (4)

The prediction in question 3a is likely to be more reliable because it is based on a temperature that is within the normal range of temperatures. The data is based on temperatures between 2°C and 17°C, with 10°C being close to the average. Therefore, any attempt to predict sales when temperatures go beyond this range (such as 20°C) are less reliable because there is no data to suggest what happens at this temperature.

(2 mark maximum for an argument that just refers to the red lines not extending to 20°C.)

5 Use Figure 8.10(b) to forecast the likely level of sales if the average monthly level of unemployment is 2 million. (1)

£540 million (accept 535 to 545)

6 Correlation is used to try to confirm causal links between two variables. Explain:

a how and why the monthly temperature might affect non-store sales levels (5)

Sales of retail outlets are affected by temperatures, with low temperatures discouraging people from visiting shops. To a lesser extent, very high temperatures have the same impact. Online retailing, in its own right, is not directly affected by temperature. However, as it is a direct competitor to retail outlets then low temperatures will encourage more people to shop online. Similarly, very high temperatures might also encourage online shopping. High temperatures may also take people 'out of the house' and therefore less likely to use online shopping, although the growing use of mobile shopping will reduce the significance of this last factor, in future years.

b how and why the level of unemployment might affect non-store sales levels. (5)

Unemployment tends to reduce people's spending power and so will lead to a decline in all forms of retailing, including non-store

sales. It could be argued that shopping online is cheaper than visiting stores, and online retailing can make it easier to compare prices. Someone who is unemployed is more likely to wish to compare prices and so unemployment is likely to increase online retailing in comparison to sales of retail shops (although both are likely to decline).

7 Based on Figures 8.10(a) and 8.10(b) and your answers to questions 6(a) and 6(b), do you believe that the weather has a greater impact on non-store sales than the level of unemployment? Justify your view. (16)

In Question 6 there appears to be sound logical reasoning to suggest why non-store sales will fall as the temperature falls, although there may be a slight fall if temperatures get very high also. There also seems to be strong logic to suggest that unemployment will have a strong impact on sales in the economy as a whole and therefore on non-store sales. Most products are bought on a regular basis, and in the UK, weather conditions do not normally make it impossible to reach shops. Therefore, it is likely that any impact that the weather has is fairly insignificant. Furthermore, online retailing may be affected by the weather because deliveries cannot be made, and therefore online sales are likely to be affected on a daily basis, rather than the average temperature for a whole month. However, unemployment reduces people's incomes and this is arguably one of the two most significant factors influencing demand (along with price).

Figure 8.10a has a (red) regression line that shows a slight decline in non-store retailers as the temperature increases. The blue points in this diagram represent the actual data, and these points are scattered quite widely around the regression line. This suggests that there is a very low level of correlation between the temperature and non-store retail sales.

Figure 8.10b has a (red) regression line that shows a more significant decline in non-store retailers as unemployment increases. The blue points in this diagram represent the actual data and these points are scattered reasonably around the regression line, but are much closer to the regression line than the points in Figure 8.10a. This suggests that there is a higher level of correlation between unemployment and non-store retail sales, although it is not a relationship which would enable one to predict non-store retail sales from unemployment data with any certainty.

Evaluation: There is strong evidence from Figures 8.10a and 8.10b that the weather does not have a greater impact on non-store sales than unemployment. The regression line in Figure 8.10b has a steeper slope, indicating that rises in unemployment have a more significant impact on sales than changes in temperature. Significantly, there is also a much closer statistical relationship so that predictions of non-store sales based on unemployment data are likely to be much more accurate than predictions based on temperature. Finally, there appears to be much a much stronger logic to support the view that unemployment affects non-store sales, when compared to the impact of temperature on sales.

8 Analyse why online selling is likely to lead to products becoming more price elastic in demand. (9)

There are two main reasons:

- Online selling encourages more competition, because the start-up costs of a business are much lower. City centre rents are very high and shops must ensure that they have high levels of inventory to attract customers. Online retailers merely need to display products on a website and can often get them delivered directly from the manufacturer to the consumer, so that there is either no need for storage facilities or a minimal need. These factors enable more businesses to enter markets, and with high levels of competition there is more choice for customers. More possible substitutes leads to demand becoming more price elastic.
- Online selling enables customers to compare prices without incurring the time and expense taken to compare prices in different shops. This gives better information for customers who can more quickly identify the lowest priced products. Consumers are more likely to be influenced by price if they know all the different prices charged by different suppliers.

9 Why are both income inelastic and income elastic products likely to be purchased online? Justify your view. (16)

For income inelastic products, which are likely to be basic, everyday products such as food and cleaning products:

- These markets are likely to be very competitive and so the opportunity to compare prices online will attract large numbers of buyers.
- Products with income inelastic demand are often well-known, core products. These products do not need to be seen or touched within a retail store, because consumers will already have all the information they need to decide on whether they are suitable. This means there is little risk of receiving an unsuitable product when purchasing online.
- People on low incomes will often buy these basic products. These consumers may be more likely to use the internet as it avoids unnecessary expenses, such as transport or car parking.

For income elastic products, which are likely to be luxuries:

- Expensive, individualised products are often made on a small scale. Thus, the manufacturers of these products will often prefer to sell them online.
- Manufacturers may also be certain that they can sell these products, and therefore would not want a retailer to take a percentage of the profits. Therefore, they may sell the products directly from their own website.
- Some consumers buying luxuries will be 'cash rich but time poor'. For these customers there may be insufficient time to visit retail outlets and so they will buy their products online.

Evaluation: It can be seen that both income inelastic and income elastic products are likely to be purchased online. For luxury (income elastic) products the convenience and time factor is likely to be the main influence, because this is the choice of the consumer rather than the manufacturer. Additional expenses, such as returns of unwanted products, are also likely to be more easily managed by the business if there is a higher profit margin. Because lower value orders tend to be charged delivery expenses by internet suppliers, the cost advantage of buying online essential products may well be negated by the delivery charges. Therefore, there may be less purchasing online of income inelastic products in comparison to those with income elastic demand.

9 Making marketing decisions: segmentation, targeting, positioning

Practice exercise 1 (60 marks), page 173

1 Which one of the following approaches to market segmentation is demographic? (1)
   a Regular users
   b Social class
   c Urban users
   d Gender.

   The answer is d .

2 A business decides to focus its marketing on a certain group of consumers. This is known as: (1)
   a market positioning
   b market segmentation
   c market targeting.

   The answer is c.

3 Market positioning, market segmentation and market targeting are three activities undertaken in marketing planning. In which order would a business organise these three elements of its marketing decision making? (2)

   Market segmentation – market targeting – market positioning.

4 Explain the meaning of 'product differentiation'. (3)

   Product differentiation is the extent to which consumers perceive one brand to be distinctive in comparison to alternative products.

5 Explain one reason why social class is a useful approach to market segmentation. (6)

   Social class and family income are closely linked. Although tastes vary among individuals, income is probably the main factor influencing the products that consumers buy. High income earners will buy more luxuries, such as expensive cars, exotic holidays, restaurant meals and upmarket housing. Those on lower incomes will tend to spend relatively more money on economy food items and public transport, and will use television as a form of entertainment rather than live concerts, for example.

   Social class may also affect tastes, regardless of income. Sporting interests (e.g. lacrosse or darts) and choices of entertainment (e.g. theatre or cinema) can be influenced by social class.

6 Analyse why 'behavioural segmentation' is growing in popularity. (9)
   • Behavioural segmentation is becoming more popular because firms have better databases. This enables them to register factors such as the customer's level of usage and frequency of purchase. Consequently, firms can target their marketing and special offers at customers who they know will be regular purchasers of the product.
   • Lifestyle is an important part of behavioural segmentation. Many lifestyles are closely linked to the types of purchases made by consumers. Therefore, improvements in knowledge of people's behaviour enable businesses to have a greater understanding of their customers.
   • Many types of segmentation, such as age, are based on very broad factors. Consequently, the behaviour of individual consumers may vary considerably within this segmentation. Behavioural segmentation is much more closely related to the character of the person and therefore may enable much more exact targeting of customers.

7 State two examples of niche markets. (2)

   Possible answers are: sports car manufacturing; producing ethnic food or clothing; folk music; fair trade products; providing for the caravan holiday industry.

8 Why might a magazine publisher target a niche market? (5)

People have specific interests and it may therefore be easy to identify a potential market segment with a particular interest. Although the size of the market may be small, brand loyalty may be high if the magazine is the only one providing for that market. With a 'monopoly', the magazine can charge a high price if consumers want the magazine sufficiently. The small market may also mean that competitors are not interested in publishing a rival magazine. Additionally, a specialist magazine may find it easy to attract advertisers, who see the magazine as the best place to advertise products that relate to this specialist market.

9 Explain two benefits of mass marketing. (6)

- Large-scale production will lead to lower costs, enabling a firm to lower its price and gain more sales or benefit from a higher profit margin.
- Advertising and promotion reach the target customers, as the most popular media can be used.
- The firm will normally be able to afford more detailed market research, helping it to improve its understanding of the market.
- The company name becomes more widely recognised. This increases brand loyalty and will help the firm to introduce new products.
- In some industries there are huge costs, such as for research and development and capital equipment. A mass market gives the firm a greater chance of recouping this expenditure.

10 Explain three factors that might form the basis of market positioning. (9)

Market positioning is where a product or brand stands in relation to the products or brands of other businesses. Some factors influencing market positioning are:

- **Characteristics of the product**. Factors such as the quality of the product will help the business differentiate itself from competitors and so this may determine the brand's position (e.g. high-quality and expensive) within the market.
- **Competition**. If the level of competition is strong then a business may want to position itself away from positions held by competitors' products. However, the presence of competition may indicate the most lucrative positions within the market and so a firm may decide to position itself directly against competition, especially if it believes that it has the superior product.
- **Product users**. The business will conduct market research into its target market. Knowledge of its target market segment(s) will influence its market positioning as the product users may want to benefit from their association with the product, for example, by gaining a reputation for being stylish or innovative.
- **Pricing**. Whether the business uses a low-price or high-price strategy will determine its position in the market.

11 Is it inevitable that businesses in a niche market will be unable to break into a mass market? Justify your view. (16)

- Demand in a niche market is limited, so the business may not be able to produce on a large scale. Small-scale production means higher costs and prices, making it difficult to compete on price with mass-market producers.
- Niche firms will gain a reputation for their particular area of the market, but the firm may lack the skills (and customers may not have confidence in their ability) to produce mass-market products.
- Markets are constantly changing, and this year's niche may be next year's mass market. In these circumstances, businesses with experience of the niche market will be ideally placed to take advantage of the growth of the market.
- Firms that provide for customer needs will gain a good reputation. Thus a successful firm in a niche market will have loyal customers and should be able to raise extra capital easily in order to move into a mass market.

Evaluation: Ultimately this should not be seen as inevitable, but will depend on factors such as the rate of change in the market, the nature of the product, the reputation of the firm and the actions of competitors. (Words such as 'inevitable' are very definite and should be used in the evaluation. It is rare for something to be inevitable, so the conclusion should lean towards it NOT being inevitable, in nearly all cases.)

Case study: Lush Cosmetics (65 marks), pages 174–5

1 What is meant by the term 'target market'? (2)

A target market is the consumers or market segment(s) to whom a business intends to sell its product

2 State two examples of behavioural segmentation indicated in the article. (2)

- People who want unusual and varied cosmetics.

- People who want freshly made cosmetics.
- People who like 'quirky' advertising and promotions.
- People who appreciate good customer service.
- People who are concerned about environmental and sustainability issues.
- Regular users.

3 Analyse two reasons why Lush introduces new products every three months. (9)

- It aims to encourage consumers to keep visiting the stores – there will always be new products to arouse their interest.
- As products are made from fresh ingredients, stock turnover is very high and therefore it is easy to adjust the range constantly.
- Consumers pay high prices for Lush products, so they will want uniqueness to justify these high prices.
- As indicated in the article, Lush changes products according to demand, using market research to discover changes in consumer preferences.

4 Analyse two reasons why Lush might have decided to open its own shops when it re-launched the business in 1994. (9)

- The Body Shop would have used other suppliers in the meantime and may have preferred to continue with them, especially as Lush had not kept up its supplies during its previous existence. Owning its own shops was a guaranteed way of gaining access to customers.
- Owning the shops allows Lush to take all of the profit from its products, rather than sharing it with distributors and retailers.
- Shops have direct contact with customers, so Lush can obtain better information on consumer wants and preferences, and get more up-to-date comments on its products.
- Owning the shops means that Lush has more control of the presenting and selling of its products to the public.

5 Analyse how Lush's market positioning allows it to achieve differentiation from its competitors. (9)

Lush's positioning features factors such as regularly changing stocks; fresh products; excellent customer service; high prices; emphasis on selling in shops where consumers can experience the products; targeting well-educated, middle-class females in urban areas. These factors allow differentiation because:

- most competitors target the mass market
- its smaller competitors do not tend to have their own outlets, but rely on independent shops to stock their products

- its products appeal to consumers who are concerned about the environment and related matters
- customers can experience the products in-store, whereas soaps from competitors are unlikely to be experienced until after the packaging has been opened at home
- its products are hard to get elsewhere, as they are unique to Lush.

6 Analyse the possible difficulties faced by Lush as a result of its decision to produce a range of 200 different products. (9)

- Market research would need constant updating, as the products are changing at frequent intervals.
- Marketing becomes difficult, as the nature of the products varies all of the time.
- Production planning is difficult, and because mass production is not possible, unit costs are high.
- Stock control and quality control are difficult with 200 different products.
- Consumers may become confused by the breadth of the range and Lush may lose goodwill if it removes products that were the favourite choices of its customers.

7 Analyse the benefits for Lush from operating in a niche market. (9)

- Lush has few direct competitors. There are a large number of companies providing cosmetics, but Lush is unique. The lack of competition enables Lush to charge a much higher price for its products. Selling relatively few products at high profit margins should enable Lush to achieve good profits.
- Lush can quickly adapt its products to meet the specific needs of the niche market, rather than compromise between the needs of many different groups of consumers. Tailor-made products, designed to meet the specific needs of a customer, are quite common. Lush produces over 200 products and updates its range every three months. This creates excitement and gives Lush a unique selling point, enabling it to charge high prices.
- Lush can target customers and promote its products effectively because it is only selling to a certain type of customer. The content of advertisements can be designed to appeal to the specific market segment being targeted. Furthermore, the media used can be selected according to which media are favoured by the market segment. Lush is largely targeting young women who are prepared to pay high prices for their cosmetics and who want environmentally friendly products.

8 Lush uses market segmentation in its planning. Evaluate the usefulness of market segmentation in enabling Lush to make large profits. (16)

- Lush has identified market segments with above average incomes, and so its specific market segmentation is enabling it to earn high added value.
- Its market segmentation has also enabled it to find a niche market in which there is no close competitor; again, not only has this guaranteed good sales but also enabled them to charge higher prices.
- The factors that their market segments value, such as fresh and innovative products, have assisted Lush in their marketing decision-making. This has increased the effectiveness of their marketing and thus boosted profit. It is also able to target its market segments through understanding the type of media that they would use.
- Lush's new product ideas have arisen because of its understanding of its market segments. Its products are targeted towards its mainly young, female market.

BUT

It could be argued that by focusing on its market segments, Lush may be ignoring a large percentage of the population (such as males). Therefore this is likely to restrict their appeal in comparison to competitors such as Boots. Because Lush has chosen to target a market segment that likes change, it may be forcing itself to change its product range frequently – an approach that can be costly, especially if the new products launched are not popular.

Evaluation: Lush's niche market segments gives it a loyal customer base that purchases regularly and that is prepared to pay high prices for products with high added value. The profit that results from such a situation enables Lush to reinvest in new, innovative products, further reinforcing its popularity. The main drawback is the need to constantly reinvent itself, but Lush regularly replaces unpopular products and so this issue is not likely to be a long-term problem. Even during the recession, Lush remained profitable.

10 Making marketing decisions: using the marketing mix

Practice exercise 1 (60 marks), page 196

1 Goods that are purchased and consumed regularly by a lot of customers and tend to be sold at low prices are: (1)
   a convenience goods
   b industrial goods
   c shopping goods
   d speciality goods.

   The answer is a.

2 Designer clothing is most likely to be a: (1)
   a convenience good
   b industrial good
   c shopping good
   d speciality good.

   The answer is d.

3 Analyse possible reasons why 70% of all new products fail within three years. (9)
   • Insufficient or inaccurate market research can lead to an unsuccessful product launch due to lack of demand.
   • Tastes may change after the launch, leading to lower sales than anticipated.
   • Competitors may introduce a new product that reduces the sales of the product in question.
   • Consumer loyalty to existing products will make it difficult for new products to penetrate the market.
   • The small scale of output of a new product will make it relatively expensive to produce and may put pressure on the firm's cash flow, limiting the financial support that can be given to the new product.

4 In the Boston Matrix, what is the difference between a 'star' and a 'dog'? (4)
   • A star is a product with a high market share in a market with a high rate of growth.
   • A dog is a product with a low market share in a market with a low rate of growth.

5 Why are some products in the Boston Matrix called 'cash cows'? (3)

Products with a high market share in a low-growth market can be 'milked' for the high levels of cash that they earn for the business. Firms will not want to compete with an established cash cow, as the low market growth means that they can only increase sales at the expense of the cash cow (usually a very popular product).

6 State one example of a product's USP. (1)

A USP could be a distinctive feature, such as the hole in a Polo mint.

7 Explain how a firm's marketing mix might have helped to create this USP. (6)

There are many ways of using the marketing mix to achieve a USP:
   • making a product that is different from rival products, such as a different clothing design (e.g. Burberry)
   • using brand names and promotions that distinguish one product from close competitors (e.g. Panasonic)
   • creating advertising images to attract people who wish to relate to that image (e.g. Ferrero Rocher)
   • making modifications to the brand (e.g. decaffeinated coffee or diet cola) to attract specific segments of the market
   • using packaging to enhance the perceived quality of the product (e.g. Ferrero Rocher)
   • a seller providing a good service (e.g. an attractive environment may encourage shoppers to a shop)
   • associating the product with a well-known name (e.g. Pepsi-Cola and famous stars)
   • using an established and popular brand name (e.g. putting the Ferrari name on items of clothing)
   • introducing an individually tailored service (e.g. a holiday itinerary to suit the needs of the individual).

8 Explain two advantages for a firm that decides to focus on its core business. (6)

- Specialisation allows the firm to concentrate on its strengths.
- The firm will know its market better if it concentrates on a limited area.
- Focusing on a core area leads to higher production levels and therefore lower costs.
- Managers can more easily control a business with a narrow focus.
- Consumers may trust a firm more if it focuses on a few products.

9 Explain one benefit of product proliferation. (4)

- It spreads risks, in case a particular product or market declines.
- It allows the firm to appeal to different market segments with different products.
- There may be more scope to increase sales in a different market than in the existing market.
- A firm will be able to deal with changes in customer tastes more easily.

10 Identify the four stages of the product life cycle that follow the launch date of a new product. (4)

Introduction, growth, maturity, decline.

11 Identify the most profitable stage of the product life cycle. (1)

Maturity.

12 Why might a business not want all of its products at this stage of the product life cycle? (5)

Although this is the most profitable stage in the short run, a company must look ahead. After maturity comes decline, and a firm must avoid a situation where all of its products are in decline. Therefore, at any point in time it should be developing some new products, have some products recently launched and have some currently in their growth stage. This provides a more secure future, as it means there will always be some profitable products in maturity, supporting the other products.

13 Identify three extension strategies and give a real-life example of each one. (6)

Possible answers are:

- attracting a new market segment (e.g. Topshop adding Topman shops)
- increasing usage among existing customers (e.g. encouraging computer buyers to use their PCs for games, office work, music, films and photography)
- modifying the product (e.g. iPhones introducing additional features and extra capacity)

- changing the image (e.g. Skoda concentrating on quality rather than price as its main selling point)
- targeting new markets (e.g. Aldi and Lidl introducing more expensive products to target customers with higher incomes)
- promotions and offers (e.g. Specsavers offering '2 for the price of 1' to boost interest in its spectacles).

14 Analyse two factors that might influence a product's marketing mix. (9)

- Cash flow. If a business is suffering from cash-flow problems, it may need to reduce spending on items such as promotion, as this can lead to significant expenditure before any revenue is received. Similarly, difficulties in cash flow may encourage a business to cut its prices dramatically, in order to bring in much-needed cash in the short term.
- The marketing budget and the cost of promotions. Firms generally base promotional decisions on cost-effectiveness and the cost per thousand customers (CPT).
- Competition. If market research shows the existence of a lot of competition, a business needs to differentiate its product from those of competitors. This is achieved through branding or patenting original ideas.
- Substitutes. Market research may reveal the existence of substitutes in the form of other products. Businesses must look beyond their own market and appreciate that other industries can impact on their success.
- Consumer opinions. Ultimately, this is the most important factor. A firm's products must appeal to the needs of customers, so continuous market research is needed.
- The market segment. Some target markets may be easier to reach through certain media. Specialist magazines are used to promote products such as cosmetics and computer games because the profile of the magazine's readership matches the market segment that the business is trying to attract.
- The sophistication of the organisation's database. If a business has acquired information on specific customers, it is more likely to use direct mail or internet contact to attract them.
- Internet. The internet is having a major impact on place, with companies such as Amazon not requiring a traditional shop from which to sell their products. The internet also popular web pages.

Practice exercise 2 (35 marks), page 200

1 What is meant by the term 'psychological pricing'? (3)

Psychological pricing is a tactic intended to give the impression of value (e.g. selling a good for £9.99 rather than £10).

2 The following costs apply to a product: wages 50p, raw materials 60p, other costs 70p.

a What price would be set if cost-plus pricing were used and a mark-up of 100% were chosen by the business to set the price? (3)

Cost per product = 50p + 60p + 70p = £1.80
100% mark-up is 100% of £1.80 = £1.80
Price = cost per product (£1.80) + mark-up (£1.80) = £3.60

b Wages rise by 10% and the mark-up is reduced to 80%. Calculate the new price. (4)

Wages rise by 10%: 50p + (10% of 50p) = 50p + 5p = 55p
Cost per product = 55p + 60p + 70p = £1.85
80% mark-up of £1.85 = £1.48
Price = cost per product (£1.85) + mark-up (£1.48) = £3.33

3 Explain two reasons why a company might use price skimming and state two real-life examples of this strategy. (8)

Price skimming enables producers to make maximum profit from early adopters, who are usually prepared to pay high prices for new products. Recent examples are the iPhone, 4G mobile phones and Porsche Macan.

It also gives an 'upmarket' image to the product by ensuring that wealthier consumers are more likely to purchase it, and therefore gains high added value. Examples are Rolls-Royce, the Ritz and Fortnum & Mason.

4 Explain two reasons for penetration pricing by a business. (8)

- Penetration pricing is a good method for introducing a product to a market for the first time. Customers will be attracted by the low price and may overcome their natural reluctance to try something new if it is priced very attractively. However, the company needs to be cautious because some customers may expect this low price to continue.

- Penetration pricing is an excellent method for boosting market share, particularly in a very closely competitive market where price elasticity of demand is elastic.

- Businesses that are targeting customers with low incomes or selling products of inferior quality will find this a useful element of the marketing mix, as it will enable them to gain some customer loyalty.

5 What is the difference between a 'price leader' and a 'price taker'? State one example of each. (6)

- A price leader is a large company, usually the one with the largest market share, which sets the market price that smaller firms tend to follow (e.g. Coca-Cola, Tesco).

- A price taker is a smaller firm that tends to follow the price set by the price leader (e.g. Panda Cola, Morrisons).

6 What is meant by a 'loss leader'? (3)

A loss leader is a product or service sold cheaply in order to encourage consumers to buy other products from that firm.

Case study: Shakeaway (65 marks), pages 200-1

1 As a brand, Shakeaway has a large market share in a fast-growing niche market. In terms of the Boston Matrix, the Shakeaway brand is a: (1)

a Cash cow
b Dog
c Problem child/question mark
d Star.

The answer is d.

2 Explain two important features of the Shakeaway product that have helped the business to succeed. (6)

- A wide range of milkshakes – a product that is traditionally offered in only a few flavours. This enables Shakeaway to meet the specific tastes of a very wide range of customers. It also allows customers to enjoy new experiences on each visit.

- The introduction of alternative products such as hot drinks, yoghurts and confectionery. Hot drinks would be particularly useful in boosting customer numbers in the winter months.

- An attractive but recognisable layout which customers might perceive to be an aspect of the product.

- Freshly made products, made to order.

3 Are Shakeaway milkshakes a convenience good, a shopping good or a speciality good? Justify your view. (8)

Convenience goods are purchased frequently, with minimum thought and planning. They are often impulse buys. Shakeaway products would tend to be impulse buys for many customers, but may not be 'frequent' purchases. Shopping habits are changing and many customers now incorporate a visit to a coffee shop or café into their planned shopping trips. In these circumstances, Shakeaway fits the description of a 'shopping good', but if the visit was not pre-planned this classification does not apply. Although Shakeaway is a fairly unique product it is unlikely to be sought out specifically by consumers. However, consumers may seek out a Shakeaway for their café visit. Shakeaway does not fit neatly in to one classification, as its category will depend on the thinking process of the individual consumer. However, on balance it is likely to be an impulse buy and thus a 'convenience good'.

4 Explain two benefits of product proliferation for Shakeaway. (6)

- Attracting customers, especially in groups, because it is more likely to be able to cater for everyone's tastes than a business offering a limited range.
- Encouraging repeat visits because there are always new flavours to be experienced.
- Providing variety, such as hot drinks and yoghurts, can broaden Shakeaway's appeal. It can also help to ensure that sales are spread more evenly over the year, making it easier to manage staff and finances.

5 Explain one way in which knowledge of the product life cycles of its products might benefit Shakeaway. (4)

- Knowing the product life cycle allows the business to plan it marketing decisions. Each stage requires different approaches such as awareness promotions at introduction, extension strategies during maturity and possible cuts in price and promotions during decline.
- Knowing the product life cycle allows the business to plan decision-making in the other functional areas. For example, staff recruitment and training will be needed during introduction and growth, and the human resource flow will need to be planned to keep high levels of staffing during maturity. Redundancy or redeployment are likely to be necessary during decline.

6 What is meant by the term 'price skimming'? (3)

Price skimming is a strategy in which a high price is set in order to achieve a high profit margin.

7 Look at the figures in the case study.
  a Calculate the average cost of production of a regular milkshake. (5)
  Cost of ingredients = £1.10 per milkshake
  Labour and other costs per milkshake = daily cost/number of milkshakes per day
  = £380/500 = £0.76 (76p)

Average cost of a regular milkshake = £1.10 + £0.76 = £1.86

  b Shakeaway uses a cost-plus pricing method. Use your answer to part (a) to calculate the percentage that Shakeaway adds on to the average cost in order to set its price for a regular milkshake. (4)
  Price of a regular milkshake = £2.99
  Mark-up (add-on) = £2.99 − £1.86 = £1.13 %
  mark-up (add-on) = mark-up/average cost × 100 = 113p/186p × 100
  = 60.8% (61%)
  or £2.99/£1.86 = 1.608 %
  mark-up = 60.8%

8 Analyse why Shakeaway originally used price skimming. (8)

- Shakeaway may have wanted to 'cream' the market, by charging high prices to 'early adopters' of the product. Early adopters tend to be happy to pay higher prices because they place value on being associated with new products.
- This approach is particularly helpful if there are high start-up costs that Shakeaway wants to recover. Price skimming tends to give a higher profit margin which can help to pay off debts.
- Price skimming can help to give a product an image of high quality. To project this image a high price is needed so that a consistent message is sent.
- If Shakeaway expected its products to have short product life cycles it would want to recover its costs quickly. High prices (price skimming) would bring in higher profit to help the firm cover its fixed costs.

9 Shakeaway believes that demand for its milkshakes is price inelastic. Analyse two reasons why this might be true. (8)

- Shakeaway has a unique selling point and, although others are beginning to enter the market, Shakeaway has the advantage of being the first maker of this type of milkshake. As a result, it will have built up considerable brand loyalty, which will help it to increase price without reducing demand by a significant amount.
- Shakeaway has been successfully employing price skimming. Its belief that psychological pricing would not help profits confirms the view that, in its experience, demand is not greatly affected by changes in price.
- The shops are based in areas of high income/ tourism. High prices do not appear to be a deterrent to customers' desire to purchase the milkshakes, suggesting that demand is price inelastic.

10 Evaluate the main factors that may lead to Shakeaway being forced to change its current strategy of psychological pricing. (12)

- Psychological pricing is expected to reduce the profit level in the future: the price chosen (£2.99) gives a mark-up of £1.13. However, if costs rise this profit margin will fall.

- Shakeaway considered that the psychological price would not have increased demand by very much because demand was price inelastic. Thus more profit could be made by selling slightly fewer milkshakes at a significantly higher price.

- In a niche market with high prices it is a contradiction to try to make the price appear cheaper with psychological pricing. The high price helped Shakeaway to get the message across that this was a luxury product.

- It can be difficult to increase a psychological price as even the smallest change takes it away from the desirable level (under £3 in this case). For Shakeaway the next obvious psychological price is £3.99, which would be a very large price rise. For such a large price rise demand may not be price inelastic.

- Competition. If rivals enter the market, Shakeaway will lose its USP. This is the factor that enables it to charge a high price. Furthermore, competitors may introduce more luxurious versions (Shakeaway mainly uses children's sweets) that will appeal to those consumers who are prepared to pay the highest prices. Shakeaway need to ensure that their prices reflect the competitiveness of the market – greater competition may mean that £2.99 is no longer a competitive price.

Evaluation: A case could be made for any of the above factors having the strongest influence. However, given the fact that costs are expected to rise and Shakeaway has incurred rising costs it is likely that it is making less profit than it was. Because its demand is price inelastic Shakeaway can increase price (above the psychological £3 barrier) without losing very many customers. However, rising competition and consumer resistance to high price rises should mean that a rise to another psychological price, such as £3.99, is not practical.

Practice exercise 3 (70 marks), page 210

1 What is the difference between 'promotion' and 'advertising'? (6)

Promotion incorporates all methods used by an organisation to draw consumers' attention to its products or services. Advertising is communication that is purchased and delivered through certain media, such as newspapers, cinemas, radio and television. Advertising is therefore an element of promotion.

2 What does the mnemonic AIDA stand for? (4)

AIDA stands for attention, interest, desire and action.

3 What is an 'impulse buy'? (2)

An 'impulse buy' is a purchase that is not pre-planned by a customer, but made on the spur of the moment.

4 Which media would you select in order to advertise the following? In each case justify your choice.

a a job vacancy for a checkout assistant in Asda. (3)

A local newspaper or local radio would be cheap and would reach the target market, as the checkout assistants would need to live locally. They are also the medium that prospective workers would use to search for jobs.

b a new model of a car. (3)

National media are needed to raise awareness, more expensive cars may be promoted via media that attract higher earners, and so on. Point-of-sale promotions and posters would increase local awareness, and brochures would provide the information desired by some buyers.

5 Explain one benefit and one problem of direct selling. (8)

Benefits of direct selling:

- It can often be accurately targeted at customers who probably have a high interest in the product.

- It allows technical expertise to be presented to the customer and gives opportunity for two-way communication between customers and the business.

Problems:

- Many customers dislike direct selling, as they believe it to be aggressive.

- It is often perceived as junk mail or an invasion of privacy.

6 Explain one benefit and one problem of merchandising. (8)

Benefit of merchandising:

- Attractive merchandising can persuade customers to make unplanned purchases (impulse buys).

Problems:

- It is only effective if other measures have been successful in drawing customers into the store.
- It can be expensive to devise measures to entice customers to buy these goods.

7 Explain the difference between sponsorship and public relations. (4)

Sponsorship takes place when an organisation (the sponsor) gives financial support to an activity, individual or firm. Public relations involves using the media to give favourable publicity for a firm or other organisation.

8 Identify two products that might use exhibitions or trade fairs as a form of promotion. (2)

Examples include manufacturing equipment, durable goods, household products, computing equipment and vehicles.

9 Identify three examples of sales promotion. (3)

Examples include competitions, two-for-the-price-of-one offers, credit terms, endorsement by well-known public figures, coupons, free offers and product placement.

10 Briefly explain one advantage and one disadvantage of using the following media for advertising:

a television (6)
b cinema (6)
c internet (6)

Possible advantages and disadvantages are shown in the table.

Medium	Advantages	Disadvantages
a Television	• Memorable, using moving images and colour • Reaches a very wide audience	• High costs • Not always easy to target
b Cinema	• Can target customer interests • Colour and sound	• Limited range of products suited to media • Relatively low audiences
c Internet	• Cheap • Customers can be very closely targeted	• Hits on a page may not mean that adverts have been read • Can be avoided by web users

11 Analyse factors that an organisation should consider when planning its promotional mix. (9)

- **Objectives of the campaign**. If the firm is trying to introduce a new product, it will focus on using media that raise awareness, such as television. Action is more likely to be triggered by merchandising activities.
- **Costs**. Small firms are likely to be limited to local media, but national companies find it much more cost effective to use national media.
- **The target market**. Magazines and local media can be more effective than national media at reaching a specific market segment.
- **Legal factors**. Restrictions on the use of media, such as limits on alcohol advertising on television, may encourage firms to use different media.
- **External factors**. Changes in the overall wealth of the country and social and political changes can all influence promotions. Customers will usually be more receptive to promotions if they are experiencing higher living standards. The style of the promotions and the images and messages used must also fit in with society's views.

Practice exercise 4 (50 marks), page 219

1 What is meant by the term 'place' in the context of the marketing mix? (4)

In this context, 'place' means the (geographical) location of the outlet, the positioning of the product or service within that outlet, and the number of outlets in which products are placed.

2 Explain two reasons why the location of a store is important. (6)

The location of a store is important because it enables the retailer to meet a number of customer needs. It may provide convenience by being located close to the consumer, accessibility in terms of the time taken to visit the store, cost-effective access through free car parking or proximity to home or work, and finally, the possibility of status if the retailer is located in a prestigious area. Ideally, the retailer should also be conveniently located for its suppliers.

3 Why do manufacturers of convenience goods see place as an important factor in the marketing mix? (6)

Impulse buys are decisions to buy products, made on the spur of the moment, rather than being planned beforehand. Thus they are typically decisions about buying convenience goods. In order to encourage this impulsive behaviour, retailers need to make sure that the point of sale is attractive because this is the factor that persuades the buyer to purchase convenience goods. This can be achieved through attractive packaging and/or displays, prominently displayed special offers or eye-catching promotions drawing attention to the convenience good.

4 Explain two ways in which a company such as Birds Eye can increase the amount of space that retailers provide for its products. (6)

- Provide free display cabinets (particularly important for a frozen food supplier, as this will be an expensive form of storage for the retailer).
- Ensure that the design of the storage is used to attract interest from consumers.
- Offer products that have high value added, so that retailers understand the value of stocking the product.
- Promise (and deliver) effective advertising and promotional campaigns, so that customers will want to visit the store to buy the products.
- Brand proliferation – increasing the number of varieties of a product will encourage retailers to allocate more space overall, so that each variation is available to its customers.

5 Describe two services that a retailer provides for its customers. (6)

- **Convenience** for customers by making a range of products easily accessible. This may be through geographical proximity, by taking orders over the telephone, by going to the customer's doorstep, or by selling products on a website.
- **Financial assistance**. This usually takes the form of credit facilities, but it may involve the retailer accepting payment in a convenient form.
- **After-sales service**. For some products, the opportunity to exchange them and receive post-purchase servicing and a guarantee is a major benefit.
- **Advice**. For technical products in particular, an expert opinion from the retailer can guide the buyer to the right purchase.

6 Explain two factors that influence the method of distribution chosen for a product. (6)

- The **size** of the retailer. Larger retailers are more likely to choose a distribution channel that bypasses the wholesaler.
- The **nature** of the product. Complicated and perishable products are more likely to be sold via specialist retailers that can provide expert advice or specialist facilities.

- **Speed** of delivery. For fast delivery of individual products, the wholesaler will be omitted, but in situations with many producers and retailers, as is the case with newspapers, it is quicker to use a wholesaler as the hub to and from which distribution can be centralised.
- **Geography**. In remote, low-populated areas, wholesalers are more likely to be cost-effective, as manufacturers will be reluctant to deliver directly.

7 To what extent do you believe that the use of multichannel distribution will continue to increase in the future? Justify your view. (16)

Multichannel distribution is when firms use more than one type of distribution channel. Possible reasons for the future growth of multichannel distribution:

- Different approaches enable a business to reach different market segments. For example, Mars uses vending machines to attract impulse buyers but also places Mars Bars in supermarkets for consumers who would see them as shopping goods.
- It enables businesses to appeal to consumers who are loyal to (or more inclined to use) a particular channel. Some customers prefer shopping in retail outlets while others prefer online shopping. Using a multichannel approach means a business can reach more customers and suit customers' needs.
- Multichannel distribution provides more flexibility for consumers. IT systems can be used to identify the stores that have an item in stock and the system can lead to goods being transferred for delivery to the consumer or to their local store. Consequently, sales are not lost if a shop is out of stock.
- Multichannel methods integrate all aspects of marketing and the other functional areas of a business. Promotions can lead to a customer visiting a website which is linked to a customer adviser who can provide (or get) more information for the customer. In many cases the adviser will have the authority to give promotional offers to the customer in order to secure a sale.

Evaluation: All these reasons will contribute to the success of a business. However, many people believe that the final argument (above) is the most significant reason because it gives a business a greater understanding of the customer. It also facilitates a sale at the exact time that the customer is showing an interest in the good (by visiting the website or contacting an adviser). Consequently, additional sales are more probable from using this approach.

Case study: Levi Strauss (50 marks), page 220

1 Analyse, the possible reasons why a new promotional mix failed to change customers' views of the Levi Strauss brand. (9)

- The promotions focused on images that were no longer seen to be relevant and attractive by Levi Strauss's target customers.
- The promotional mix did not focus on Levi Strauss's American image. This approach would have proved to be popular with customers.
- The promotional mix failed to change the brand image from its 'rugged edginess' to a new image that would be placed in the middle of the market.

2 Analyse two ways in which the marketing mix could be employed in order to encourage customers to buy complementary clothing. (9)

- Displaying complementary products such as shirts and jeans together in retail outlets.
- Giving incentives such as discounts to customers who bought complementary products together.
- Putting greater emphasis on the sales of shirt and other products that complement jeans and trousers, so that customers buy a more even balance of complementary products. At present Levi Strauss are much more successful at selling jeans than product such as shirts.

3 Do you think that Levi Strauss are right to target the Indian and Chinese markets, in order to increase their global sales levels? Justify your view. (16)

Benefits of targeting China and India:

- China and India are the two most populated countries in the world, and therefore offer excellent growth opportunities. This benefit is accentuated by the strong economic growth that these two countries have experienced in recent years when compared with more mature economies, such as the USA.
- There has been little attempt to introduce denim products to date, and therefore it is possible that Levi Strauss would acquire significant levels of monopoly power and a competitive advantage from being the first provider of this type of product in China and India.
- An American image may appeal to certain market segments in these countries – particularly those segments that want to emulate the American lifestyle.

Problems with targeting China and India:

- Levi Strauss would withdraw its existing brand – Denizen – from China and India. This brand is established and the new brands may not reach the level of sales that the company has already achieved with the Denizen brand.

- Denizen may be more appropriate for the target market. Introducing a more upmarket brand may therefore prove to be a costly error.
- In effect, Levi Strauss would be starting from scratch with a new brand. Although this name may have some recognition in China and India, it will be more expensive to establish the brand, because there will be little or no existing brand loyalty for the Levi Strauss brand.

Evaluation: There are pros and cons to this decision. The main benefit is the sheer size of the target markets, but this will also attract much higher levels of competition. However, Levi Strauss is a worldwide brand and may therefore be in a strong position to resist competition. It may be advisable for Levi Strauss to cater for the broader market in these countries by retaining the low price Denizen brand and using Levi Strauss as an alternative upmarket brand. This approach should enable the firm to attract a very broad range of customers.

4 Levi Strauss has largely focused on promotion and place in order to improve its profitability. Do you think it has focused on the right elements (Ps) in the changes to its marketing mix? Justify your view. (16)

- Denim is no longer fashionable and so there should have been a greater emphasis on **product** in order to make sure the material was changed.
- Consumers want lower **prices** – but Levi Strauss have continued to focus on skimming pricing.
- Consumers perceive the company's main **product** to be dated; Levi Strauss should have focused more on updating products.
- **Place** is an important aspect of the marketing mix for Levi Strauss. However, its retail outlets were not considered to be attractive by its target market.
- The nature of **products** was changing – with a much greater focus on formal wear and 'athleisure'. Levi Strauss did not appear to be catering for more formal wear, although it was promoting and offering more sporting items, such as shirts displaying the logo of San Francisco 49ers.

Evaluation: Levi Strauss appeared to have got the product wrong, by not moving with changes in tastes in the market. Consequently, the other elements of the marketing mix were less likely to be successful because they were not being used to sell products that customers desired in sufficient quantities. Although it emphasised place, its products were not displayed in attractive environments, and the skimming pricing approach did not appeal to sufficient customers.

Practice exercise 5 (60 marks), page 230

1 What is meant by the term 'integrated marketing mix'? (6)

The marketing mix describes those elements of a business's approach to marketing that enable it to satisfy its customers. In an integrated marketing mix, each of the seven Ps reinforces the other elements. For example, a firm trying to promote an image of high quality would design adverts to reflect this quality and ensure that the product is well-made and appealing. It is also likely to follow a skimming pricing approach and ensure that the physical environment in which the product is sold is suited to its image.

2 Explain two ways in which the product life cycle might influence the marketing mix. (6)

- During the introduction stage the product will be heavily promoted and the business may use penetration pricing to gain market share, unless it wants to establish a reputation for prestige through skimming pricing.

- During growth there will be emphasis placed on broadening the range of promotions to attract new market segments. The business will try to increase the availability of products to many different outlets so that sales can grow.

- In the maturity stage the emphasis will tend to be placed on extension strategies, so that the product can stay in maturity for as long as possible. These strategies will take the form of special offers, temporary cut in prices and modifications to the product. These methods will attract a broader customer range and ensure that the product keeps up with changes in tastes.

- When the decline period commences the business may cut back on promotions in order to cut costs. Thus the product will still create profit. Alternatively, it may cut price in order to try to overcome the decline.

3 Explain two ways in which marketing objectives might influence the marketing mix. (6)

- A marketing objective to increase sales growth would encourage measures such as an emphasis on promotion and price cuts to gain more sales. There may also be product modifications to try and add new interest in the product among its target market.

- An objective to attract new market segments can be facilitated by product modifications and new forms of promotion. These would emphasise messages and use media that would be attractive to the new market segments being targeted.

- A marketing objective to create higher added value on products would be facilitated by price skimming. However, for this to be effective it would need to be integrated with methods such as placing the product in up-market retail outlets and modifying the product so that it has greater appeal to customers who are prepared to pay high prices.

4 Explain two factors that might reduce the effectiveness of 'process' in the marketing mix of a service. (6)

- Poor communications. If customers are not kept informed then the process element of the marketing mix will be less satisfactory. For example, many delivery companies will now give a quite precise expected time of delivery for a parcel. A company that does not meet this standard will lose customers because of the ineffectiveness of its process.

- Slow response. Most firms have a time limit set for the speed of response to a customer query. Slow response will alienate customers who will then seek to purchase products from competitors, where their needs will be dealt with more promptly.

- Low quality training. If staff receive inadequate training, or are not empowered to make decisions, then customers will become frustrated and so the process element of the marketing mix will lower the attractiveness of the good or service being offered.

5 Analyse how 'physical evidence' can lead to a more successful marketing mix for a service. (8)

- Staff uniforms and the appearance of staff will give greater confidence to customers, particularly if the service requires appearance and presentation. For example, people may judge hairdressers by their hairstyles.

- In the case of a hotel, the quality of the landscaping of the grounds and the facilities provided in the hotel's leisure areas will have a significant impact on people's initial perception of the service they will receive. First impressions can be very important influences on a customer's overall impression of the quality of a service.

- A business's website may be the main point of contact between a customer and a business. An attractively designed website, that is easy to navigate and user-friendly when seeking information or making orders, will be a crucial factor in influencing the customer's perception of the quality of the business.

6 What is the difference between 'digital marketing' and 'e-commerce'? (4)

Digital marketing is the anticipating and satisfying of consumer wants through different forms of technology. E-commerce is an element of digital marketing in that it describes the buying and selling of goods and services through the use of electronic media.

7 Explain one advantage of digital marketing for a business. (4)

- Reduced costs. Digital marketing may reduce the need for expensive promotions, because businesses can use their websites for much more specific targeting of their customers. Digital marketing now accounts for more than 50% of all promotional activity.

- Quicker response. Digital marketing enables a business to respond quickly to the external environment. Within minutes of a news item being reported, digital marketing can utilise this news to capture customers' interest.

- Marketing can be personalised and targeted much more specifically to the needs of different market segments. More significantly, a business can use its detailed profile of individual customers to target messages based on their knowledge of the individual's tastes and preferences.

8 Explain one possible problem that might arise when a business introduces e-commerce. (4)

- Initial cost. Establishing the IT systems, storage facilities and delivery infrastructure can be a very expensive undertaking. Although running costs are much lower than for retail outlets, the initial costs can still be quite high.

- Security. E-commerce requires a business to hold a lot of personal details of customers on its IT system. Therefore it can be vulnerable to hackers or computing errors. Security errors can have a very damaging impact on a business's reputation.

- Lack of direct contact with the product. For some products, such as fashion items and cosmetics, customers prefer to have direct contact with the product before purchasing it. As a rule, e-commerce does not offer this facility. Although it is possible to return products, this can be time-consuming and costly for the customer and/or the e-commerce business.

9 'People' is only an important element of the marketing mix for services. It has no relevance for goods. Do you agree? Justify your view. (16)

- In some cases, the people involved in providing a service are fundamental. For personal services, such as hairdressing, the quality of the person involved in providing the service represents all or most of the experience of the customer, and so it is absolutely vital.

- For some services, such as restaurant meals, customer experience will depend on the quality of the product (the food) as well as the service provided by staff (the waiters and chefs). Although the people element is of vital importance, a high quality service will also depend on the quality of the goods with which the people providing the service are working.

- In the case of some services, such as car maintenance, it may be impossible to recognise the quality of the service itself, unless there is a problem such as a breakdown of the car after the services has been provided. In these instances the customer's perception of the services are certainly going to be influenced more by the quality of the staff who had direct contact with the customer, such as the receptionist and the person providing peripheral services, such as a courtesy car.

- For customers buying goods there are still service elements to the process, such as delivery, technical advice and marketing. A high quality product may not be perceived as such by the customer if it is damaged or delayed during the delivery process. Effective marketing can also influence customer perceptions of the worth of a good and thus the satisfaction that they receive from that good.

Evaluation: People in a business play an important role in meeting the needs of consumers. To argue that people have no relevance in the provision of goods is incorrect. The quality of the people involved in providing a good is an important influence on the level of satisfaction that a customer receives, because a poor receptionist, website designer or lorry driver can all reduce the satisfaction that the customer receives from a good. However, there tends to be a more direct relationship between people and customers when services are provided and so the quality of the people involved in providing a service can be more significant than it would be for a good. The importance of people is also influenced by the needs of the customer and the nature of the good or service. For example, some customers may value good service in a restaurant more than the quality of the food, while for others the quality of the food will be paramount. For a customer selecting a plumber, fixing a leak quickly may be more important than the extent to which the problem is fixed permanently.

Case study: The Eden Project (70 marks), pages 230–1

1 What is meant by the term 'price skimming'? (3)

Price skimming is a strategy in which a high price is set in order to yield a high profit margin.

2 What is meant by the term 'public relations'? (3)

Public relations involves gaining favourable publicity through the media in order to help boost the image of a product or business.

3 What is 'word-of-mouth' advertising? (2)

Word-of-mouth advertising takes place when customers make favourable comments to their friends and relatives, thus boosting the reputation of a product.

4 Explain two possible reasons why Cornwall is a good place to locate the Eden Project. (6)

- Cornwall has a reputation as a family holiday destination. The project is seen as an attraction aimed at families, particularly children.
- There is a lack of competition in the form of rival attractions, especially those that are suitable for rainy days.
- The existence of complementary attractions, such as the Lost Gardens of Heligan, will allow consumers with an interest in plants to benefit from visiting Cornwall with the specific aim of viewing these sites.

5 Explain two reasons why the entrance ticket for a child is approximately half the price charged to an adult visitor. (6)

- The pricing is based on market forces. There will be insufficient demand from children if they are expected to pay the same price as adults.
- A policy of price discrimination is being operated. Children (or families) are less able to afford high prices and the tickets cannot be transferred, so the Eden Project charges lower prices to enable them to visit the project. Individual adults are charged higher prices.
- In order to support one of the aims of the project (to educate people about the environment), the Eden Project has deliberately set a lower price for school pupils.
- A low price will encourage more children to visit. This will establish a firm base of loyal customers who, it is hoped, will continue to visit throughout their lifetime.

6 To what extent was it wise for the Eden Project to have spent only a limited sum on promotions and advertising? (14)

It was wise for the following reasons:

- Efficient use of public relations has enabled the Eden Project to gain a lot of coverage in the media, thus reducing the need for 'paid-for' promotions.
- The unique nature of the project and public interest in the actual construction process also acted as free publicity; overall there is a high level of public awareness of the project.
- The website has attracted many visitors, hence reducing the need for other, more expensive forms of promotion and advertising.
- The Eden Project organisers believe that direct mail advertising in the local area and viral (word-of-mouth) advertising are effective ways of reaching the public.

Reasons for it being unwise are:

- The lack of use of mainstream media such as national newspapers and television will reduce public awareness of the project.
- The promotional methods chosen rely on capturing the interest of people who are already likely to have an interest in an environmental project. This may lead to a failure to meet the educational targets of the organisers.
- A reliance on local direct mail means that the project will tend to attract visitors who have already decided to visit Cornwall, restricting the size of its target market.

Evaluation: On balance, it appears to have been a wise decision, although market research into the types of visitor may reveal a failure to attract certain market segments. The number of visitors has been very high and the project has met targets in regenerating the local economy. With its USP there is less need to spend money on promotion, so focusing on other aspects of the marketing mix (notably the product) was probably a wise decision.

7 Would the price elasticity of demand for a visit to the Eden Project be elastic or inelastic? Justify your view. (16)

- To many customers the Eden Project is unique. Consequently, these customers will not be put off visiting if the price is high. For such customers, the lack of a close substitute will cause demand to be price inelastic.

- For the education market there is no comparable attraction in the UK, so schools may often see it as a necessity if they are looking for a visit that matches the services provided by the Eden Project.

- While visiting the Eden Project, no alternative shops are accessible. The shop can take advantage of its 'monopoly' situation in order to charge high prices, as demand will be inelastic. The shop stocks local crafts and other products that are unique and therefore likely to attract a premium price.

- Tourists generally enjoy buying souvenirs and tend to be prepared to pay higher prices for products while on holiday. The high profile of the project will also encourage consumers to visit the Eden Project, regardless of price.

- The lack of competition in the form of rival attractions, especially those that are suitable for rainy days, suggests that demand would be price inelastic.

- For children and families the price may seem excessive, so the Eden Project offers lower prices for those groups, suggesting that demand is price elastic.

Evaluation: Overall, most factors suggest that demand is price inelastic. However, there is a hint that demand is price elastic for children and families, so lower prices are charged to these groups.

8 To what extent are product and the physical environment the most important elements of the marketing mix for the Eden Project? Justify your view. (20)

Reasons why product and physical environment are important factors:

- The product is unique, arguably from a worldwide perspective, and this originality means that people will travel long distances to visit it.

- The setting (the physical environment) is a vital element of the product that people are paying to enjoy. The product is unique because the physical environment is unique.

- The product appeals to different people in different ways. It may attract people because of its biodomes and plants, its environmental

message, its restaurant and crafts or as a source of learning. It is unusual for a product to possess so many features, each of which might be the key factor encouraging suppliers to buy it.

- The Skywire is targeted at people who might be looking for high adrenaline experiences

Reasons why the other five Ps are important factors:

- The Eden Project's pricing is vital to maximise returns by using skimming pricing for souvenirs and the restaurant. Overall pricing is set high, because demand is believed to be price inelastic. However, offering discounts to children, people making advanced bookings and eco-friendly travellers, may encourage visitors who are more sensitive to price.

- Promotions are used to attract local people and the website has many visitors, although the article suggests that promotion is fairly limited as an element of the marketing mix.

- Public relations are a key element of the marketing mix, with publicity in national newspapers helping to raise and maintain interest in the project.

- Place has a mixed impact on the project. Journey times from the UK's major population centres are long and can be unreliable. However, Cornwall is popular with tourists and there are few major 'built' attractions and so the Eden Project can attract people who have decided to take a holiday in Cornwall.

Evaluation: Overall, most of the key factors suggest that product and physical environment are the most important elements of the marketing mix in terms of attracting visitor numbers. This is reinforced by the fact that 'place' and 'price' may actually be a deterrent to many customers, although 'place' is vital for attracting some tourists and residents of Cornwall. However, price seems to be an important element in terms of maximising revenue. Promotions also appear to be quite low, with the Eden Project relying on PR and word-of-mouth advertising. On balance, the evidence suggests that product and physical environment are the most important elements. However, as with most tourist attractions, 'people' are likely to be important in ensuring repeat visits by customers.

Case study: The marketing mix at Ryanair (90 marks), pages 232–4

1 In the context of the marketing mix, what is meant by the term 'process'? (2)

Process describes the procedures or flow of activities by which services are delivered to the customer.

2 Explain why the physical environment might be a weakness in Ryanair's traditional marketing mix. (6)

Physical environment may be a weakness in Ryanair's traditional marketing mix because it kept facilities at the airport to a minimum and so it would have compared unfavourably to airlines such as BA. Long queues at the airport would have reduced the quality of the customer experience. Free meals are not provided and toilet visits can be charged, further adding to the discomfort of passengers during flights.

3 What is meant by digital marketing? (3)

Digital marketing is the anticipating and satisfying of consumer wants through the use of different forms of technology.

4 Explain how Ryanair uses 'penetration pricing'. (5)

Ryanair uses penetration pricing by offering cheap flights to the customers who were prepared to book early. This encouraged early booking and enabled Ryanair to fill its flights earlier than other airlines. Ryanair also used very low pricing to attract new customers. Invariably, these were offered for one-way flights and so customers would pay more for the return flight, having been tempted to use Ryanair because of the low 'headline' price.

5 Explain how Ryanair uses 'price skimming'. (5)

Ryanair uses skimming pricing as a natural result of its policy of penetration pricing. By filling most of its seats early, Ryanair is able to charge high prices for the remaining few seats. This is based on the logic that customers who book close to the flight time may have fewer alternatives and a more pressing need to be on the flight. Skimming pricing can also be used for customers who have taken cheap one-way tickets. By making these offers in one direction only, people will have to pay the return price demanded and so Ryanair can set this price high.

6 Explain the possible reasons why Southwest Airlines did not attempt to bring its low-cost approach to Europe before Ryanair used the idea. (6)

- Southwest Airlines may have believed that Europe was not ready for this approach. People fly more frequently in the USA and it may have believed there was no scope for low-cost flights at the time Ryanair started.
- Southwest Airlines may have regarded it as an unnecessary risk. It has been very successful in the USA and understands that market, and therefore may prefer its expansion to take place in America.
- The company may have lacked the resources to enter a new market. The expensive infrastructure (planes, bases in airports and trained staff) may have been beyond its means,

especially as low prices would have meant low profit margins.

- It may have found that it lacked suitable suppliers in Europe, so it was unable to reproduce its low-cost approach in another continent. There may also have been difficulties in controlling and monitoring European activities.

7 Explain why 'people' will become a more important element of the marketing mix in Ryanair's new marketing mix. (6)

Ryanair is now focusing on trying to attract customers who are prepared to pay a higher price. This will require Ryanair to provide a better quality experience for customers. To achieve this aim for a service, it is essential that the business improves the interface between its staff and its customers. Ryanair must improve the quality of the service it provides by having more and highly qualified staff who can deal with problems in airports, thus reducing queues. It must also offer better facilities on the planes and a more attractive and user-friendly website. All of these aims will require appropriately skilled people.

8 Ryanair charges low prices to early customers and higher prices to people who book flights later, because it believes that demand for early flights is price elastic whereas demand for late flights is price inelastic. Analyse the reasons for this difference in price elasticity of demand over time. (9)

Ryanair believes that low prices are necessary to attract early customers. At this stage, the consumers have plenty of alternatives and so they can shop around in order to find the best price. The existence of lots of alternatives means that demand is price elastic. At this point the alternatives might also include not taking a holiday, if there are no reasonably priced holidays available. Furthermore, for Ryanair's regular low-cost customers, price is the most important factor. However, as the date and time of departure become closer, consumers have fewer alternatives and less time to investigate them. Therefore, demand becomes price inelastic, so Ryanair charges a high price in order to maximise the revenue from those seats, even if it leaves some seats unsold. With online bookings, in particular, it is easy to modify the price on a regular basis – as the flight time approaches, prices can be adjusted upwards or downwards in accordance with the number of seats still available.

9 Analyse the benefits to Ryanair from its decision to make greater use of technology in its marketing mix. (12)

- Internet bookings saved 15% of the cost of normal bookings – primarily because no commission is paid travel agents.
- Technology reduces the paperwork required by customers at airports and therefore cuts the size of queues. This improves the customers experience in the physical environment.
- More data capture from its use of technology will enable Ryanair to modify its marketing mix so that it can specifically target individual customers with tailor-made offers.
- The purchasing process should become much easier because the new website is more user-friendly and allows customers to book flights more quickly. It also offers flexibility so that customers can amend flights if they wish.

10 Evaluate the potential difficulties faced by Ryanair in trying to change its marketing mix in order to widen its appeal. (16)

- The introduction of pre-booked seats and higher quality customer service may lead to an increase in the turnaround time of Ryanair's flights. This will increase Ryanair's costs, and possibly eliminate one of its USPs.
- The new marketing mix requires 'heavy investment in information technology and digital marketing'. Ryanair will need to consider whether the financial returns of this new approach will be sufficient to pay the costs of this heavy investment.
- Brand image is very hard to change, particularly in the case of businesses whose reputation has been built on its pricing. It may be a very expensive undertaking to create a marketing mix to radically change the image of Ryanair in people's minds. There may also be a lack of trust in Ryanair's ability to provide a service that warrants a higher price than its existing, low-cost low-price offering.
- Ryanair may lack the expertise to modify its marketing mix. The culture of its existing staff is focused on saving costs rather than promoting the quality of the airline. The business has already had to introduce its first-ever marketing director and recruit staff to design its new website.
- It may be difficult to modify the marketing mix without alienating its loyal customers who regularly fly with Ryanair because of its low prices. For many goods and services, differences in quality can be easily recognised by customers. However, its existing customers may not receive an improvement in quality if they do not value factors such as pre-booked seats, and may think that the service is worse because customers paying higher prices will take the best seats.

Evaluation: Changing a business's marketing mix is a difficult process, particularly as the new approach Ryanair places a very different emphasis on the seven Ps. Its original marketing mix was based almost solely on low price. Its planes were of sufficient quality to guarantee safety, but in every other respect Ryanair's main marketing approach was to emphasise, at every opportunity, its approach to cutting costs so that customers could benefit from low prices. It was also renowned as the airline with the smallest customer service department.

This new marketing mix must use promotions – a new skill – and also emphasise its people and physical environment. Traditionally, these have been seen to be Ryanair's main weaknesses, along with the airports from which it flies (a factor that will be difficult to change). It may be difficult to persuade customers that Ryanair can turn its original weaknesses into its main strengths.

11 Some analysts believe that it is inevitable that low-price providers, such as Ryanair, Ikea and Aldi, must move into target markets that involve higher prices. Do you agree? Justify your view. (20)

YES, because …

- Businesses are usually advised to capitalise on their strengths. If a business has devised a successful model it is advisable to stay with that model as long as it can still enable the business to achieve its objectives.
- According to Porter, low-cost, low-price strategies are an effective way of differentiating a business from its competitors. A business that establishes this advantage at an early stage can use it as a barrier to entry, so that it can maintain a large market share of this niche. There are many businesses, such as Wal-Mart, Primark and Poundland, which continue to operate on a large scale using this as their approach.
- Because of the low profit margins, providers may be more secure against competition than those working at high profit margins. It would be very difficult for a smaller business to penetrate a low-price market because high profits are made through the volume sold, rather than the high value of individual items. Consequently, it is a model that favours larger businesses.
- Companies such as Ryanair have used heavily discounted pricing strategies to undermine the potential profits of new entrants to a market, knowing that they can raise their prices again, once the new threat is driven out of the market.

NO, because ...

- Higher prices should enable a business to work on much higher profit margins. This approach will appeal to most stakeholders who will benefit from the potential of a high profit resulting from this approach.

- As living standards improve, people tend to focus more on the quality of the goods and services they desire, because their basic needs have already been met. Over time, there has tended to be a steady increase in living standards throughout the world. Therefore, in the long term, a high price strategy is likely to be more sustainable.

- Focusing on a limited range of prices will restrict the potential customer base for a business. If the business wishes to continue to expand, it should try to offer products that fit into a wide range of price bands. A business that commences with low-priced products will therefore need to move into higher price ranges in order to continue its expansion.

Evaluation: Changing its target market so that it can charge higher prices should enable a business to increase its scale of operations and potentially its profit margins. However, this may be a difficult strategy if the business is too closely associated with low-priced products. It may also be undesirable as it will no longer be playing to its strengths. Some businesses overcome this problem by integrating with other firms who offer a different range of products. In this way, a firm may provide a complete range of products, using different brand names to take advantage of their images. For example, Volkswagen offer products at a range of prices by using different brands. Skoda and Aldi charge more basic prices while Volkswagen and Audi set higher prices.

In conclusion, there will be pressures for a business to move away from a low-cost, low-price strategy, particularly if living standards continue to increase (an assumption that is challenged by many people). However, it is certainly not inevitable. There are many businesses, such as Google, that operate at high profit margins, but there are others, such as Wal-Mart, that continue to thrive by charging low prices.

11 Setting operational objectives

Practice exercise 1 (30 marks), page 245

1 What is the formula for calculating unit costs? (2)

$$\text{Formula for unit costs} = \frac{\text{Total costs}}{\text{Units of output}}$$

2 Which one of the following objectives is not an operational objective? (1)

a improving quality

b lowering energy costs

c identifying new markets

d improving speed of response.

The answer is c.

3i 'Those features of the product that allow it to satisfy and delight customers.' This is a definition of: (1)

a dependability

b flexibility

c quality

d unique selling point.

The answer is c.

3ii In order to cope with an increase in customer demand for a product, a business should ideally have: (1)

a delivery flexibility

b mix flexibility

c product flexibility

d volume flexibility.

The answer is d.

4 The business aims to reduce the time taken to deliver a product. This is an example of: (1)

a an added value objective

b a dependability objective

c an environmental objective

d a speed of response objective.

The answer is d.

5 The business aims to increase the difference between price and cost of materials. This is an example of: (1)

a an added value objective

b a dependability objective

c an environmental objective

d a speed of response objective.

The answer is a.

6 Explain two benefits of setting operational objectives. (6)

- To give direction to the operations department so that all employees are working to achieve the same purpose.
- To provide a yardstick against which performance can be measured. This allows the department to assess its successes and failures.
- To improve efficiency by scrutinising the reasons for success (or failure) and using this knowledge to make improvements.

7 A business is scheduled to deliver 50 items to its customers. Eight items are not delivered. The remaining items are all delivered, but six of them arrive late. What is the punctuality percentage for these deliveries? (2)

Late deliveries are 8 + 6 = 14.

Therefore 50 − 14 = 36 arrive on time.

Punctuality % = 36/50 x 100 = 72%

8 Explain two ways in which quality can be measured. (8)

- Customer satisfaction ratings. A survey of customers reveals their opinions on the quality of good/service they have received. These ratings are usually on a scale of 1 to 10 or 1 to 5. By using a consistent scale a business can gain useful information covering a wide range of its functions and personnel.
- Customer complaints. Usually this is measured as the number of customers who complain as a percentage of the total number of customers. Although this is a rather negative measure of quality it is based on an honest opinion that is not requested by the business and therefore may be unbiased.
- Level of product returns. If a high percentage of products sold are subsequently returned by customers this indicates a lack of quality. However, this measure needs to be treated with caution because many products may be returned because they are the wrong size rather than a genuine fault.

9 Explain why improved flexibility might increase the costs of a business providing office supplies. (7)

Flexibility is the ability of an organisation to change its operations in some way. It can take the form of product flexibility, volume flexibility, mix flexibility and delivery flexibility. Product mix flexibility can increase costs because it requires sophisticated machinery that can be adapted to produce either a completely different product or an adaptation of the original product. This adaptability can also lead to a slower rate of production that increases unit costs. Volume flexibility requires spare capacity to cope with sudden increases in output, but spare capacity increases fixed costs per unit. Finally, delivery flexibility may require last-minute changes to delivery schedules, which may reduce the efficiency of the schedule (because most scheduling is planned by dedicated software).

Practice exercise 2 (35 marks), page 246

1 Calculate Fine Furniture's unit costs for 2015. Did the company achieve its unit costs objective for 2015? (3)

Fine Furniture plc's unit costs were £32,400/180 = £180 per unit. This failed to meet the target of £175 per unit.

2 To what extent might Fine Furniture plc's senior management be satisfied that it has achieved its operational objectives? (16)

- Labour productivity is 180/30 = 6 items per week, below the target of 6.5.
- The customer satisfaction rating of 8.4 is significantly higher than the 7.5 target.
- Customer complaints (1.2%) are better than the target (2%).
- Order punctuality of 95% exceeds the target (92%).

Analysis should be based on identifying the relative importance of these measures of performance (including unit costs from Question 1). For example, noting that unit costs are more important than labour productivity because it incorporates the effect of labour productivity on efficiency but also considers other areas of efficiency.

Analysis should also consider the extent to which different performance measures have been achieved (or missed) and the implications of this for the business. For example, customer satisfaction is much higher than its target and could have a very beneficial effect if the product is sold on the basis of its quality.

Evaluation: Fine Furniture plc is performing above target in terms of the targets involving customers. Customers will be pleased with the punctuality of the service and the quality of customer service provided. However, the company's failure to achieve higher productivity is leading to increased production costs. This will need to be improved in order to remain competitive.

3 Fine Furniture plc is looking for advice on the operational objectives that it should set for 2016. In the light of your answer to question 1 and the performance of Fine Furniture's main competitor, answer the following question: To what extent does Fine Furniture need to change its operational objectives for 2016? Justify your view. (16)

(The answers below are just examples. Answers should be assessed on the quality of the justification given.)

Modified targets are as follows:

- Unit costs = £160 per unit. This is significantly lower than the current level, but as its main competitor is achieving £150 per unit (£42,000/280), it must try to get closer to this performance.
- Labour productivity = 7 items per week. This involves a slight increase on present targets but does not require a dramatic improvement and will enable it to match its main competitor.
- Customer satisfaction rating = 8.4. It is achieving this level and is at a significantly higher rating than its competitor.
- Customer complaints = 1.2%. It is achieving this level but it is a difficult level to surpass.
- Order punctuality = 95%, a level that Fine Furniture is currently achieving, but which is 5% above the achievement of its closest competitor.

Evaluation: These targets will enable Fine Furniture plc to match or surpass its main competitor in each operational area except unit costs. However, Fine Furniture currently appears to be providing good quality at a relatively high cost. This may be its USP, so it may be unrealistic and unnecessary for it to surpass its competitor in every area.

Case study: Operations at Toyota (55 marks), pages 246–8

1 Analyse how Toyota's new GBL system will help to improve its flexibility and dependability. (9)

- 30% reduction of the time a vehicle spends in the body shop. This will lead to lower production time, thus improving volume flexibility because increased demand can be met more quickly.
- 70% reduction in the time taken to complete a major model change. This will improve mix flexibility by potentially broadening the range of versions of a model.
- 50% cut in the cost to add or switch models. This will improve product flexibility by making it easier to produce new models and/or mix flexibility if the new models are variations on the original model.
- 50% reduction in initial investment.
- 50% reduction in assembly line footprint.
- 50% cut in maintenance costs.
- The higher speed of production will make it easier to meet delivery times and thus improve dependability

Note: The GBL system is not described in the article, but is based on the features described in the article. Thus any approach that shows how these features help flexibility and dependability should be credited too. Examples include: local suppliers; short lead times; localised production; and any quality measures.

2 Analyse how Toyota's new GBL system will help to lower its unit costs. (9)

- 30% reduction of the time a vehicle spends in the body shop. This will lead to lower production time, thus lowering the unit costs as the same resources can produce more cars per hour.
- 50% reduction in initial investment. This will lower fixed costs and thus reduce unit costs of production.
- 50% reduction in assembly line footprint. The size of the production area will be reduced, reducing waste (of space) and lowering rent or land costs.
- 50% cut in maintenance costs. These cost savings will mean lower unit costs for each car produced.

Note: The GBL system is not described in the article, but is based on the features described in the article. Thus any approach that shows how these features help lower unit costs should be credited too. Examples include: short lead times; localised production to save transport costs; quality measures that cut costs of replacement;

cost savings of over £1 billion from purchasing materials; using kaizen to continuously improve methods.

3 Explain one reason why the achievement of quality is a key objective for Toyota. (5)

Quality is important so that the manufacturing process operates without disruption, enabling Toyota to lower costs.

A major benefit of quality is that it encourages consumers to buy the product and to pay a high price. Word-of-mouth advertising is positive and enables Toyota to add more value to its cars. This leads to long-term growth.

4 Toyota's operational objectives place a very high priority on the achievement of its environmental objectives. To what extent do you believe that this emphasis on environmental objectives will improve Toyota's competitiveness as a car manufacturer? (16)

Environmental objectives are helpful to Toyota because they enable the business to minimise waste. This can take the form of lower energy use, reduced wastage generated by the vehicle itself, and reduced waste during the production process. Toyota has also reduced costs by recycling energy and materials, and reusing 99.9% of its packaging.

Toyota has been able to make significant cuts in costs such as energy use (70% per vehicle) and water use (75% per vehicle). These cost savings help to reduce the price of the finished product.

As consumers become more discerning and aware of the environment, they seek out businesses with a good environmental record. If Toyota is achieving demanding environmental targets, particularly with respect to the environmental friendliness of the finished product, these customers are likely to increase their purchases of Toyota cars and the prices they are willing to pay.

Evaluation: Toyota must weigh up the benefits against the costs of introducing and implementing these targets. As consumers become increasingly aware of the environment, it is likely that such targets will become more important. Furthermore, as businesses are run by individuals, these targets may be set because the managers of the company believe them to be right rather than because they are a way of increasing profits. In Toyota's case, its environmental objectives have enabled it to make some very impressive achievements, all of which either reduce its costs or improve the value of its vehicles.

5 Toyota's operational objectives are influenced by both internal and external factors. Do you consider internal or external factors to be the more important influence on Toyota's operational objectives? Justify your view. (16)

Toyota's operational objectives have been categorised into three different areas. The relative impact of internal and external factors appears to depend on which category an objective fits within.

- Productive efficiency targets are largely dependent on the quality of the machinery used by the workforce, so the internal factors are crucial, although capacity utilisation is largely influenced by external market demand. Its policy of localisation is an internal factor but its success depends heavily on the quality of local suppliers near plants – this is an external factor. It has been able to cut material costs by £1 billion – a sign of efficient internal operations (although this may reflect lower prices in the external environment).

- Quality targets depend heavily on the HR and operational activities within a business and therefore internal factors dominate. However, as operations are often outsourced there may be a reliance on the quality of external suppliers, although problems in this aspect of operations could be attributed to poor internal control of outsourcing.

- Similarly, environmental objectives largely depend on the efficiency and willingness of a business to set challenging targets. However, the growing importance of environmental objectives has developed through greater external awareness of their importance.

Evaluation: Both internal and external factors have an influence, but predominantly it appears to be internal factors that are driving operational issues at Toyota, especially in terms of quality and environmental objectives. The exceptions are the environmental objectives and the influence of market factors on capacity utilisation and thus efficiency.

12 Analysing operational performance

Practice exercise 1: Data response (30 marks), pages 253–4

1 Calculate the capacity utilisation of Factory K. (2)

1,120/1,550 x 100 = 72.3% (or 72%)

2 Calculate the labour productivity of Factory L. (2)

1,330/7 = 190 units per worker

3 Calculate the unit costs of Factory J. (2)

£4,600/1,000 = £4.60 per unit

4 Based on the data in Tables 12.5 and 12.6, analyse two possible reasons why the unit costs of Factory M are lower than the unit costs of the other factories. (8)

- Factory M has much higher capacity utilisation and so it is using its fixed (non-current) assets much more effectively. This lowers AFC and thus helps to reduce average cost which is AFC + AVC.
- Labour productivity is 265 units per worker. This is much more efficient than the other factories – the next best performer is Factory J with 200 units per worker. With similar wages in each factory this means that wage costs per unit are much lower for Factory M. Wage costs are about 40% of TC so this is a significant saving.
- 'Other costs' per unit are £2.04 for Factory M. The next best factory is J, with £2.70, so again Factory M is the most efficient in terms of lower costs per unit.

5 Weekly demand for the company's products is fairly consistent, averaging 6,100 units per week. The Operations Director decides to close Factory L. Do you agree with this decision? Justify your view. (16)

- Future demand is forecast to average 6,100 units. After closing a factory, Brilliant Products plc should ensure that it can produce this amount each week, with some spare capacity for fluctuations. Closing Factory M leaves capacity of 8,050 – 1,900 = 6,150. This only allows for minor weekly fluctuations in demand. It may be more sensible to close a smaller factory, such as J or K to avoid potential shortages.
- Capacity utilisation of Factory L is low at 70% but it is higher than Factory J (63%) and so Factory L performs better than J in this measure of operational performance.
- Labour productivity in Factory L is much lower than M and slightly lower than J, but it is marginally better than Factory K.
- Unit costs are £4.96 in Factory L, which makes it the most expensive factory of the four.
- Factory M performs best in all three measures of operational performance and has the greatest capacity. Therefore it should not be considered when deciding on which factory to close.

Evaluation: Ultimately, weaknesses in labour productivity and capacity utilisation will lead to higher unit costs. Given that there is no comment on quality, the best way of measuring performance is unit costs because this is the factor that has the most significant impact on price and profit margins. Factory L has unit costs that are 12p per unit higher than Factory K (the third worst performer in this respect) and so it should be closed. However, its 'other costs' per unit are high and so it might be worth investigating the cause of this situation to see if it can be improved. The three remaining factories will operate with higher capacity utilisation; if low capacity utilisation is the main cause of its high costs then the decision should be reconsidered. The crucial factor is total capacity – if closure of Factory L leads to unfulfilled consumer demand then Factory K might be a more suitable choice for closure.

13 Making operational decisions to improve performance: increasing efficiency and productivity

Practice exercise 1 (60 marks), page 265

1 Using the information in the table, labour productivity would be measured by: (1)
   a Column 1 divided by Column 2
   b Column 1 divided by Column 4
   c Column 3 divided by Column 2
   d Column 3 divided by Column 4.

   The answer is a.

2 Using the information in the table, efficiency would be assessed by comparing: (1)
   a Column 1 with Column 2
   b Column 1 with Column 4
   c Column 3 with Column 2
   d Column 3 with Column 4.

   The answer is b.

3 In Table 13.1 (page 261), the firm is at maximum productive efficiency when output is: (1)
   a 1 unit
   b 8 units
   c 9 units
   d 12 units.

   The answer is c.

4 Using Table 13.1, the fixed costs per unit at 4 units of output are: (1)
   a £60
   b £119
   c £179
   d £240.

   The answer is a.

5 Analyse two possible economies of scale that might occur in a national newspaper publisher, or another firm of which you have knowledge. (9)
   - Technical economies. A national newspaper publisher will be able to afford sophisticated and highly productive equipment that will lead to quicker and more accurate production. Expensive computer facilities can improve flexibility, allowing more regular updates of stories and shorter lead times.
   - Purchasing economies. The large newspaper can buy its print materials in bulk, enabling it to undercut the prices of rival papers or enjoy a higher profit margin.

6 Analyse two possible diseconomies of scale that might occur in a national newspaper publisher, or the firm that you chose in question 5. (9)
   - Coordination. As the newspaper grows, it becomes more difficult to control the activities of different managers. In newspaper publishing this problem is particularly likely to happen if the publisher owns a variety of regional newspapers.
   - Communication. In a large publisher there may be too many layers of hierarchy or a wide span of control, both of which can impair the effectiveness of communication. A lack of feedback may mean that employees are not aware of their performance.

7 Distinguish between labour-intensive production and capital-intensive production. (4)
   - Labour-intensive production describes methods of production that use high levels of labour in comparison to capital equipment.
   - Capital-intensive production methods use a high level of capital equipment in comparison to other inputs, such as labour.

8 Analyse two factors that would influence a farmer when deciding whether to use labour-intensive production or capital-intensive production. (9)

- The business's finances. Capital equipment, such as a combine harvester, is expensive to install, so a farmer with low profits or cash-flow difficulties may not be able to afford capital-intensive methods, especially as farm labourers tend to be low paid.
- The nature of the product. Usually, capital-intensive methods are more suited to large-scale production of standardised products; labour-intensive methods are more suited to one-off, unique products or services. For some types of farming, such as livestock, it may not be possible to use equipment.

9 Read the fact file on computer games. To what extent was it inevitable that firms providing games for consoles, such as the Xbox or PlayStation, would change from being labour-intensive to capital-intensive? (16)

- Creativity and imagination are key elements of a computer game. These are readily available in firms of all sizes, so small firms can compete with larger firms in terms of the original ideas. However, most creative workers in the games console market are attracted to work for large firms.
- Consumers now want more sophisticated programmes. This requires teams of 20 to 40, rather than one or two people, making small firms uncompetitive, even when they have a very original idea.
- Games need to gain a certain market share before they become financially viable. The risk of failing to achieve this level of market share is too high for small firms.
- A typical development budget for a game is now $8 million. This is beyond the reach of small firms.

Evaluation: The combination of high costs and the need for high quality effectively means that only firms that can afford to lose millions of dollars on a game are able to stay in the market. Resources find their way to the highest rewards and so skilled workers are attracted to the larger firms in this industry.

10 Read the fact file on computer games. Analyse two reasons why it will be easier for small businesses to compete with larger firms in the market for games played on smartphones and tablets. (9)

- Typically, games consoles attract committed gamers. However, the Nintendo Wii and, more significantly, mobile devices have attracted 'casual gamers', who want to play during brief periods of relaxation. These customers do not require the sophisticated (expensive) programmes that are needed to appeal to committed gamers.
- In the mobile gaming market there are fewer opportunities for economies of scale and so small businesses can compete alongside larger competitors.
- Casual users who play games on mobile devices do not require high quality graphics and sound. These were the features that required high levels of capital equipment and gave competitive advantage to larger firms; this advantage does not matter so much in mobile gaming.
- The market for mobile games has grown quickly, increasing the opportunities of all businesses (including small businesses) to make profit. In 2013–14 this market generated annual revenue of almost $21 billion; a figure that is expected to reach almost $29 billion by 2016.

Case study: Productivity and efficiency in dairy farming (50 marks), pages 266–7

1 Based on the information in Table 13.4, what size of dairy herd is most efficient? (1)

301+

2 Based on the information in Table 13.3, calculate labour productivity in 1995. (2)

12,502 million litres/75,200 workers = 166,250 litres per worker
(or 0.166 million litres)

3 Based on data in the article and your answer to question 2, has productivity per cow improved more than labour productivity? Show your working. (5)

Labour productivity in 2011 was 11,893 million/38,160 = 311,661 litres per worker. This is nearly double the

figure for 1995. Table 13.3 shows that the average yield per cow increased from 5,320 to 7,480. This increase is about 40%, but is much lower than the labour productivity increase.

4 What evidence is there to suggest that dairy farming is NOT an efficient industry? (6)

- Farms with herd sizes of less than 150 produce an output that is less valuable than the input of factors of production. Although farms with more than 150 cows create a positive return, the average large farm's output is only slightly larger than its input.
- Dairy farmers have found it difficult to make enough money to survive, with a 60% decline in dairy farmers in 16 years.

- Low profits have given farmers little opportunity to modernise – this has led to efficiency remaining low.

5 Choose one of the bullet points in the final paragraph of the case study. Explain how the factor described might lead to an increase in efficiency in dairy farming. (5)

- The smaller, less efficient farms will leave the industry so that only the larger, more efficient farms remain. There will also be opportunities for these larger farms to grow further by taking over the farms that have left dairy farming; thus offering opportunities for further economies of scale.
- The milk wholesalers will compete in order to get supplies of milk, so that they can operate close to full capacity. However, they will want to give contracts to the most efficient farms who can produce the milk at competitive prices.
- Direct selling enables dairy farmers to specialise in high added value products, such as specialist cheeses. As inputs are being used to produce a greater value of outputs, this is recognised as a sign of improved efficiency.

6 Explain two reasons why dairy farming is becoming more capital intensive. (6)

- The move towards larger farms means that it is more likely that dairy farmers have the finance to invest in machinery in order to improve efficiency.
- Large herd sizes mean that equipment, such as milking machines, are more likely to be fully utilised and therefore more advantageous to the farmer because they reduce unit costs to a larger extent.
- Equipment has enabled farmers to increase the average yield of cows. It has also improved labour productivity by replacing workers with machinery. The extent of these efficiency gains is shown in Table 13.3.

7 Analyse the possible impact of the current low profits in dairy farming on the future efficiency of dairy farming. (9)

- Current low profits are driving farmers out of dairy farming. This is tending to hit the least efficient and smaller dairy farms most. Consequently the industry is being left with the larger, more efficient farms and so the efficiency of dairy farming as an industry should improve in future years.
- Current low profits are creating a climate in which dairy farmers know that they must improve efficiency if they are to survive. This has led to significant improvements in the use of machinery which has led to improvements in both the yield of cows and labour productivity.

- Many dairy farms have discovered that the best way of improving efficiency is to find ways of adding value. This is likely to lead to a continual drive towards direct selling through farm shops and farmers' markets, so that farmers can achieve greater profit from their output.

8 To what extent is the efficiency of a dairy farm outside the control of the dairy farmer? Justify your view. (16)

The efficiency of dairy farmers is influenced by both internal and external factors:

- Internal – the size of farms has increased, leading to greater economies of scale and thus lower unit costs of production.
- Internal – more capital intensive output is being used within dairy farming and this is improving the cost effectiveness of production.
- Internal – significant cuts in the labour force have helped to improve the cost effectiveness of output.
- External – the demand for milk and dairy products, such as cheese, has declined steadily over a long period of time and this has been a major negative influence on the ability of farmers to achieve a good price. Consequently, there is little scope for value added, which is a major measure of efficiency.
- External – competition between wholesalers has tended to cut the price offered a farms, although the increase in the capacity of the wholesalers may make them more inclined to offer better prices.
- External – competition between supermarkets has led to significant cuts in the real price of milk to consumers over a long period of time. The strong bargaining power of the supermarkets has led to pressure to cut the price paid to farmers for the milk that they supply.
- External – high fodder costs for feeding cows have increased the unit costs of dairy farms and led to lower efficiency.
- External – higher prices for specialist products, sold through direct selling, has enabled farms to improve their efficiency through achieving high added value.

Evaluation: The efficiency of dairy farming has been influenced by both internal and external factors, with many of the internal factors being in response to the external factors. For this reason, it could be argued that the external factors have been the key influence. Arguably the two most significant factors have been the decline in demand for dairy products accompanied by their use as loss leaders by supermarkets, which has further intensified the extent to which the price of milk has fallen in real terms. However, greater economies of scale and more efficient use of technology have been the dairy farmers' response to these external developments.

Practice exercise 2 (15 marks), page 272

1   Which of the following factors is most likely to increase the level of spare capacity in a firm?   (1)
    a   the firm's product becoming more fashionable
    b   closure of a factory
    c   new competitors entering the market
    d   an unsuccessful marketing campaign.

    The answer is c (although d is possible).

2   A business that produces 600 units has a spare capacity of 25%. Its output falls to 480 units. Calculate its new level of capacity utilisation.   (4)

    600 units of output leaves spare capacity of 25% so 600 units = 75% of full capacity
    Full capacity = 100%/75% × 600 = 800 units
    New output = 480 units
    Therefore, capacity utilisation = 480/800 × 100 = 60%

3   Explain how a more flexible workforce might help a business to overcome a capacity shortage.   (4)

A more flexible workforce might help because capacity is a measure of the normal maximum possible output. Flexible staff may work additional hours so that output can be higher than 'capacity' for a period of time. Also, flexible workers from other parts of the business may help the factory to increase output temporarily, until the capacity shortage problem is overcome.

4   Explain two ways in which a firm can reduce its capacity.   (6)
    • Selling all or part of its factories/retail outlets in order to reduce its maximum possible output.
    • Making staff redundant so that the maximum amount of output that can be produced is cut.
    • If the business only wants a temporary reduction it can put workers on a shorter working week; for example, by requiring part-time workers to work fewer hours or by reducing numbers of temporary workers.

Case study: Center Parcs builds a new resort to solve capacity problems (45 marks), pages 272–3

1   What is meant by the term 'capacity'?   (2)

    The maximum possible output that a business/factory can produce in a given time period.

2   Analyse two benefits for Center Parcs of having high capacity utilisation.   (9)
    • It reduces unit costs. The higher the level of capacity utilisation, the more efficiently a business is using its resources. At 97.2% capacity utilisation, Center Parcs is able to spread its fixed costs, such as rent, over a wide range of customers. This enables it to charge competitive prices.
    • It allows price rises. Knowing that it can fill most of its accommodation means that Center Parcs can charge higher prices. Customers will be eager to pay high prices and book early because they know that it is unlikely that they will be able to find spaces if they book later.
    • Customer views of quality. High capacity utilisation suggests that Center Parcs is popular with customers. This will encourage any customers who are more hesitant about ordering to book a holiday, because it gives the impression that Center Parcs provides a good service.

3   Analyse two possible problems for Center Parcs if its capacity utilisation fell dramatically.   (9)

    • If fixed cost remains unchanged, the fixed cost per unit will be higher, and so the unit cost for the business will be greater than it needed to be.
    • Variable costs may fall if the under-utilisation is due to a decline in sales that was expected. But there may also be less scope for bulk-buying and other economies, so variable costs per unit may rise.
    • Workers can become demoralised by a lack of work and a feeling of vulnerability. Redundancies may make it harder for Center Parcs to attract skilled workers if demand rises again.
    • Spare capacity can portray a negative image of the business to its customers. Furthermore, the low capacity may weaken Center Parcs' ability to charge high prices as customers may know that it is struggling to sell accommodation.

4   Center Parcs achieved annual sales of £304 million a year with capacity utilisation of 97.2%. Assuming that the remaining 2.8% of holidays could be sold for the same price, what would Center Parcs' annual sales revenue have been if it had operated at 100% capacity utilisation?   (4)
    100% = x
    97.2% = £304m
    Therefore, x = 100/97.2 × £304m = £312.75 million
    (Accept £312.8 million or £313 million.)

5 Center Parcs could increase its capacity by increasing the amount of accommodation provided at its existing sites. Why might it be reluctant to take this approach? (5)

This might reduce the quality of the holiday experience, as it may make the site too crowded. First, it is taking away an area of land for recreational use and thus lowering the attractiveness of the park's environment. Second, it would also put more customers onto the site and they would be competing for the same facilities. This is likely to lead to longer queues and thus reduce the number of activities that customers can experience.

6 To what extent do you believe that Center Parcs' pricing policy is the most important factor in achieving high capacity utilisation at Center Parcs? (16)

- It charges higher fees in the school holidays. A four-night midweek stay in four-bedroom accommodation in August costs £2,499; the equivalent break in mid-November costs £799. This encourages people to book away from the peak times, so that bookings are more evenly spread throughout the year. By carefully assessing what customers are willing to pay at different times of the year, and setting low prices at unpopular times and higher prices at more popular times, Center Parcs is able to increase capacity utilisation.

- With over 60% of turnover coming from repeat business, there is an indication that most customers are very satisfied, leading to high demand each year. Customer satisfaction ratings show that 96% rank their holidays as good or excellent. The pricing must be seen as reasonable by most customers.

- Pricing of individual activities is also used to keep capacity utilisation high. The pools are provided free of price while low popular activities, such as table tennis, are charged at £5 an hour. To reduce excessive use of the popular facilities, such as laser combat, £22 an hour is charged.

- Finally, high prices are used to improve the quality of the facilities, again encouraging bookings.

Although prices are used to keep capacity utilisation high, there are other factors too:

- Center Parcs provide a unique experience in the UK and so demand is likely to be high.

- Planning permission problems severely restrict the number of sites and so supply will remain relatively low, ensuring high utilisation rates.

- Center Parcs have invested in updating their accommodation and facilities. These changes have ensured that they are meeting the changing needs of customers, such as hot tubs, televisions and spas, while eliminating or reducing less wanted facilities, such as squash courts.

Evaluation: It could be argued that the overall level of capacity utilisation is linked more closely to supply and demand factors. High demand has resulted from Center Parcs' understanding of its customers' needs, while supply has been restricted by planning permission and related issues. However, the use of pricing has enabled Center Parcs to manage capacity utilisation of individual facilities, by setting high prices for popular times and activities so that demand does not exceed supply. For less popular times and activities, lower prices have ensured higher capacity utilisation.

Practice exercise 3 (20 marks), page 278

1 What is meant by the term 'lean production'? (2)

Lean production is production based on the range of time-saving and waste-saving measures inspired by Japanese manufacturing companies.

2 What is meant by the term 'just-in-time production'? (2)

Just-in-time production is a system whereby items of inventory arrive just at the time they are needed for production or sale.

3 Study the fact file on easyCar and analyse the characteristic of lean production that the company uses most often. Justify your choice. (7)

easyCar seems to be focused on minimising waste of resources and time. Initially, staff costs were reduced by saving time on washing cars, refuelling and transporting customers between their homes and the branch. Costs were also saved through minimal advertising, the booking system, the efficient use of cars (90% utilisation) and mass purchases of just one model. All of these factors derive from two aspects of lean production: muda (minimisation of waste) and time-based management. Recent approaches mean that easyCar acts as a booking agent and so there is no need to even hold an inventory of cars, as these may belong to private individuals.

4 Analyse how just-in-time methods can improve the efficiency of a manufacturer of packaging materials, such as cardboard boxes. (9)

- JIT works on the pull system so the packaging manufacturer knows that there is a customer for the product it is making, thus significantly reducing the problems of making items that do not sell.

- Space is saved because there is no need to store packaging and boxes –items can be delivered directly to the customer.

- It allows the manufacturer to offer more flexibility and variety to customers, if its manufacturing process allows this. Requests by customers for unusual packaging material can be provided, because items can be tailored to customer requirements. With 'push' systems of production it would be too risky to manufacture unusual items.

Case study: Comparison between Marks & Spencer and Zara (55 marks), pages 278–80

1 Explain two benefits to Marks & Spencer arising from its approach to large-scale retailing. (8)

- Bulk-buying economies of scale – traditional mass production techniques allow the business to buy its raw materials or stock in large quantities, thus helping to keep unit costs low and either make the product cheaper or gain higher profit margins on each item.

- Mass production enables Marks & Spencer to use flow production. The continuous method of production means that machinery is used efficiently and staff can carry out specialist roles, enhancing their skills and speed.

- Fewer deliveries are made and mass production leads to higher stock levels. This means that the business is less likely to run out of stock, so it is unlikely to lose customer goodwill and may even capture disgruntled customers from other businesses.

2 Explain why Marks & Spencer's approach is more suited to socks and underwear than to fashion items. (6)

Marks & Spencer's approach enables the company to plan production carefully and on a large scale. This helps the company to keep costs low and monitor the quality of its products. However, it involves long lead times and relies on accurately forecasting the future tastes of its customers. For fashion items this can cause problems because the firm may be left with large quantities of stock. However, as a rule socks are not 'fashion' items and so it is probable that all of the stock will be sold eventually. Thus there is no need for short lead times.

3 Zara's production and supply of clothing operates on a just-in-time basis. Analyse two factors that might lead to problems in using this approach. (9)

- Weather problems and other unexpected external events create more serious problems if 'just-in-time' is being used. Any unexpected delays, such as the late receipt of raw materials, create a greater problem because no back-up items are being held, 'just in case' of difficulties. This could mean that the shops run short on items, which could seriously damage the company's reputation.

- Just-in-time means that independence is given to suppliers and individuals within the organisation. Consequently, Zara needs to trust these stakeholders fully and runs the risk of a much lower level of control of certain aspects of its operations.

4 To what extent is the success of Zara's operations management dependent on its strategy of empowering some of its key employees? (16)

- People-centred management is critical because the whole system at Zara relies on the skills of individuals. A greater empowerment of workers exists compared with other stores, particularly with the designers and shop managers.

- There is also a greater need for trust rather than control, as speed is more important than quality. Consequently, workers need to be able to set their own targets, devise their own methods and assess their own achievements.

- More consultation is needed, so that Zara can understand both its customers and the capabilities of its employees.

- Workers take greater responsibility – the constant modifications to the product range mean that workers cannot establish a routine; they must be flexible and adaptable.

Evaluation: All of the features above are necessary to Zara's success. It is heavily reliant on the performance of individuals and, although some characters such as the designers are vitally important, it is important that all staff recognise the need to take the initiative and to react in a flexible way to the demands of customers.

5 Evaluate the advantages and disadvantages to Zara of its shorter product development times. (16)

Advantages:

- Zara's shorter product development time means that it can react much more quickly to changes in fashion, which is especially useful if customers want a replica of a garment that they have seen recently.

- Zara only holds a few examples of each item in stock, so any mistakes will not be excessively costly in terms of wasted stock.
- The focus on speed satisfies consumers who value products for fashion rather than durability, so there is less pressure on Zara to spend time and effort on quality.
- The shorter product development approach encourages customers to visit shops more frequently, as there is an expectation that new items of stock will keep arriving in stores.

Disadvantages:

- The system relies heavily on the skills of certain staff – notably the ability of the shop managers to anticipate demand for items accurately and the ability of designers to

produce or reproduce popular fashion items at a low cost.

- The constant change of stock may upset customers who find that a product line has been finished before they were able to buy it.
- The approach increases costs as it prevents Zara from using suppliers in countries with very low costs.

Evaluation: An approach of shorter product development times has worked well for Zara, as indicated by its growth and the number of companies benchmarking against it. However, it is dependent on customers wanting a certain type of clothing. If society changes and customers become concerned less about fashion and more about the durability of their clothing, Zara's approach will not succeed. In recent years the trends have suggested that Zara's formula will actually become more successful.

Practice exercise 4 (35 marks), page 288

1 What is meant by the term 'technology'? (2)

In business, technology describes the applications of practical, mechanical, electrical and related sciences to industry and commerce.

2 What do the initials EPOS stand for? (2)

EPOS stands for electronic point of sale.

3 Distinguish between CAD and CAM. (4)
- CAD is computer-aided design – the use of computers to improve the design of products.
- CAM is computer-aided manufacture – the use of computers to undertake activities such as planning, operating and controlling production.

4 State two ways in which robots can be used in a business. (2)

Robots can be used for: handling operations; welding; assembling; packaging; measuring; inspecting; hazardous applications.

5 Analyse two advantages to a retailer of using technology in its inventory control. (8)
- Computer programs linked to statistics on patterns of consumer purchases enable a firm to anticipate changes in stock inventory levels more accurately and thus reduce the possibility of running out of stock or building up unnecessarily high levels.
- Re-ordering becomes much easier, as retailers can link their tills to stock control systems. These systems automatically contact the supplier when the re-order level is reached.

- Organisations with many branches can use IT to locate stock inventory and, if necessary, switch stock from one branch to another, according to consumer needs.

6 Analyse two benefits of technology to a car manufacturer. (8)
- Ideas for products and processes can be created and compared more quickly using technology, and ideas can be simulated through computer programs, saving considerable sums of money by eliminating the need to produce and test prototypes.
- The use of fully automated production lines that are controlled by computers increases productivity and flexibility. It also reduces the risk of human error. Greater miniaturisation in production allows very small components to be manufactured that could not be made by humans.
- The internet can benefit a car manufacturer by reducing the need for staff and expensive premises. Potential customers can access details of cars through the internet and place their orders directly, thus saving the expense of having a large sales force.
- The internet allows access 24 hours a day, and credit card payments can be made immediately. This enables the car manufacturer to make its products available at times that suit the customer.

7 Explain three ways in which the use of information technology might create difficulties for a firm. (9)

- It can lead to job losses for workers, particularly those in traditional skilled crafts. This causes stress and can lead to demoralisation and demotivation of workers. Even those workers whose jobs are not immediately threatened will be affected by the fates of their colleagues and, as a consequence, productivity may fall.

- It is expensive to introduce. Firms must also consider whether to spend money continually on IT in order to keep up to date, or allow the business to fall behind competitors, but save on IT costs.

- The constantly changing nature of IT means that there is a continual need to replace hardware and software. Continuous training for staff is also needed and adds to costs. The efficiency of businesses that are unable to keep pace is under threat.

Case study: Automation for dishwashers (30 marks), pages 288–9

1 Explain one reason why employees may oppose the introduction of robots on Bosch Siemens' dishwasher production line. (5)

Employees may believe that the robots will replace them on the production line. Furthermore, as robots become more sophisticated, they are likely to be taking away the more highly skilled jobs that pay well.

2 Analyse two reasons why employees may support the introduction of the robots. (9)

- The robots may be taking away the more routine, boring jobs, leaving the workers with the more interesting roles to fulfil.

- Robots can be programmed to work in difficult conditions such as high temperatures or handling heavy loads. Using robots may improve health and safety for the employees.

- The greater profitability of the business should enable it to pay higher wages to its workforce. The employees may benefit from greater job security if the business is more profitable.

3 Bosch Siemens identified a number of benefits to the business arising from the introduction of the robots. Evaluate the major advantages to Bosch Siemens of introducing these robots. (16)

- Improved quality will be a great help to Bosch, as this is one of its unique selling points. The high quality will enable it to offer guarantees for ten or more years without fear of excessive compensation to customers whose dishwashers have deteriorated before the guarantee ends.

- The gentler handling of components and the consequent elimination of waste, along with the greater productivity achieved, will reduce the cost of making the dishwashers. This will allow Bosch either to charge a more competitive price or to increase its profit margin.

- Greater reliability and flexibility will enable Bosch to meet sudden increases in demand for its dishwashers, if necessary.

- Bosch will be able to fulfil its obligations to its employees by improving their working conditions.

Evaluation: Which of these benefits is/are the major advantage(s) will depend on the aims of Bosch. As a business with a reputation for quality, it is probable that Bosch will see improved quality as the main benefit, although higher productivity will boost its profitability in a more clear-cut way.

14 Making operational decisions to improve performance: improving quality

Practice exercise 1 (30 marks), pages 298–9

1 Which of these factors is a tangible feature of quality? (1)
   a durability
   b exclusiveness
   c image
   d reputation.

   The answer is a.

2 Which of these factors is an intangible feature of quality? (1)
   a additional features
   b after-sales service
   c brand
   d reliability.

   The answer is c.

3 'Right first time' is a feature of: (1)
   a inspection
   b kaizen
   c quality assurance
   d quality control.

   The answer is c.

4 Which one of these costs would not be a direct consequence of a failure to control quality? (1)
   a prevention costs
   b product recall costs
   c reworking costs
   d scrappage costs.

   The answer is a.

5 What is meant by the term 'quality'? (2)

   Quality describes the features of a product or service that allow it to satisfy (or delight) customers.

6 Explain why firms have tended to move from quality control to quality assurance. (6)

   Quality assurance is considered to be superior because it gives greater responsibility for the product to individual workers. This will lead to higher levels of motivation and productivity, and greater consistency in the level of quality. Consequently, customers will be more willing to buy the products. Quality control relies on inspectors identifying quality issues after they have occurred. This costs money. With quality assurance, costs are also reduced by the decline in need to rework and scrap products.

7 Analyse two difficulties a business might face when trying to improve the quality of its products. (9)
   • Costs. Quality procedures require a great deal of administrative expense to set up and operate. Therefore, the business must ensure that the financial benefits arising from the higher quality achieved exceed the costs needed to achieve higher quality.

   • Training. This can be a major issue in the introduction of a new quality system, as it is with the introduction of any new operating system. Training may be quite extensive and costly. Recent changes in quality systems tend to involve workers far more in guaranteeing quality, so high-quality training has become more and more important.

   • Disruption to production. In the short run, the training programme provided can be quite disruptive to existing production methods. Workers will need to be trained before the new system is introduced and so, in order to undertake their training, they may need to be taken off the current production line.

8 Analyse two possible benefits to a business that result from the high quality of its products. (9)

- The cost of waste materials or scrapping of products is reduced, enabling a business to cut its prices and become more competitive. Alternatively, it may keep prices the same and benefit from higher profit margins.

- High quality will lead to brand loyalty and high sales volume, so that the business can expand its scale of operations.
- High quality will improve the product's reputation and may give the business a competitive advantage. Better quality will enable the firm to charge a higher price and so enjoy greater added value.

Case study: Constance Products plc (50 marks), page 299

1 Analyse the reasons why a shift to quality assurance led to 'increased morale of the workforce'. (9)

- After quality assurance was introduced, the jobs of the workforce became more varied and interesting.
- Workers were given greater levels of responsibility, a factor recognised as a motivator by Herzberg. In this case, the extra responsibility became a motivating factor for the workers after nine months.
- The system brings a greater recognition of the worker's role, a motivating factor recognised by Herzberg.
- Workers had more control over their daily routine and approach to work, which would have increased morale.

2 Identify one measure of quality that could still be improved, and analyse two ways in which Constance Products might improve that aspect of its operations. (9)

Answers might focus on one of the following:

- Scrap rate. Additional training of the workers, to ensure that the product is not passed on to the next stage of productions unless it is in perfect condition, should help to alleviate this problem. The machinery or production process could be investigated to see if they might be causing the problems. Better materials from suppliers might also be a way of rectifying this problem.
- Customer complaints. Careful research to ensure that Constance Products is providing exactly what the customer requires may help reduce complaints. The business should also scrutinise the quality of its components and raw materials bought in from its suppliers.

3 To what extent did quality suffer during the early stages of the change from quality control to quality assurance? (16)

- Training was needed to give the workforce the necessary skills and this created a drain on finances. Constance Products found that its workers were less productive during the training period.

- A change of culture, from one of clear direction and control to one of greater autonomy for the workers, could have created uncertainty in the workforce. If workers were attracted to the organisation because of its original culture, this change might have led lower morale.
- There was a two-week loss of production – unless the organisation anticipated the potential loss of production during this time, it could have created problems in its relationship with customers.
- There was much slower production during the first few weeks, again possibly leading to a loss of customer goodwill.

Evaluation: Most of the problems indicated are short-term issues that may gradually disappear as time passes. However, Sarah pointed out that Constance Products had a relatively unskilled workforce, hinting that they might be less capable of operating a system that involves empowerment of workers. In the long run, the ability of the workers could be the key difficulty.

4 Evaluate the overall success of the new system once it had been fully established. (16)

Benefits of the new system:

- Morale increased significantly, as workers enjoyed greater responsibility and more interesting jobs. Furthermore, they were about to receive productivity bonuses, suggesting that improvements had been made in output per worker.
- Delivery times were improved from 1.4 days to 0.7 days.
- The percentage of deliveries on time rose from 93% to 99%.
- Ratings of customer satisfaction increased from 88% to 96%.
- Employee satisfaction ratings rose from 63% to 92%.

Problems were:

- Two weeks' production was lost in order to redesign the production line.

- The first few weeks were a disaster, with everyone working slowly while they adapted to the new system. In the table, five of the six measures of quality show a deterioration in the early stages. This could have been disastrous for the company's reputation.
- The scrap rate rose from 1% to 3% and was 5% in the early stages of implementation.
- Customer complaints rose from 2% to 3%, but reached 7% in the early stages of implementation.

Evaluation: In four of the six measures of quality there were improvements. These were most noticeable in employee satisfaction ratings, which increased by a very impressive percentage. There were significant improvements in the percentage of deliveries on time and in the delivery time, and overall customer satisfaction also increased. Although there were some declining ratings, these were relatively small, and so, overall, the introduction of quality assurance appears to have been a success.

Case study: Quality of the visitor experience: Alice Holt 2013 (34 marks), pages 300–1

1   A Net Promoter Score (NPS) greater than 80 is considered to be exceptionally high. Analyse two possible reasons why a visitor attraction, such as Alice Holt, is able to achieve such a high score.   (9)
- There is no entry fee and so visitors are likely to feel that it provides value for money.
- There are some facilities which involve spending money, such as the café, but these seem to be reasonably priced – the average visitor to Alice Holt only spent £4.07 compared with £6.13 for other Forestry Commission sites.
- Forestry Commission sites, such as Alice Holt, are likely to attract visitors who know what to expect (e.g. trees) and therefore should experience something that they know, in advance, that they will enjoy.
- The variety of facilities should help visitors to enjoy the experience.

2   Analyse two ways in which Alice Holt might improve its attractiveness to visitors.   (9)
- Improving the café, as this feature has the lowest satisfaction rating. Research should focus on the causes of this rating, for example, whether it is price, quality or choice. Once this has been established, appropriate improvements can be made.
- The other low rating applies to the car parking. Again, the reasons for this rating (such as price, quality of the surface and convenience of its location) should be established.
- Go Ape is the most highly rated facility but is only used by a minority of visitors. A reconsideration of the price charged might help to boost overall attractiveness by increasing use of this facility.

3   Evaluate the key factors that led to Alice Holt achieving a high rating for quality from its customers. Justify your view.   [16]
- It provides a peaceful environment, a factor which may appeal to its target markets, such as families with young children.
- The cost: entry is free and the average visitor to Alice Holt only spent £4.07.
- Most of the facilities were rated highly and so these would have contributed to a high satisfaction rating, albeit in different ways:
- The two most highly rated facilities were the most active pursuits – Go Ape and cycling. However, the number of people commenting on these facilities – 33 and 41 respectively – suggests that they are activities that are paid for, as relatively few visitors out of the 241 surveyed expressed an opinion.
- The most widely used facilities (excluding car parking) are the play areas and equipment, and the choices of paths for walking. These facilities were used by the majority of visitors and also showed high satisfaction ratings.

Evaluation: The high rating for quality appears to arise from a combination of different factors, all of which contribute. The low cost appears to be a key factor, as there are relatively few opportunities in the United Kingdom for non-cost leisure activities. For a minority, the high rating is caused by specialist, more active leisure pursuits. However, a high overall rating requires popularity from a high percentage of the visitors. Therefore, arguably it is the two mainstay activities – the play areas and forest walks – that are the key factors leading to a high rating overall.

15 Making operational decisions to improve performance: managing inventory and supply chains

Practice exercise 1 (65 marks), page 313

1 A business is scheduled to deliver 1,000 items of a product to a customer on 21 July. On 20 July the customer requests a modification to the order so that the delivery on the next day will be of a different version of the product. This is an example of: (1)
   a delivery flexibility
   b mix flexibility
   c product flexibility
   d volume flexibility

   The answer is b.

2 Mass customisation is: (1)
   a an approach to production that uses 'push' methods
   b based on companies keeping high levels of inventory so that customers have a wide choice of products
   c offering individually tailored products to customers on a large scale
   d a production system that customises goods but not services.

   The answer is c.

3 Customisation where the consumer is unaware of the customisation is: (1)
   a adaptive customisation
   b collaborative customisation
   c cosmetic customisation
   d transparent customisation.

   The answer is d.

4 Which one of the following is most likely to be based on mass production methods? (1)
   a producing to order
   b mass customisation
   c built to stock
   d tailor-made production.

   The answer is c.

5 Explain one problem facing a business that uses mass customisation. (4)

   Mass customisation requires an expensive management information system. This cost could be prohibitive to a small business.

   This approach is based on flexible suppliers. Because suppliers do not know what to supply in advance, each order is likely to be small – increasing costs for both the supplier and the producer.

6 Explain two factors that are necessary for mass customisation to take place. (6)
   • A market in which customers value variety and individuality. Ideally this variety should be based around one or two standard products, so the individuality can be achieved by customising a standard product rather than making a totally different product.
   • A large-scale market so that there is sufficient scope for manufacturers to achieve economies of scale, in order for it to compete with high volume producers who do not provide customisation.
   • An ability to respond quickly to market changes, because the individuality that customers desire is likely to change rapidly.

7 Analyse how a hotel might use temporary or part-time staff in order to improve flexibility. (9)

- Volume flexibility can be achieved because the contracts of temporary staff are such that the hotel may call on workers when there are many guests staying, to cope with sudden increases in numbers.

- Volume flexibility can also benefit the hotel during off-peak periods. It will not require temporary staff to work if relatively few guests are staying at that time, thus cutting costs when there is a low level of revenue being earned.

- Product flexibility can be achieved because a hotel may be able to call on a wide number of people who work on temporary or part-time contracts. This can give the hotel a broad spectrum of skills, so that different services can be provided in accordance with the needs of the customers. For example, some temporary staff may have kitchen skills while others may have entertainment skills.

8 Explain two factors a business might consider when deciding on whether to outsource its production. (6)

- The business's level of spare capacity. A business with high levels of spare capacity is unlikely to outsource production, but one that is close to full capacity will find outsourcing to be advantageous

- Quality. Is the business more capable of producing a high quality product than the company to which it is outsourcing production? If so, it might be unwise to outsource.

- Cost. Will outsourcing lead to a significant reduction in costs, because of the expertise of the company to which production is being outsourced? If not, then the business should consider manufacturing the good itself.

9 Explain two benefits to a clothing manufacturer as a result of improvements in its flexibility. (6)

- It can increase the volume of sales, because customers may like the idea that styles can be quickly modified to suit their tastes.

- It can reduce the risk of holding high levels of unsold inventory once an item is made but which are then considered to be unfashionable by customers.

- Flexibility usually meets the needs of the customer, whether it is a newly designed product or one that is delivered promptly, and therefore a clothing manufacturer is likely to be able to charge a higher price for its products.

10 Explain how a business might improve its speed of response. (5)

Speed of response may be improved by having an effective and up-to-date information technology system so that customer requirements can be dealt with quickly. Ideally there should also be a flexible workforce prepared to focus on priority tasks, such as working late to complete an order.

11 Analyse two reasons why aeroplanes are built to order. (9)

- The manufacture of an aeroplane is a very time-consuming and expensive undertaking. Consequently, an aeroplane manufacturer will want to be certain that the aeroplane has a buyer before it commences production. Build-to-order provides this guarantee.

- Individual airlines like to have their own distinctive aircraft and often use the layout of their aircraft to promote their airlines. Some airlines will want a large number of seats to fill, while others will want more luxurious accommodation fitted on to the plane.

- Holding an inventory of aeroplanes is impractical because of the huge investment that it represents. Similarly, airlines will only want an aircraft to be completed at the time that it needs it. Most airlines believe that they can accurately predict future numbers and therefore will place orders years in advance of production.

12 Evaluate the pros and cons of mass customisation for a fast-food provider, such as Burger King. (16)

Pros:

- It enables a restaurant to benefit from economies of scale while still meeting individual taste of consumers.

- It gives the restaurant a better understanding of its customers. Mass production companies will only know how many consumers like what they are offered, whereas mass customisation companies will know which products the customers prefer.

- Mass customisation provides more varied jobs for staff who are preparing meals and therefore should increase the level of motivation of the workforce

Cons:

- Mass customisation can cause difficulties if a customer rejects the meal that is offered, because it is specifically tailored to the needs of that customer. Therefore it is less likely to be suitable for other customers.

- Mass customisation increases costs, particularly in terms of information technology, flexible capital equipment and additional

- training for staff. These additional costs may not be paid for by the benefits received.
- Suppliers need to be very flexible. If the restaurant supply chain lacks flexibility, it can lead to discontented customers who are unable to purchase the dishes that they prefer.

Evaluation: Fast-food restaurants may find it difficult to match the low costs of competitors who do not provide mass customisation.

However, they will be able to provide meals that are more specific to the wants of the customers. Because customers are becoming more familiar with mass customisation, it is likely that they will be prepared to pay a premium price for a customised meal, even from a fast-food restaurant. This should lead to higher levels of profit, particulars as customisation can often operate at only slightly higher levels of cost than mass production providers.

Case study: Dell [Part 1] (30 marks), pages 313–4

1 Explain how mass customisation reduces inventory costs for a company such as Dell. (5)

Mass customisation reduces inventory costs because computers are made to order. The components are only purchased after an order has been made and they arrive just-in-time for assembly, so no storage is needed. There is also little need for storage of finished computers as they are dispatched directly to the customer. These factors lead to minimal storage costs.

2 Analyse two reasons why Dell experienced problems when trying to match supply to demand. (9)
- The basic unit of the computers sold in the USA were made in Taiwan. In effect, this meant that Dell had to hold high levels of inventory of its base units, in anticipation of demand, because the delivery times from Taiwan were much longer than from the USA.
- Sales grew quickly and Dell found it difficult to keep pace with the demand. In time it opened up new outlets in many different sites around the world, such as Ireland, Malaysia, China and Brazil. However, prior to these new factories being built it became difficult to meet customer demands quickly.
- Increasing competition also made it hard to estimate the level of demand for Dell's own computers.

3 To what extent was 'outsourcing' beneficial to Dell's aim to achieve sales growth? (16)

The value of outsourcing to Dell:
- Initially it was beneficial because it allowed Dell to continue to grow quickly and meet growing demand, as it expanded beyond the USA.

BUT this did lead to difficulties in managing inventory because of the time that it took for basic units to be supplied from Taiwan.
- The new assembly factories in places such as Ireland helped Dell to improve production and delivery costs (in fact these were Dell factories, but this is not stated in the case and so this is a valid point).
- Outsourcing enabled Dell to focus on its core capability of customising basic units.

BUT this did lead to Dell outsourcing so many of its activities that it lost some of its core capabilities and even helped companies, notably Asus, to develop the skills that would allow it to set up as a competitor to Dell.
- Outsourcing customer support to call centres in India would have reduced Dell's costs of providing customer support.

BUT this led to its rating as the best computer customer service provider being hit because of problems leading to poor quality service. This could have been a major issue for a mass customisation firm such as Dell.

Evaluation: Initially, outsourcing proved to be beneficial to Dell because it allowed it to expand beyond the USA market. However, the article indicates that Dell appeared to rely too much on outsourcing so that its core capabilities were lost. Also some outsourcing, such as customer services, did not operate efficiently and damaged Dell's reputation. On balance the outsourcing has been a contributing factor towards Dell deciding to change its strategy, although whether this change proves to be an advantage or a disadvantage remains to be seen.

Practice exercise 2 (40 marks), page 318

1 Identify the three different forms of inventory. (3)
- raw materials
- work-in-progress
- finished goods.

2 Explain two advantages of holding high levels of inventory. (6)
- This allows the business to buy in bulk, saving costs and benefiting from economies of scale.

The price can therefore be set low or the company can have high profit margins.

- High inventory levels enable a business to react quickly to sudden increases in demand. They also avoid a firm being tarnished with a bad reputation caused by its failure to meet customers' needs.

3 Explain two problems of holding high levels of inventory. (6)

- High inventory levels will increase storage costs. This can be a major expense for an organisation operating in a high rental area, such as a high street.
- There will be more likelihood of pilferage or damage to inventory. With perishable inventory the items may become out of date, especially if demand falls unexpectedly.
- Firms need money to buy the inventory and this reduces cash flow. For a company experiencing a cash shortage, high levels of inventory can be very damaging.

4 Explain two factors that will influence the re-order level of a product. (6)

- The lead time of the supplier. If the supplier takes a long time to deliver its products then the organisation that is buying will want to have a high re-order level to ensure that it does not run out of inventory.
- The demand for the product. If demand is high, the inventory will deplete rapidly and so a high re-order level is needed.
- The buffer inventory level. If the organisation wants to maintain a high minimum inventory level, perhaps because demand is unpredictable or inconsistent, then it will need to set a high buffer inventory level.
- If the business is aware that its inventory control is inefficient, it may decide to operate a higher buffer inventory level than usual to avoid running out of inventory.

5 State three possible reasons for inventory wastage. (3)

- Waste of materials during the manufacturing process.

- Materials wasted because finished products are faulty and need to be scrapped.
- Pilferage or theft by employees or customers.
- Damage to inventory during storage or production.
- Obsolescence – inventory becoming out of date or outmoded.

6 What is meant by just-in-time inventory control? (2)

Just-in-time is a Japanese philosophy that organises operations so that inventory arrives just in time for it to be used in the production process.

7 Analyse two benefits of just-in-time inventory control for an electrical goods manufacturer. (9)

- The production area is less cluttered, reducing the risk of accidents and damage to inventory. For a manufacturer of electrical goods, this could involve bulky materials and electrical items that would add to the risk of accidents.
- The costs of storage will be reduced if the manufacturer holds less inventory, with noticeable savings because these goods may be bulky. This reduces the necessary size of warehouses and storage areas. In addition to saving rent, it can also lower wage costs and insurance.
- Inventory will be unlikely to perish and become out of date if it goes immediately on to the production line. Although electrical goods are unlikely to perish they may become obsolete or be seen to be out of date quite quickly.

8 Why might suppliers dislike supplying to a company that operates on a just-in-time basis? (5)

The suppliers will be under constant pressure to deliver small, regular amounts to such a company. This means that the supplier has to be very efficient, producing just the amount required. If orders are unpredictable or irregular, this will be very difficult to achieve.

Ironically, the supplier will probably have to hold high inventory levels, just in case a sudden order is received.

Case study: Inventory out of control (55 marks), pages 318–9

1 In the first eight days, inventory control operated smoothly. Use this information and Figure 15.2 to work out the value of:

a the maximum inventory level (1)

6,000 units

(Accept answers between 6,800 and 7,000 because of the situation in Week 28, but this is not the normal maximum level.)

b the buffer inventory level (1)

1,000 units

c the re-order level, assuming a lead time of 2 days (3)

3,500 units

Re-order level = minimum inventory + use during lead time

Daily use = 5,000 units over 4 days = 1,250 units per day

1,000 + (2 x 1,250) = 3,500

2 Briefly explain two factors that might have caused the company to run out of inventory on day 13. (6)

- Magni Pizzas failed to order at the re-order level. The delivery took place three days after inventory had run out and so it suggests that the order was placed four days too late.
- The supplier may have failed to deliver on time – it may have been three days late because of a strike or communication failure.

Note: The rate of use of inventory is the same throughout the first 13 days – 1,250 items per day, and so any answer that suggests that this was caused by a sudden increase in demand is wrong.

3 Explain why the zero levels of inventory during the period between days 17 and 28 were caused by different factors from those that led to the zero level of inventory on day 13. (8)

- The inventory-outs between days 17 and 28 did not follow the same pattern as the day 13 inventory-out. The slope of the lines indicates that the use of inventory was much higher in this period. This indicates that increased demand was a factor in the inventory-outs during this period. It is possible that this increase arose from consumers buying extra pizza bases because they had been unable to purchase them while Magni had run out of inventory previously.
- A second, less significant, factor was the inventory delivery on day 16, which was just over 2,000 units whereas other inventory deliveries had been 5,000 units. This suggests a mistake in the order – either the order placed was too low or the amount delivered was less than that requested.

4 Explain one possible reason for the change in the chart after day 28. (4)

- The order level for day 28 was much higher than usual (over 6,500 units were delivered). This was probably an attempt to prevent future shortages of inventory.
- The slope of the line after day 28 suggests a much lower use of inventory, the result of a fall in demand. This was probably caused by customer dissatisfaction and the subsequent loss of goodwill because of Magni's frequent inventory-outs over the previous two weeks. Buyers may have found alternative suppliers or were not buying because they did not expect Magni to have any inventory. However, it may have just been a fall in demand caused by external factors.

5 Evaluate the implications of the situation shown in the chart for Mich's business. (16)

- Mich has two major supermarket contracts with weekly orders. One of these supermarkets has already threatened to end the contract unless immediate action is taken. Depending on the date of the letter, this will have serious implications for Mich as these large orders are probably a major element of his sales.
- Even if Mich rectifies this situation his business will have lost the goodwill of his customers. The supermarkets in particular will probably be trying to identify alternative suppliers and so any future problems will have more serious repercussions.
- The effect may depend on the cause. If Mich can establish that the situation was the result of BIPB plc's failure to deliver then his customers will be more understanding. It is also possible that rival pizza producers will have suffered from a lack of supply in this case. However, if as seems likely, Hugo is the cause of the problem, then the repercussions are more serious.
- The problems created for his customers will also be a factor. Individual consumers may tolerate a lack of inventory, but an absence of pizzas delivered to a shop may have damaged the shop's reputation too.

Evaluation: The overall impact will depend on the level of difficulties experienced by Mich's customers. However, it may also be influenced by the actions that he takes now. Taking responsibility and providing compensation will go a long way to easing the problems. Most significantly, the service provided over the next few months may alleviate the fears of customers and rectify the problem.

6 To what extent could the problems shown have been prevented? Justify your view. (16)

- If the problems were caused by Hugo, one has to consider whether this situation was foreseeable. Mich should have briefed Hugo fully on the workings of the business and ensured that he was fully trained. If this was the problem then it could have been prevented.
- Hugo may have been unreliable. Was this something that Mich could have anticipated? It seems risky to entrust a business to one person, although Hugo may always have been reliable in the past.
- If the problem was caused by unreliable suppliers then it would have been difficult to forecast, especially as the business had run smoothly for many years.

Evaluation: The prevention of the problem ultimately depends on the cause. However, if as seems apparent, Hugo was to blame, then the problem should have been easy to resolve. The initial problem arose from a four-day delay. It is hard to envisage that this could have happened without Hugo being able to do something. The later difficulties, which arose from much faster depletion of inventory, were not easy to foresee. Consequently, these problems may not have been as easy to prevent.

Practice exercise 3 (35 marks), page 328

1 What is meant by the term 'supply chain'? (2)

A supply chain is a network of sellers of raw materials, manufacturers who transform those materials into products, and wholesalers and retailers who get those products to customers.

2 What impact does 'sale or return' have on the level of risk for the supplier and the buyer? (5)

'Sale or return' is a system whereby, if a retailer does not sell a product, the product can be returned to the supplier (usually the producer or wholesaler) without payment being made. Usually the retailer carries the risk of a product not being sold, but this system transfers that risk from the retailer to the producer/wholesaler.

3 Identify and analyse three ways in which a supplier might help to improve the operational performance of a business that it supplies. (12)

- A supplier may be able to undercut the prices of other suppliers. This will enable the business that it supplies to keep its costs low. As a result it can charge a lower price and achieve high sales volume.
- High quality raw materials can enhance the quality of the finished product, enabling the manufacturer to gain brand loyalty and a reputation for quality.
- A flexible supplier will be able to meet new orders at short notice, and possibly modify its supply to meet last-minute changes. This will speed up the process of manufacture and also help the manufacturer to provide a more flexible service to its customers.
- A supplier may offer credit terms, such as 'sale or return'. This can reduce the level of risk for a business. Although it also reduces the profit levels of a business (because the supplier is taking the risk) sale or return can be particularly helpful for a small business that cannot afford to take risks.

4 Evaluate possible reasons why oil companies have tended to keep to a more traditional approach to supply chain management, whereas car manufacturers have adopted the modern approach to supply chain management. (16)

The traditional approach to supply chain management is based on 'Viking' – 'volume is king'. Large-scale purchases from a single supplier would lead to low unit costs.

The modern approach is to use a number of suppliers, focusing more on flexibility and reliability.

Oil companies:

This industry deals with a relatively homogeneous product that is difficult to differentiate. Although demand is price inelastic for oil and petrol as a whole, it is very price elastic for a particular brand, because each brand has a number of very similar substitutes.

- Price competition encourages a 'Viking' approach, with large orders placed to get discounts.
- There is consistent demand for this product over time and so holding large inventory poses little risk of holding supplies that will not be sold.
- The product is standardised (in fact legislation requires this to be the case). Therefore, businesses holding large inventory will not find the product becoming out of date.
- In order to keep control of prices the industry is vertically integrated, with oil companies owning all stages of production (from discovery of reserves to extraction to refining to delivery and finally selling to the customer).

Car manufacturers:

Increasingly cars are being sold on the basis of quality and reliability rather than price. This has led to a movement away from 'Viking' in this market.

- Suppliers are often specialists in certain components, so a car manufacturer will buy from many suppliers because of the variety of components.
- Buying from many (competing) suppliers increases the buying power of the car manufacturer, and so costs can be driven down by this factor rather than bulk-buying.
- Flexible production methods have enabled customers to have greater choice, particularly in terms of the fittings and additional features on a car.

- Car manufacturing has become a 'pull' industry, with production being provided to meet specific customer orders. This requires JIT production with reliable suppliers, often based close to the main assembly plant.

Evaluation: The products provided are the key influence on the different approaches of these two industries. Oil is a standardised product provided by a few large firms. Price is of vital importance to customers and so the traditional approach serves their needs. Buyers of cars have a different priority, on the whole, with growing emphasis on speed of delivery and product or mix flexibility. Customers are prepared to pay more for this flexibility and so the modern approach to supply chain management suits this industry more.

Case study: Dell [Part 2] (40 marks), pages 328–9

1 Explain why Dell wanted to simplify its supply chain. (6)

- Dell offered variations to customers and so it needed to source different computers from different suppliers. The lack of economies of scale from bulk buying opportunities from one supplier would have led to increased unit costs.
- This situation also made the supply chain more difficult to manage, as Dell dealt with so many different suppliers. This would have also increased their costs.

2 Analyse the implications for Dell's inventory control as a result of its decision to sell more goods through normal distribution channels, such as supermarkets and electrical retailers. (9)

- Products had been made to order (a 'pull' system) and so Dell held minimal inventory levels. Computers were only ordered when they were needed to supply customer orders.
- Supermarkets and electrical retailers were on a 'push' system. This required Dell to produce more standardised products that would appeal to customers who made decisions to buy a particular computer when visiting a retailer.
- Retailers would tend to place regular orders for a limited range of goods, so Dell knew in advance what orders and therefore items of inventory they should hold.

3 Analyse two benefits to Dell from providing outsourcing services to companies such as Lufthansa. (9)

- It plays to Dell's new strengths, which it has acquired through takeovers of other businesses.
- Lufthansa is a secure business that requires regular servicing of its maintenance and IT support for its booking system for the next five years. This type of contract provides a very low level of risk Dell, in contrast to the high-risk, competitive market that it has been operating within.

- Cash flow and profit levels are much more predictable for Dell, although profit may not be so high because of the limited risk to Dell of this type of work.

4 Was Dell right to choose to focus on a strategy of cost leadership in the PC industry? Justify your view. (16)

When Dell started mass customisation its cost leadership strategy was successful because:

- Computers tended to be highly priced items and so Dell could differentiate itself from competitors through its cost leadership strategy.
- Because it saved costs in terms of low inventory and less requirement of space, Dell was able to combine its cost leadership strategy with the offer of mass customisation, providing differentiated products suited to the needs of each customer. For customers, this was an unusual and very attractive combination.
- This strategy was unlikely to succeed in the long term as low-cost countries would be able to take sales from a USA-based business, such as Dell. The high levels of wages and other costs in the USA mean that the USA is not a suitable base for a business trying to achieve international cost leadership.
- Over time, high added value became the key to high profits. For example, using a focused differentiation based on high quality, Apple made more profit than the combined profits of all of the market leaders in the cost leadership market for computers.

Evaluation: Originally, Dell's approach was excellent because it combined Porter's low-cost and differentiation strategies. However, as the computer market became more international, it was unlikely that Dell could compete with businesses from low-cost economies which could still provide the skilled labour required to build computers. It was also unable to establish itself in the high added value segment.

16 Setting financial objectives

Practice exercise 1 (55 marks), page 346

1 Which one of the following is not a type of financial objective? (1)
   a capital expenditure objectives
   b cost objectives
   c productivity objectives
   d revenue objectives.

   The answer is c.

2 A business spends £50,000 on a project that increases its total profit from £10,000 to £15,000. The rate of interest is 2%. What is the return on investment (%)? $5-1k = \dfrac{4k}{50000} \times 100 = 8\%$ (1)
   a 8%
   b 10% $\dfrac{5000}{50,000} \times 100 = 10\%$
   c 28%
   d 30%.

   The answer is b.   a .

3 Explain two reasons for setting financial objectives. (6)
   - To act as a focus for decision making and effort by giving a target for all employees and managers to aim towards.
   - To improve efficiency by motivating workers to achieve targets.
   - By measuring the performance of different sectors, the business can determine those areas which are operating most effectively.

4 Explain one possible difficulty of setting financial objectives. (4)

   It can be difficult to assess a target performance, particularly for a new activity such as an investment in a new product, because there will be limited experience to draw on. Also, external changes, such as the level of economic growth, or market changes, such as new competition entering the market, can have a major and possibly unexpected impact on financial outcomes.

5 Analyse possible reasons why a profitable firm might suffer from cash-flow problems. (9)
   - A business may have given a very large dividend to its shareholders. This represents a significant-outflow of cash and so the business has little or no ready cash that it can access easily.
   - A business may build up its inventory levels, in anticipation of future growth in sales. This may mean that all of its liquid assets are in the form of inventory rather than cash.
   - A profitable business will want to grow further in order to make even higher profits. This will require expenditure on non-current assets, such as machinery and equipment. If this is financed from the business's own resources it will lead to a dramatic fall in cash, until the new machinery etc. begins to generate high profits.
   - A firm may give credit to its customers. Therefore the business will experience an increase in debtors (receivables). These will be an asset but it will mean that the profit has not yet been received in the form of cash.

6 Explain two possible disadvantages of prioritising cost minimisation as a major financial objective. (6)
   - Achieving cost reductions through reduced raw material costs may mean that the business is buying lower-quality materials. This may lower the quality of the finished product and hence lead to reduced sales revenue.
   - Lowering wage costs to achieve cost minimisation may mean that the workforce becomes demoralised. This can lead to problems such as a higher labour turnover, absenteeism and lower labour productivity.

7 Explain why it is important to have cash-flow objectives. (5)

   In the long run a firm's survival depends on its ability to make profit. However, poor cash-flow management can be (is) the cause of many business failures because a lack of cash may mean that a business cannot pay its payables (creditors) or the interest on an overdraft. This can lead to the closure of the business and so it is vital that the business identifies cash-flow objectives to prevent this problem.

8 Why is investment in capital goods important for a business? (4)

Capital equipment is the expenditure that provides the foundation for production of goods and services. Because it wears out it is vital that businesses replace it regularly and ensure that it helps the business to produce goods and services that will continue to meet changing customers' wants.

9 Explain why spare capacity might influence a company's capital expenditure objective. (4)

A business needs to have sufficient capacity to meet anticipated levels of demand. A business with high levels of spare capacity may be able to cope with increases in demand by using its spare capacity. Therefore its capital expenditure objective will be a low level of spending. In contrast, low spare capacity will mean a need to plan high levels of capital expenditure, particularly if demand is expected to increase.

10 State three external factors that might influence financial objectives. (3)

External factors include: political factors; the state of the economy; environmental changes; actions of competitors.

11 State three internal factors that might influence financial objectives. (3)

Internal factors include: corporate objectives; resources available; human resources and their skills; the nature of the product.

12 Analyse two reasons why shareholders might prefer a capital structure objective that increases debt rather than increases equity capital. (9)

- Capital structure targets involve the balance between debt (loans) and equity (share capital).
- Debt capital describes sources such as bank loans and debentures. These forms of finance need to be repaid and so they can increase a business's risk, especially if the assets purchased are likely to take a long time to pay for themselves. However, the interest paid is often fixed and tends to be lower than the percentage dividend paid to shareholders.
- Equity capital describes shareholders' funds. These shares are not repaid by the company – instead each shareholder gets a percentage of the profit distributed. This may be low in times of low profit.
- Each issue of shares means that the profit is divided between more shareholders and so this will mean that shareholders will prefer debt capital to be used for additional finance. If interest rates are low (as at present in 2015) then it will also be a cheaper source of finance. This will lead to more profit to be shared amongst fewer shareholders, so this will be the preference of shareholders if profits are high and interest rates are low.

Case study: Google and Apple (45 marks), pages 347–8

1 Use Table 16.6 to answer the following question: In 2011 how much profit was available to Google's shareholders? (1)
  a $37,905 million
  b $24,717 million
  c $11,632 million
  d $9,737 million.
  The answer is d.

2 Using Table 16.4, calculate the debt to equity ratio of Apple in 2013. (2)
  $39,793m : $163,350m ∴ ratio is 0.24: 1

3 Using Table 16.4, calculate the debt to long-term funding (%) of Google in 2013. (3)
  $7,803m/$118,723m x 100 = 6.6%

4 Explain one possible reason for the significant increase in Google's 'cost of sales' between 2011 and 2013. (4)

Cost of sales have almost doubled. Most of this can be attributed to the fact that revenue has increased by almost 60%. Therefore the scale of the business has increased, thus increasing all of its costs too. (However, the percentage increases are very different, suggesting that Google may not be controlling its cost of sales very effectively.)

5 Explain one possible reason why Apple's debts have risen so dramatically between 2012 and 2013. (4)

Apple has increased its long-term funding significantly, to finance expansion plans. With low interest rates on loans Apple might have chosen to borrow the money rather than sell shares (particularly as its profitability suggests it can pay back this debt fairly quickly from its profits).

6 Analyse two possible reasons why the debt to long-term funding ratios are so low for these two businesses. (9)

- Both businesses have been very profitable. This has enabled them to pay dividends AND retain high levels of profit. Retained profit is classified as equity capital because it 'belongs'

AQA A-level Business 1 Answer Guide **89**

to the shareholders who agreed not to take it as dividends. Therefore, any business with high levels of retained profit will have a low debt to long-term funding ratio.

- Debt capital must be paid back, often in the medium term. Fast-expanding companies, such as Google and Apple, might not want to use a form of finance that needs repayment – share capital is permanent and therefore the companies will not have the problem of having to repay debt with share capital.

- Sources of finance for a particular use, such as new product development, should be matched to the time period over which that use will return the sum of money required. It can take a long time for major projects, such as new product development, to pay for themselves and so share capital is the best option.

- Share capital is risk capital. If projects are considered to be risky they should be financed by share capital, if possible.

7 Based on the data in Table 16.5, calculate Apple's targeted gross profit (%) for the 1st quarter of 2014. [3]
Targeted gross profit is: $20bn/$55bn x 100 = 36.4%

8 Based on the data in Table 16.5, calculate Apple's actual gross profit in $billions for the 1st quarter of 2014. [3]
Actual gross profit = 37.9% of $57.6bn = $21.8bn

9 Use Table 16.6 to calculate Google's operating profit for 2013. [2]
Operating profit = $12,214m + $1,752m = $13,966m

10 Use your answer to question 9 and Table 16.6 to calculate Google's administrative expenses for 2013. [2]
Administrative expenses = $34,001 mn - $13,966 mn = $20,035 mn

11 Assume that Google had targeted 15% increases in its revenue and profit levels between 2012 and 2013. To what extent was Google's financial performance a success in 2013? Justify your view. [12]
Targets = 15% growth in revenue and profit between 2012 and 2013.

- Revenue
$$\% \text{ increase} = \frac{59,825 - 50,175}{50,175} \times 100 = 19.2\% \text{ increase}$$

- Gross profit
$$\% \text{ increase} = \frac{34,001 - 29,670}{29,670} \times 100 = 14.6\% \text{ increase}$$

- Operating profit
$$\% \text{ increase} = \frac{13,966 - 12,760}{12,760} \times 100 = 9.5\% \text{ increase}$$

- Profit for year
$$\% \text{ increase} = \frac{12,214 - 10,788}{10,788} \times 100 = 13.2\% \text{ increase}$$

Evaluation: Google has succeeded in increasing sales revenue by well over 15%. However, this performance has not been matched by its profitability, perhaps indicating that the sales growth has been achieved through lower prices and thus lower profit margins. The operating profit is seen to be the best measure of the business's overall performance and this figure is well below 15%, confirming that Google's profits have not kept pace with the growth in its sales revenue.

17 Analysing financial performance

Practice exercise 1 (15 marks), page 358

1 What is meant by the term 'variance analysis'? (2)

Variance analysis is the process by which the outcomes of budgets are examined and then compared with the budgeted figures. The reasons for any differences (variances) are then found.

2 What is the difference between a favourable variance and an adverse variance? (4)

A favourable variance will lead to a higher profit than budgeted/expected – for example, lower costs or higher revenue than budgeted. An adverse variance will lead to a lower profit than budgeted – for example, higher costs or lower revenue than budgeted.

3 Explain two reasons why an adverse variance might not be a sign of poor management by the budget holder. (9)

- The original cost allocation may have been inadequate. If a budget holder had no say in setting the budget, it is feasible that the failure to hit the target was the responsibility of the manager who set the budget rather than the one who then managed the situation.
- External factors may change. An increase in the rate of inflation, increased competition for resources, a problem with suppliers and a change in interest rates are all potential factors.
- Internal changes, such as wastage by another department or a sudden increase in sales volume, may lead to a department having to spend more on its activities.

Practice exercise 2 (10 marks), page 359

1 Rewrite the budget, taking into account the changes listed below: (10)

- Ten students have asked to switch from 'entertainment tickets' to 'dinner tickets'.
- The expenditure budget changes to take into account the 10 extra dinner tickets sold and the 10 extra welcome drinks that are provided to dinner ticket holders.
- The band has negotiated a 5% increase in its fee.
- Publicity costs have fallen to £55.55.

Income budget

Income	Price (£)	Number	Total (£)
Dinner tickets	25.00	110 (100 +10)	2,750.00
Entertainment tickets	10.00	35 (45 – 10)	350.00
Total			**3,100.00**

Expenditure budget

Expenditure (incl. VAT)	(£)
Publicity	55.55
Dinners	1,265.00[a]
Welcome drinks	181.50[a]
PA and lighting	276.25
Band	924.00
Sub-total	2,702.30
Contingency 10%	270.23[b]
Total	**2,972.53**

[a] increased by 10%

[b] 10% of the new sub-total

Profit budget

	(£)
Income	3,100.00
Expenditure	2,972.53
Profit	127.47

Case study: Frank Roseland, dairyman and newsagent (40 marks), pages 359–61

1 The budgeted profit for 2016 is: (1)
 a £19,000
 b £36,000
 c £45,000
 d £63,000.

 The answer is d.

2 The variance for the 2015 expenditure budget is: (1)
 a £19,000 – favourable
 b £19,000 – adverse
 c £38,000 – favourable
 d £38,000 – adverse.

 The answer is d.

3 What is meant by the term 'profit budget'? (2)

 A profit budget is the agreed, planned profit of a business or division over a period of time.

4 The actual outcomes in 2015 were very different from the budgets that Frank set. To what extent was this due to Frank's inexperience in setting budgets? Justify your view. (16)

 • Milk sales were considerably higher than budgeted due to a competitor retiring. It was unlikely that this could have been foreseen and therefore this was a chance event rather than being due to Frank's inexperience in setting budgets.

 • Milk sales were also higher because Frank realised that he could charge a much higher price. Greater experience of budgeting would probably have meant that he recognised this fact in the first place (his competitor charged higher prices) and incorporated it into his initial budgets.

 • Grocery almost doubled against budget. This could not have been foreseen, as it resulted from an initiative that Frank took towards the end of the financial year, as he came to understand his business more fully.

 • Frank underestimated the workload and within two months he needed to employ another part-timer to collect and deliver items, which also meant that he had to buy another van. This would appear to be an example of inexperience, as Frank should have foreseen such a significant change happening so soon after he took over the business. However, some of this increase in business was due to the retirement of a competitor and the deal with the farmer, which could not have been foreseen.

Evaluation: There were significant differences between the budgeted and actual figures in Frank's first year. In part these were due to Frank showing initiative in grasping opportunities that could not have been foreseen, but there are also examples of situations that could have been predicted if he had spent a little more time talking to customers, suppliers and his father. On balance, the major changes have come about because of the rapid expansion of the business. This could not have been foreseen, as the changes were caused mainly by external factors happening during that first year of trading. Therefore, the differences were primarily not a result of Frank's inexperience in setting budgets.

5 Evaluate the overall usefulness of budgeting and variance analysis in helping Frank to manage the finances of his business. (20)

 • His early review of his budgets enabled him to identify some unexpected trends, such as milk sales falling faster than expected. He was thus able to tackle this problem before it created severe difficulties for his business.

 • Frank was able to review his prices. He had been reluctant to add on 67% to his milk costs in order to set the price, until he could see whether this was acceptable to customers. His early budgets confirmed that this pricing policy would be all right.

 • The budgeting process identified/confirmed that the main growth area for Frank was in sales of groceries, encouraging him to seize the opportunity of working with the local farmer.

 • The variance analysis of his income budgets confirmed that Frank should focus on milk and groceries rather than newspapers.

 • The variance analysis of his expenditure budgets indicated that Frank was controlling costs well, as the increases were closely linked to the extra sales he was recording, although it showed weaknesses in some of his planning, such as staffing.

 HOWEVER:

 • There were many changes taking place that undermined the accuracy and usefulness of his budgeting and variance analysis. Examples included the new supermarket taking away some of his sales of milk; customers being prepared to pay higher than expected prices; the retirement of a competitor.

 • Frank showed initiative in expanding the business into new areas that had not been allowed for in the original budgeting.

Evaluation: The significant changes in budgets and the wide variances suggest that the budgets were of limited use to Frank. However, it did demonstrate the need to treat budgets flexibly. Analysis of the reasons for variances indicated to Frank the direction that he should take and, allowing for the changes in income budgets, the variances did confirm that Frank was controlling most costs appropriately. However, the discrepancies between the budgets and their outcomes severely restricted their usefulness.

Case study: Budgeting the Eden Project (35 marks), pages 361–2

1 What is meant by the term 'budget'? (2)

A budget is an agreed plan establishing, in numerical or financial terms, the policy to be pursued and the expected results of the policy.

2 Identify one favourable variance from Table 17.14. (1)

Soil and plants, including nursery.

3 Calculate the variance between the total budget and the total actual costs as a percentage of the budgeted cost. (3)

Variance = 12.0 (adverse)
Variance as a percentage = $-12/74 \times 100 = -16.2\%$ (adverse)

4 Explain one reason why firms find it easier to estimate revenue budgets than capital budgets. (4)

Revenue budgets are targets for income. Most firms will have undertaken market research or possess past data that will enable them to predict sales accurately. Capital budgets are for major projects, often one-offs such as the Eden Project. Firms will have limited experience of such projects and will therefore find it more difficult to predict costs and revenues. Major projects are more likely to be hit by unexpected events, such as the heavy rainfall in the first three months of the Eden Project.

5 Analyse two factors that caused the actual expenditure for setting up the Eden Project to exceed the budgeted figure. (9)

- Reshaping the ground showed a major adverse variance. A project of this scale had never been attempted before, so this variance was probably caused by an underestimate of the difficulty of completing this task.
- Unexpected events, such as the heavy rainfall in the first three months, led to the builders having to stop construction for three months. This added to the project's costs considerably, as staff still needed to be paid during this period.
- The need to employ consultants to overcome these problems would have been a major factor leading to the high overspend on the part of the budget entitled 'Design, engineering, legal advice etc.'.

- The wages and training overspend could have been due to the unexpectedly high number of visitors. This would have led to the organisation needing to employ and train more workers than was originally planned.

6 To what extent did the Eden Project benefit from the time spent on its budgeting? (16)

- The project benefited initially because the budget showed the level of support needed from the European Union and the Millennium Commission. It was particularly useful in persuading the Millennium Commission to agree to further support when early problems arose.
- The budgeting process enabled the organisers to evaluate the feasibility of the project. Their projections showed that it could be successful and therefore the project went ahead.
- The time spent on budgeting enabled the Eden Project to predict costs to a reasonable degree of accuracy. Most of the cost variances were small, thus helping the management of the project to run the business efficiently.
- In some areas there was considerable overspending, suggesting that the time spent on these budgets was less useful. However, it is questionable whether the actual time spent on budgeting was a factor in determining its accuracy.
- More time spent on the revenue budget would have helped most, as there was a considerable underestimate of visitor numbers.

Evaluation: Overall, the main benefit of budgeting was that it enabled the Eden Project to gain funding and receive additional help with early construction problems. However, more time might have been devoted to forecasting sales revenue. The lack of accuracy in this area caused difficulties, as the original budget underestimated the number of employees needed. Ultimately, this would have been a critical weakness, if the low estimate of visitor numbers had led to the conclusion that the project was not going to be worth undertaking in the first place.

Practice exercise 3 (33 marks), pages 370–1

1 Which of these formulae is correct? Net cash flow equals: (1)

   a Opening balance + cash outflows

   b Closing balance – cash inflows

   c Cash inflows – cash outflows

   d Opening balance – closing balance.

   The answer is c.

2 Which one of these items is a cash inflow to a business? (1)

   a Wages

   b Capital costs

   c Dividends received by shareholders

   d Rent from property owned by the business.

   The answer is d.

3 Draw a diagram to show the cash-flow cycle. (4)

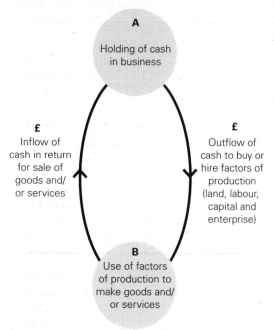

A
Holding of cash in business

£
Inflow of cash in return for sale of goods and/ or services

£
Outflow of cash to buy or hire factors of production (land, labour, capital and enterprise)

B
Use of factors of production to make goods and/ or services

4 Explain the meaning of the term 'cash-flow forecast'. (2)

   A cash-flow forecast is an estimate of the expected cash inflows and cash outflows over a period of time.

5 Explain two problems that a firm might have when trying to predict its cash flow. (8)

   Problems include:

   • changes in consumer tastes leading to unpredictable demand levels

   • inadequate market research

   • economic changes such as high economic growth or changes in interest rates affecting demand

   • changes in levels of competition

   • poor forecasting of costs

   • unpredictable changes in costs.

   The first three factors will affect cash inflows. These in turn will mean different levels of production and so predicted cash outflows will also be incorrect.

   The final two factors will only affect cash outflows, although the changes to outflow could be positive or negative.

6 What is meant by the term 'liquidity'? (2)

   Liquidity is the ability to turn an asset into cash without loss or delay. It measures how easy it is for a business to pay its debts quickly.

7 Calculate the working capital cycle based on the following information: (3)

   a Goods are held in stock for 23 days.

   b Debtors are given 15 days to pay.

   c Creditors give the firm 28 days to pay.

   23 + 15 – 28 = 10 days

8 Analyse how control of receivables and payables might overcome a firm's cash flow problems. (9)

   Receivables should be kept to a minimum as they mean a delay in receiving cash. This makes it harder for firms to pay their own debts. Prompt invoicing and regular reminders of the need for payment towards the end of the credit period can help to ensure that customers pay promptly. This activity needs to be supported by chasing up late payers. Many firms will obtain a credit rating on potential debtors to ensure that there is little risk of non-payment. However, a firm can also ensure that it provides a good service to its customers, so that they are more likely to pay willingly.

   In theory, payables should be delayed as long as possible. In this way a business is holding cash owed to other business. If 28 days' credit is given then payment should be made on the 28th day. However, caution is needed – a business may get a reputation for late payment and suppliers may refuse to supply it in future.

9 Why is it sensible for a firm to make sure that its level of working capital is not too high? (3)

   If the level of working capital is very high, it means that assets are tied up in unproductive resources. Fundamentally, profit arises from the use of non-current assets to produce goods and services, and therefore a reasonable balance should be struck between non-current assets and working capital.

Case study: Fun for Kids Ltd (40 marks), pages 371–2

1 Look at Table 17.18. What are the missing values in the cash flow forecast at (a) and (b)?

a 34.7 (£34,700) (1)

b 48.3 (£48,300) (1)

2 Explain two sources of information that would have helped Siu to construct this cash-flow forecast. (6)

- Other businesses in this field. However, competitors may not provide information that helps Siu and advice from businesses in other areas may be less relevant.
- Suppliers of materials may be of particular use because they will want to help Siu's business to succeed.
- Market research to estimate demand – this would need to be more objective than asking friends.
- Bank manager for advice and information on the possibility of an overdraft – again the bank manager would want a successful customer.

3 Evaluate the main reasons why this cash-flow forecast may be inaccurate. (16)

- Siu has no previous experience of this type of business.
- There is no evidence of market research. Does Siu know the probable demand (based on firm orders) or is she relying on guesswork? She appears to be relying on friends' opinions, which may be biased.
- The unusual site means that it is difficult to estimate future demand. The premises may be deemed too impersonal (or they may be a USP).
- Are the cost estimates reliable? Some payments (such as rent) will be known, but items such as gas and electricity may be difficult to estimate.
- Are the predicted increases in customers in July and August realistic? These customers do not appear to be part of the usual target market.

Evaluation: As this is a new business with no established customer base, the estimates of sales revenue are probably the most unreliable part of the forecast. Siu's lack of experience is also a major factor that may cause inaccurate forecasts.

4 Discuss the possible implications for Siu's business if she decides to offer credit terms to her customers. (16)

- There is likely to be poor cash flow in the short term, as there will be a period with no inflows of cash.
- However, if this leads to an increase in sales, long-term profits may increase. Siu expects this offer to increase sales by 10%.
- If credit is offered, the firm may earn interest from its customers, leading to greater inflows of cash in the long run.
- Offering credit increases the risk of bad debt. At present, Siu has no risk of bad debts as payment is received in advance.
- Credit facilities increase administration costs – the credit has to be arranged and monitored. Because the business is quite large for a start-up, Siu may need to employ someone to carry out this task, increasing her costs and possibly eroding the benefit gained from any extra sales gained from offering credit terms.

Evaluation: The main implications will be a decline in cash flow, but a potential increase in profits. Siu must weigh up these two issues. At present, cash flow is reasonably stable, but with annual sales of about £200,000, one month's credit will reduce cash flow by about £17,000 in a typical month. The business's surplus cash flow is very close to this level after the 1st quarter and so offering credit will probably not, but may require an overdraft. However, a 10% increase in sales should be worth it and the increased profit will limit the possibility of cash-flow issues.

Practice exercise 4 (25 marks), page 384

1 What is meant by the term 'total variable costs'? (2)

Total variable costs are sum of those costs that vary directly with output in the short run.

2 Calculate the contribution per unit. (4)

Contribution per unit = selling price – variable cost per unit
= £11 – £3,000/500 = £11 – £6 = £5 per unit

3 Calculate the total contribution from 500 units. (3)

Total contribution = contribution per unit × number of units
= £5 × 500 = £2,500

4 Calculate the break-even quantity. (5)

Break-even quantity = fixed costs/contribution per unit
= £1,200/£5 = 240 units

5 How much profit is made if all 500 units are sold? (4)

(500 × £11) – (£1,200 + £3,000) = £5,500 – £4,200 = £1,300

The contribution method is total contribution – fixed costs:

(500 × £5) – £1,200 = £2,500 – £1,200 = £1,300

6 What is the margin of safety if 500 units are sold? (2)

500 – 240 = 260 units

7 Calculate the break-even quantity if the variable costs rise to £7 per unit and the fixed costs increase to £1,400. (5)

Break-even quantity = fixed costs/contribution per unit
= £1,400/(£11 – £7) = £1,400/£4 = 350 units

Case study: Rocking horses (35 marks), pages 384–5

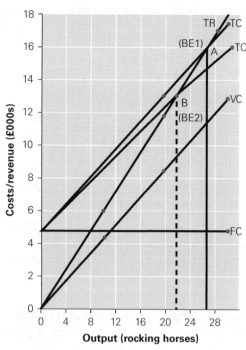

Figure 17.14: Break-even chart for rocking horses

1 On the break-even chart show the break-even point and the break-even output. (2)

See Figure 17.14 above.

2 Raw material costs are expected to fall by £40 per horse.
  a Amend the total cost line to show this change and show the new break-even output. (3)

See Figure 17.14 above.

  b Calculate the original break-even output using the formula. (4)
Breakeven output = fixed costs/contribution per unit (selling price – variable costs per unit)
Therefore, breakeven output = £4,800/(£600 – £420)
= £4,800/£180 = 26.7 horses.

  c Assuming that variable costs fall by £40 per horse, calculate the new break-even output using the formula. (2)
Amended break-even output = fixed costs/ contribution per unit (selling price – variable costs per unit).

Variable costs fall by £40 per unit (from £420 to £380).
Therefore, breakeven output = £4,800/(£600 – £380)
= £4,800/£220 = 21.8 horses.

3 Based on the original costs, calculate the loss that is made from selling 26 rocking horses. (5)

Total revenue = £600 × 26 horses = £15,600
Fixed costs = £4,800

Total variable costs = £420 × 26 horses = £10,920
Total costs = £4,800 + £10,920 = £15,720
Profit = £15,600 – £15,720 = (£120), a loss of £120
Alternative calculation: profit = total contribution – fixed costs
Contribution per horse = £600 – £420 = £180
Total contribution = £180 × 26 = £4,680
Profit = £4,680 – £4,800 = (£120), a loss of £120.

4 Calculate the profit that would be made if variable costs fall by £40 per horse. (3)

Total revenue = £600 × 26 horses = £15,600
Fixed costs = £4,800
Total variable costs = £380 × 26 horses = £9,880
Total costs = £4,800 + £9880 = £14,680
Profit = £15,600 – £14,680 = £920
Alternative calculation: profit = total contribution – fixed costs
Contribution per horse = £600-£380 = £220
Total contribution = £220 × 26 = £5,720
Profit = £5,720 – £4,800 = £920

5 Discuss the possible ways in which Chris might be able to change this loss into a profit. (16)

Possible answers are:
- The company could diversify or expand into other wooden products that can be crafted by hand.
- It could increase the price. This is a niche market and a contribution of £180 per horse is much too low; often there is considerable scope for value added in niche markets.
- Cost savings will add to the profit. Could Chris make savings in fixed costs?
- It could increase the production schedule to cover the whole year. Winter may not be the best time to sell rocking horses, and producing horses all year may lead to a reduction in the fixed cost per horse.
- It could produce more horses – the breakeven output is 26.7 but only 26 are produced.

Evaluation: Each of the above suggestions could play a part in turning this loss into a profit, but the greatest potential seems to lie in increasing the price. Market research should be undertaken to discover the market price. It seems unlikely that £600 is a sensible price, even if Chris's costs are too high.

Practice exercise 5 (15 marks), page 391

1   Financial accounting is: (1)
    a   used externally and focuses on past data
    b   used externally and plans for the future
    c   used internally and focuses on past data
    d   used internally and plans for the future.

    The answer is a.

2   Management accounting is: (1)
    a   used externally and focuses on past data
    b   used externally and plans for the future
    c   used internally and focuses on past data
    d   used internally and plans for the future.

    The answer is d.

3   Which one of these items is the best example of financial accounting data? (1)
    a   Budgets
    b   Cash-flow forecasts
    c   Decision trees
    d   Income statements.

    The answer is d.

4   Which one of these items is the best example of management accounting data? (1)
    a   Break-even charts
    b   Balance sheets

c   Capital structure data
d   Cash-flow statements.

The answer is a.

5   What is the formula for calculating gross profit margin? (2)

$$\text{Gross profit margin (\%)} = \frac{\text{Gross profit}}{\text{Sales revenue}} \times 100$$

6   Analyse two internal factors that might influence a firm's operating profit margin. (9)

- Labour turnover. A high turnover of labour will disrupt production. It may lower labour productivity and increase the costs of recruiting staff. It might also be a sign of low morale, which will also increase unit costs.

- Capacity utilisation (%). High capacity utilisation will lead to fixed costs being spread over more units of output and so this will lead to lower fixed costs per unit. This should improve operating profit.

- High added value. Effective use of the marketing mix can improve the brand image and enable a business to charge a higher price, even where costs are kept the same. This leads to a higher profit margin and will help to improve the operating profit margin.

Case study: Google's financial performance (50 marks), pages 391–2

1   What is the difference between 'profit' and 'profitability'? (4)

Profit is the difference between revenue and costs. Profitability measures the ability of a business to generate profit, by comparing profit to the size of the business.

2   Explain one reason why it would be difficult to compare Google's profitability with a competitor. (5)

Comparing Google to a competitor would be difficult because it has no close competitor. In its main market (as a search engine) it has a 90% market share and so it is much larger than its competitors. It has also diversified into other activities which its search engine competitors have not.

3   Analyse two external factors that might have influenced Google's profitability. (9)

- The economy. Low growth can lead to fewer transactions and so businesses which use Google for advertising purposes are likely to cut back on expenditure on these adverts. This will mean that Google receives a lower sales revenue and therefore is likely to suffer from lower profitability.

- Expectations of ethical behaviour. Google's original ethical stance was not to operate in countries such as China, which restricted internet access. This affected its potential to generate revenue. The decision to accept some restrictions from the Chinese government has enabled Google to target the Chinese market, but has led to dissatisfaction amongst ethical consumers in countries such as the USA.

- Legislation to protect consumers. Google's large market share gives it opportunities to take advantage of its customers. The European Union is currently investigating Google's potential abuse of its dominance of the search engine market. In theory, this can lead to the breaking up of a business or heavy fines.

4   Based purely on financial data, has Google improved its profitability between 2011 and 2013? Use the data in Tables 17.25 and 17.26 and your own calculations to support your view. (12)

The profit margins for 2013 are as follows:
Gross profit (%)   = 56.8%
Operating profit (%)   = 23.3%
Profit for year (%)   = 20.4%

The gross profit margins show a steady decline over the three years, with the percentage falling from 65.2% in 2011 to 56.8% in 2013. This may indicate that Google is finding it difficult to control its cost of sales, such as raw materials. However, it may also have been caused by a relative fall in prices leading to lower added value on its goods and services.

The operating profit margins show a similar decline, with the percentage falling from 30.7% in 2011 to 23.3% in 2013. This indicates that profit is not just declining because of lower gross profit; administrative expenses are also a factor leading to lower profits. However, both of these margins indicate that the decline in performance is slowing down. For example, operating profit margin fell by 5.3% between 2011 and 2012 but only fell by 2.1% between 2012 and 2013.

The income statements show that net costs of finance and one-off costs are falling each year, and so the fall in the profit for year margin (%) is smaller than it is for the other two margins. This % has fallen from 25.7% to 20.4%. and only fell slightly in 2013. In relative terms, these costs are being controlled well.

Conclusion: All three measures indicate that Google's profitability has declined between 2011 and 2013. Google has been very efficient in generating additional revenue in this time, with sales growth exceeding 50%. However, its profit margins have fallen because costs of sales have nearly doubled in this period. To a lesser extent profitability has also been reduced by the fact that administrative expenses have increased by just over 50%.

5   'A company's profitability is the ideal way to measure its overall performance.' To what extent do you agree with this statement? Use examples from Google, or any other companies with which you are familiar, to support your arguments. (20)

- Profitability is an excellent measure of business performance because it describes a business's ability to make profit and takes into consideration the size of the business. An examination of Google's performance shows that its profitability is declining; however, it also shows that with an operating profit in excess of 20% it is a very successful business in comparison to most other large businesses. For shareholders, profitability is the key measure of performance, because they usually invest money in business in order to achieve financial returns. Furthermore, high profitability means that a business such as Google can expand, providing more sales for its suppliers and more job security and possibly higher pay for its employees.

- Businesses may also have other objectives, such as growth, social aims, job security for staff and ethical behavior in respect of its products, suppliers and communities. If growth is the key objective, then sales revenue may be a more significant target than profitability. Similarly the other objectives, such as job security, will mean that different objectives are prioritised by the business and therefore profitability will not be the best way to measure its overall performance.

- The business should meet the needs of many different stakeholders. To succeed, it must enjoy good relationships with its suppliers, customers, its employees and the local community. Although profitability may provide opportunities for each of these stakeholder groups, the business may need to prioritise other targets in order to satisfy such a diverse group of interests. In this case profitability may not be the best measure of performance.

- Profitability can be influenced by external factors beyond the business's direct control. For example, the liquidation of a major supplier can damage a business's ability to produce and influence its profitability. On the other hand, favourable economic circumstances can increase the profit for a business and its competitors. Even if a business is performing less well than its competitors, it might still be enjoying very high profits.

- In the short run a business may deliberately take actions, such as investment in research and development, which may reduce short-term profitability. However, in the long-term new products may arise from this R&D and so profitability will benefit from these changes. Therefore it is important to use profitability as a long-term measure rather than a short-term measure of performance.

Evaluation: Profitability is a key business objective and therefore it is a very important measure of a business's performance in most circumstances. However, it is important to assess it over a long period of time in order to get a more accurate appreciation of the business's financial performance. A business must suit the needs of many stakeholders and so judging its overall performance will require many different measures, of which profitability will be just one measure. Furthermore, any conclusions drawn must take into consideration any external factors that may distort these measures.

18 Making financial decisions: sources of finance

Practice exercise 1 (50 marks), page 405

1 Which of these sources of finance is an internal source? (1)
   a Debt factoring
   b Loan capital
   c Overdraft
   d Venture capital.

   The answer is a.

2 Which of these sources of finance is short-term? (1)
   a Loan
   b Overdraft
   c Retained profit
   d Venture capital.

   The answer is b.

3 Which one of these sources of finance is an external source? (1)
   a Crowdfunding
   b Retained profit
   c Sale and leaseback
   d Sale of assets.

   The answer is a.

4 What is the difference between 'short-term' and 'long-term' finance? (3)

   Short-term finance is normally intended for use and repayment within 12 months. Long-term finance is used for capital expenditure, with repayment required after a usual minimum of three years.

5 Explain the difference between internal finance and external finance. (4)

   - Internal finance comes from profits generated in a business or from the sale of assets already owned by it.
   - External finance, such as a bank loan, comes from outside the organisation.

6 Explain two benefits of using retained profit as a way of raising finance. (6)

   - It provides an inexpensive source as no interest payments are required (although the opportunity cost should be considered).
   - It is flexible because it can fund short-term and long-term projects and the sum involved can vary at short notice.
   - It allows the business to expand rapidly without incurring further debt.
   - It is relatively risk-free as no repayment is required and no certain, regular payment is to be made in return.

7 What is meant by 'ordinary share capital'? (3)

   Ordinary share capital is money given to a company by shareholders in return for part ownership of the company. This entitles the shareholder to voting rights and a share of the profits.

8 Explain two reasons why a firm might decide to use internal rather than external finance. (6)

   - The level of profit. This might be high enough for the business to use its own funds rather than rely on outsiders to provide finance.
   - The amount of risk involved. External providers will want to avoid risks that are outside their control, so risky activities are more likely to be financed from internal sources.
   - The level of borrowing by the company. A company with high levels of borrowing will be unattractive to new lenders, so it is more likely to need to use internal finance.
   - The amount of money required. The higher the level of funding needed, the less likely it is that the business will be able to get hold of all of the funds from one particular source.

9 Explain one reason why a firm might choose a short-term source of finance. (4)

   - The finance is needed for a purpose that will provide a quick return to the business. The essential principle is that the length of time that money is borrowed should match the length of time that will be needed to earn enough profit to repay the loan.

- The money is only needed to cover a temporary shortage, such as the need to buy high levels of raw materials in advance of earning money from selling the final product. Similarly, a seasonal business may be short of money for a certain part of the year, but knows that it can repay the money during its peak season.

10 Describe the main differences between a bank loan and a bank overdraft. (6)

- A bank loan is a sum of money provided to a firm or individual for a specific, agreed purpose, usually at a fixed rate of interest.
- A bank overdraft is taken up when a bank allows a customer to overspend up to an agreed (overdraft) limit for a stated period of time. Usually, a variable rate of interest is charged.

11 Explain two possible disadvantages of using a bank overdraft. (6)

- A bank overdraft has a variable rate of interest and so it can be difficult to predict the sum to be repaid and therefore budget it accurately as an expense, during a period when interest rates are changing.
- In general bank overdrafts carry a higher rate of interest than bank loans (because no

security is required) and so it can add to a business's expenses.

- In theory, a bank can ask for a bank overdraft to be repaid on demand. This is unlikely but it does make a business vulnerable if it is experiencing financial difficulties (especially as this is when repayment may be demanded).
- It is a short-term source of finance and so it is not suited to the purchase of items such as machinery and vehicles.
- It will require documentation, such as a cash flow forecast, to show how it will be repaid.

12 Analyse two possible benefits of debt factoring for a business. (9)

- It improves cash flow by providing a business with immediate cash in return for its receivables (who may have not paid the cash for a long time).
- It reduces the risk of bad debt, because the factoring company is responsible for chasing up debtors who do not pay. However, debts will only be factored if a credit check is made on customers' credit records.
- It lowers administration costs. A business does not have to devote resources to administer the repayments and to chase up late payers or bad debts, which may even require legal action.

Practice exercise 2 (50 marks), page 405

1 'The level of profit will always be the most important factor influencing the sources of finance that a business uses.' Do you agree? Justify your view. (25)

- The level of profit will be an important factor because it is usually the main source of finance for a business, once it has been established. Although it is considered to be most appropriate for long-term finance, in emergency situations it can also be used to overcome short-term cash-flow problems.
- Retained profit is a cheap source of finance as there is no interest payments required. However, there is an opportunity cost to the owners and therefore it is usual for profit to be divided between shareholders' dividends and retained profit. Thus the level of profit available may be restricted and therefore the business needs to find other sources.
- The level of profit can also be important when trying to acquire other sources of finance. For example, the willingness of the bank manager to lend a business money may be dependent on its financial performance, as measured by its profit.

- The purpose of the finance is also an important factor in determining the source. For long-term projects such as construction of the new factories, a long-term source of finance is required, such as retained profits, share capital and bank loans. However, to improve cash flow it would be more sensible to use a bank overdraft or debt factoring.
- The amount required can also be a key factor. For major expansion programmes it would be impossible to use retained profits, because there would be insufficient finance available. In this situation additional share capital would most likely be required, although bank loans may be a possibility.
- The level of risk would also need to be considered: high-risk projects may not appeal to external funders, except perhaps venture capitalists, and so high-risk projects are often financed by retained profits.
- Shareholders' opinions are also critical. Many shareholders will have purchased shares in order to receive profits in the form of dividends. Therefore if the managers constantly try to retain all the profits for the

business's expansion, shareholders may become disillusioned and vote against these proposals at the annual general meeting.

Evaluation: The level of profit is a very critical factor, because not only is it a major source of finance in its own right, but also it influences the ability of a business to obtain finance from other sources, such as the bank. However, retained profit is not suitable for short-term finance and its use does depend on the agreement of shareholders. Furthermore, it may be insufficient to meet the needs of the business, in which case other sources would be more important at that time.

2 From 2009 to 2014, bank lending to businesses has fallen. This decline in lending has been much greater for small businesses than large businesses. This trend is expected to continue. Evaluate the possible implications for the financing of small businesses if this trend continues. (25)

- Small firms may continue to struggle to raise sufficient finance because the main banks will continue to dominate their market and continue to be reluctant to take risks because of their experiences in the recession.

- There may be greater regulation by the government in order to encourage bank lending, such as the Funding for Lending scheme. However, this is less likely, as it does not appear to have been successful to date.

- The government-owned Business Bank may take a more proactive role in providing finance for small business. However, this would need a change in the current terms of the bank and is likely to be both a business and a political decision.

- The continued emergence of challenger banks, such as Aldermore, to an extent where they become serious rivals to the main high street banks. If this does happen, it may force the larger banks to reconsider their current approach to lending to small firms.

- The entry of established foreign banks into the UK market in response to the perceived gap in profitable lending to small firms. Internet banking would not require these firms to have branches and so this will become more feasible over time.

- The development of more innovative ways of lending, such as crowdfunding. If current investors in crowdfunding find they are receiving excellent returns then this could become a driving force behind this method of financing of small businesses.

Evaluation: If the small business sector has little bargaining power this situation may remain the same, particularly as small firms rely on the high street banks to manage their accounts and overdrafts. However, improvements in communications and technology are making

it easier to raised finance through different approaches, such as crowdfunding, and so this may become accepted as a mainstream way of attracting finance. Ultimately, external factors are going to be important – stricter regulation of bank lending and weak economic performance will mean that banks continue to be reluctant to lend to small firms. However, improvements in the banks' own finances will lead to less regulation and this should lead to more lending to small firms. However, by then the challenger banks and crowdfunders may have established a major foothold in the market.

Case study: CurriesOnline (35 marks), page 406

1 What is meant by the term 'bank loan'? (2)

A bank loan is a sum of money provided to a firm or individual for a specific, agreed purpose, usually at a fixed rate of interest.

2 Explain two possible benefits for CurriesOnline of agreeing to raise finance from venture capitalists. (8)

- There appeared to be insufficient capital available from within the business, so an external source is required.

- Venture capitalists are prepared to take risks and this venture is identified as high risk because of its cash flow problems.

- The high potential profit will prove attractive to venture capitalists and should mean that the payment is feasible.

- Venture capitalists often provide expertise as well as money. The CurriesOnline team appear to lack business experience in both general terms and with reference to this particular market.

3 Analyse reasons why the business was unable to secure a bank loan when it started. (9)

- The business may lack security. Although the owners appeared to own some assets, these may have been insufficient to cover the size of loan that they required.

- The director indicated that they had an idea of how much they needed, but this did not appear to have been based on any analysis that could be seen by a bank manager, who would want much greater evidence to support a loan of this size. Venture capitalists are prepared to take risks and this venture is identified as high risk.

- The business made the initial mistake of 'not planning finances long term'. This lack of planning would have meant that a bank would not offer a loan. Shamin indicates that 'after eight months trading' they were able to 'develop a much better business plan and cash-flow forecast'.

- Early weaknesses in cash flow – such as underestimating development costs and website maintenance – indicate that this venture may have been very high risk in its early days.

4 How should CurriesOnline finance its expansion plans? Justify your view. (16)

- Retained profits. The owners want to retain control of the business, and retained profit is the ideal way to keep ownership of the business. However, the case study does not indicate whether there is sufficient profit to meet the business's needs.

- Use the funds offered by friends. This will dilute ownership but it is likely to keep it within a group of friends who share the values of the founders. The offer from friends also indicates that they are supportive and interested in the business and so they may take an active role.

- Use venture capitalists. If the business is still seen as high risk this might be the only option as venture capitalists are prepared to

take risks. They may also provide valuable experience to help the business succeed.

- Extend the bank loan. After eight months the business was able to get support from the bank in the form of a loan. If it explains its expansion plans to the bank manager, with supporting evidence to show how the loan will be repaid, it may be able to get a larger loan.

- Sell ordinary shares. This will dilute ownership, but if the expansion plans are large it may be the only feasible way to attract funding. Crowdfunding might be suitable for an innovative business such as this, particularly as it will be able to describe how its business model is working at present.

Note: Expansion plans require long-term sources of finance and so short-term sources, such as bank overdrafts, are not valid.

Evaluation: Any expansion plans are likely to require a compromise involving the existing directors. A high profit may mean that there is sufficient retained profit, but this seems to be unlikely at this stage. Low profit will also mean a bank manager may be reluctant to provide a larger loan. In effect, the owners may need to sacrifice their desire to retain control. In this situation the best option may be to accept the offer of finance from friends, if this provides enough money. However, venture capitalists, who can also bring in experience, appear to offer a much better method of securing the long-term finance needed to support the expansion.

Case study: A golden opportunity (40 marks), pages 406–7

1 Explain the meaning of the term 'venture capital'. (2)

Venture capital is finance that is provided to small or medium-sized firms that seek growth but may be considered as risky by typical share buyers or other lenders.

2 Explain two reasons why the business will need short-term finance, and outline when this will be necessary. (10)

- The business will need to build up high inventory levels because of the seasonal nature of jewellery sales. At this point in the year it will need short-term finance. Predominantly this occurs in the run-up to Christmas.

- Immediately prior to and after the opening of the new store, inventory levels will need to have been built up in order to provide an attractive environment for potential customers. As a consequence, short-term finance will be needed to help build up supplies of jewellery.

- Heavy marketing expenditure is often needed as a new store opens, and this will provide a drain on the business's cash, leading to a requirement for short-term finance. This will be needed prior to the opening of the store and perhaps until it has established a reputation in the area.

3 Is the money needed to open the London store an example of capital expenditure or revenue expenditure? Briefly explain your reasoning. (3)

Capital expenditure – because it is long-term finance for non-current (fixed) assets.

4 James planned to raise £2 million to open the London store. Analyse two possible problems of using a bank loan to finance this plan. (9)

- £2 million is a significant sum of money and therefore the interest payments will be quite high, particularly for a new start-up. Start-ups often find that it takes some time before they can generate a profit. Assets can be repossessed if interest payments are not met.

- A bank loan must be repaid. Depending on the length of time agreed, this could provide a future drain on the business's finance: the shorter the agreed loan period, the greater the problem.
- Usually the repayment of the bank loan is agreed in advance, so there is little flexibility in repayment terms. Consequently, if a business runs short of cash, it will still be required to make payments.

5 Discuss the arguments for and against James using ordinary share capital in order to raise the £2 million finance needed to open the shop in London. (16)

Arguments for using ordinary share capital.

- There is no capital available from within the business, so an external source is required.
- Ordinary share capital is often described as risk capital, and this venture is identified as risky because it is in a different geographical area and the move is based on a single piece of research.
- No profit is expected for three years and it is in the nature of ordinary shares that returns will be in the long term rather than short term.
- The high potential profit will prove attractive to potential shareholders and should mean that shareholders will be attracted. After three years the expected profits are £800,000 per annum which is an exceptionally good return on an investment of £2 million.

Arguments against using ordinary share capital include:

- By giving up part of the ownership, there is the potential for James and his family to lose control of the business. This is a particular risk as the family have complete control at present but may lose control of the existing Leeds business just to raise £2 million for the expansion in London.
- Ordinary shareholders will be entitled to dividends for the remainder of the existence of the business. These dividends may provide the new shareholders with high returns for their financial support, even though the profits may have been created by the efforts of James and his family.

Evaluation: The market research indicates that this business will be very successful and a profit of £800,000 per annum will be made within three years. It would be unwise to give ownership to ordinary shareholders if the money can be found from loan capital or the family, because the estimates show that retained profit will be able to fund the London store within a few years. There is also the possible loss of control of the business. However, if there are no other sources then ordinary shares will help the business to make high profits.

19 Making financial decisions: improving cash flow and profits

Practice exercise 1 (40 marks), page 413

1 The features of a bank overdraft usually include: (1)
   a a fixed interest rate
   b repayments on a monthly basis
   c the opening of a separate bank account – the overdraft account
   d no need for collateral security.

   The answer is d.

2 A system where the debts owed to a business are purchased by another business is known as: (1)
   a a loan
   b factoring
   c leasing
   d sale and leaseback.

   The answer is b.

3 Explain why delaying payments might not be a good solution to a cash-flow problem. (4)

   Delaying payment is not a good solution because it does not prevent the root cause of the cash shortage. Furthermore, it may damage the business's reputation. If suppliers are not paid they will not supply materials and will probably take legal action. In future other businesses will no longer trade with this business or insist on immediate payment, which will put even more pressure on the business's cash flow.

4 Explain the differences between 'sale of assets', 'sale and leaseback' and 'leasing'. (6)

   • 'Sale of assets' takes place when finance is raised by disposing of an item that the business owns – usually a non-current (fixed) asset that is no longer needed.

   • 'Sale and leaseback' occurs when a company raises money by selling an asset, but continues to use that asset by making regular lease (rental) payments to the new owner.

   • 'Leasing' means that a company does not own an asset but merely rents (leases) it from its owner.

5 Select two causes of cash-flow problems. Analyse the best method of solving each of these two causes, justifying your choices. (10)

Cause	Solution
Seasonal demand	Introduce a more flexible workforce or introduce new products to spread sales more evenly throughout the year. This will ensure that the business is less likely to have a period of the year in which it is likely to have fewer inflows of cash.
Over-trading	Good market research to predict sales more accurately and plan appropriate sources of finance to cope with the expected increase. This improved understanding will prevent the business holding excessive levels of inventory.
Over-investment in non-current (fixed) assets	Hire or rent non-current assets according to need, or sell excessive levels of fixed assets if the business owns too many. As with over-trading, good research should help a business to prevent this issue.
Poor inventory management	Closer scrutiny to avoid wastage and excessive holdings (e.g. introduce IT-based systems or 'just-in-time' management). These methods will match supply to demand more closely and thus enable a business to hold more of its current assets as cash.
Credit sales	Limit the use of credit if it does not boost sales or use an overdraft to cover the period before payment is received. Credit sales will always put pressure on cash flow, but if it leads to increased sales it should increase profit. Consequently it may be worth the risk
Unforeseen change	Improve market research and forecasting so that supply and demand can be matched. This will prevent excessive holding of non-cash liquid assets.

6 Analyse how an electrical goods manufacturer might improve its cash flow by improving its working capital management. (9)

- The electrical goods manufacturer may have many parts required for the manufacturing process. Effective inventory control may enable a firm to hold the optimum level of inventory. Generally, this involves minimising levels of inventory by employing methods such as just in time. Usually this requires close cooperation with suppliers who can meet tight deadlines, ensuring that the firm never runs out of inventory. These low levels of inventory will reduce the need for storage space and minimise the chances of damage, deterioration and obsolescence. However, the need to keep low levels of inventory must be matched by the need to ensure that customers' wishes are met, so a balance needs to be kept.

- Receivables should be kept to a minimum as they mean a delay in receiving cash. This makes it harder for firms to pay their own debts. Prompt invoicing and regular reminders of the need for payment towards the end of the credit period can help to ensure that customers pay promptly. This activity needs to be supported by chasing up late payers. Many firms will obtain a credit rating on potential debtors to ensure that there is little risk of non-payment. However, a firm can also ensure that it provides a good service to its customers, so that they are more likely to pay willingly.

- For payables the manufacturer should use the credit period to its maximum in order to improve its holding of cash. However, it must ensure payment is made on time, in order to avoid legal action and/or a bad reputation for paying.

7 Analyse two reasons why it might be difficult to improve a business's cash flow. (9)

It can be difficult to improve cash flow in the circumstances outlined in answer to question 5. Possible reasons are:

- Seasonal demand. The demand for some products and services is seasonal, but companies typically incur costs of production in advance of the peak season for sales. This will cause a significant, but predictable, cash-flow problem for any seasonal business.

- Overtrading. Firms may become too confident and expand rapidly without organising sufficient long-term funds. During rapid expansion this means that the business needs to buy more and more materials, but lacks money because its customers have not yet bought the goods. This leaves the business short of cash.

- Over-investment in fixed assets. Firms may invest in fixed assets in order to grow, but leave themselves with inadequate cash for day-to-day payments. The more successful a small firm, the more eager the entrepreneur will be to purchase new shops or equipment. If not managed carefully, this can leave the business drained of finance and in danger of cash-flow problems.

- Credit sales. The marketing department will want to give credit to customers, to encourage them to buy, but this can lead to a lack of cash in the organisation if sales are not leading to immediate receipts of cash.

- Poor stock inventory management. Organisations might hold excessive stock levels, using up cash that could have been used for other purposes. There is an added danger that high levels of stock inventory may mean that the stock becomes worthless as it becomes out of date or unfashionable.

- Poor management of suppliers. Cash flow can also be influenced by the credit period given to a business by its suppliers. A poorly managed business may not negotiate a suitable credit period with suppliers.

- Unforeseen change. Cash-flow difficulties might also arise from internal changes (e.g. machinery breakdown) or external factors (e.g. a change in government legislation). These could be attributed to management errors or poor planning (if they should have been predicted), but may just be bad luck.

- Losses or low profits. Although cash flow and profits are very different, the two are linked. A business whose sales revenue is less than its expenditure will usually (but not always) have less cash than one that is making a healthy profit.

Case study: Khalid Ahmed's computer peripherals (55 marks), pages 414–5

1 How is the 'closing balance' calculated? (4)

Closing balance = opening balance + net cash flow for period

2 How did debt factoring help Khalid's cash flow? (5)

The competitive nature of his market means that Khalid had to offer credit to his customers, so that he could compete with organisations such as PC World. To prevent himself running short of cash, he was able to convert these debtors receivables (customers who owed him money) into cash straight away, so that his cash flow was not adversely affected.

3 The bank manager advised Khalid to take out an overdraft. Based on the data in Table 19.1, explain the reason for this advice. (5)

Although Khalid was looking for a bank loan, the bank manager recognised that within a year of commencement Khalid would have a credit balance in his bank account. By 2016 quarter 4, he would have a positive bank balance, but the seasonal nature of his business might mean that he could fall into deficit in quarter 3 of 2017. Therefore a short-term bank overdraft, rather than a loan, would be useful to cover shortages of cash.

4 Analyse two different factors that might be causing Khalid to experience cash-flow problems. (9)

- Khalid was reluctant to borrow money. This made it difficult for him to maintain a healthy cash flow as the business expanded.
- Khalid's expansion into a larger store not only cost extra money for the store but also necessitated higher stock levels.
- Computer sales were seasonal, leading to cash-flow problems at certain times of the year – mainly from September to November, when Khalid had to buy stock in the run-up to Christmas but had not yet sold the computers.
- Khalid was forced to offer credit terms to stay competitive with larger companies selling computers, such as PC World.

5 Khalid decided to use a five-year bank loan to buy a shop rather than continuing his lease of the previous store. To what extent do you believe that this was a sensible decision? (16)

Arguments in favour of this decision:

- Buying a shop means that Khalid has an asset that he owns. This could be sold or used as security for a loan in future years if more money was needed.
- Having a short-term lease can cause problems when the lease expires, as Khalid may have no property from which to base his business. In the case study, Khalid was being forced into making the decision to buy or lease because the lease on his current shop was about to expire.
- Owning a shop means that Khalid no longer has to pay rent. His current lease at £30,000 a year was a heavy expense.

Arguments against the decision include:

- Owning a property means the assets of the business are tied up. Khalid was seeking to borrow £200,000. This might have been more usefully employed in increasing the level of

stock inventory or improving other aspects of the business.

- Khalid will have to pay interest on the £200,000, and if interest rates are high this can add to the burden. In the short term it will certainly increase expenditure and damage his cash flow, as he has not only to pay the interest but also to repay the loan.

Evaluation: The decision will be influenced by some factors that are not known, such as the rate of interest on the loan and the likely profitability and cash flow of the business after 2017. Based on the fact that Khalid is expecting to have a closing balance of £55,000 at the end of 2017, it looks as if he can afford this transaction and therefore will be in the more financially secure position of owning an asset and having the money available to repay the loan if necessary. On balance, it would appear sensible for him to buy the shop. However, more firms are leasing property to give themselves more flexibility with non-current assets.

6 Khalid has experienced cash-flow problems in the early years of his business. Do you believe that these problems will occur after the end of 2016? Justify your view. (16)

There are still seasonal variations in sales, often leaving Khalid with low cash balances, particularly in quarter 3. As the business expands, this will require increased expenditure in quarter 3 before higher sales revenue in quarter 4, so the threat of poor cash flow may well remain.

It is stated that the market is competitive and Khalid is a small shop competing with larger organisations. Consequently, he will be vulnerable to actions taken by those businesses, particularly if they decide to provide more generous credit terms to their customers, as Khalid will find it hard to match them in this respect.

Primarily, however, Khalid may find that he no longer has cash-flow problems, as he has established a firm base and in 2017 he is forecast to stay in the black in every quarter. A closing balance of £55,000 in quarter 4 of 2017 is very healthy. In future years, Khalid is likely to be able to sustain a credit balance, even during those quarters in which cash flow is more problematic, as he is expected to achieve this in 2017.

Evaluation: Ultimately, the risk of Khalid experiencing cash-flow problems is likely to hinge on his decision about whether to buy the shop. If Khalid purchases the shop, the drain on his cash may well create further cash-flow problems, although it is likely to increase profitability in the longer term.

Practice exercise 2 (30 marks), page 420

1 Which of the following situations would be certain to lead to an increase in profits? (1)

  a A price increase for a good with price elastic demand

  b A price increase for a good with price inelastic demand

  c A price decrease for a good with price elastic demand

  d A price decrease for a good with price inelastic demand.

The answer is b.

2 Explain one way in which the operations management function might help to improve a business's profits. (4)

Improving capacity utilisation will lead to better use of assets, particularly non-current assets. This will spread fixed costs over a wider output and thus reduce unit costs of production.

Using just-in-time production methods to help lower inventory levels will reduce waste and save costs, such as storage. Again, lower costs will improve profit as these measures will not affect the selling price.

3 Explain two problems that might arise if a business attempted to improve its profits by cutting costs. (7)

- If costs are being cut because inferior raw materials are being used, the quality of the product may suffer, leading to a decline in sales. It is possible that there will be more waste, increasing costs.

- If the workers are paid lower wages, they may become demotivated. The firm may attract less efficient workers, reducing production levels, as the better employees move to other firms.

- Reducing overheads, such as rent, office expenses and machinery costs, may damage sales. For example, a retail outlet may be reluctant to move to lower-rent premises if the location is less accessible to customers. In this case, the savings in costs may be much lower than the decline in sales revenue caused by the less favourable location.

4 Analyse two changes to external factors that might help a business to increase its profits. (9)

- Demographic changes. For example, a growth in immigration has led to increases in demand for many products. In some cases it has led to new businesses, such as shops supplying foodstuffs for Polish immigrants. This change has also led to lower labour costs for many businesses, such as builders and farmers.

- Consumer incomes. Increases in incomes will help most businesses to sell more goods and services. It may also enable a business to charge higher prices, as people on high incomes may be less price-conscious. (For firms providing inferior goods, a decrease in consumers' incomes will lead to higher sales volume.)

- A reduction in competition can boost a business's profit. For example, the liquidation of businesses such as Comet (electrical retailing) and Phones4U (mobile phone retailing) have boosted profits for Dixons Carphone plc because they were close competitors. A lack of competition allows a business to set higher prices and sell a higher volume of goods.

Note: Questions 4 and 5 require opposing arguments. If an external factor, such as higher incomes, causes higher profits, then the reverse of this change (lower incomes) will cause lower profits. Different external factors are described for questions 4 and 5, but the reverse of any of these answers can be used as an answer to the other question.

5 Analyse two changes to external factors that might lead to a business experiencing a fall in its profits. (9)

- Market conditions. If the CMA prevents a merger between two businesses this may lead to lower profits because smaller businesses are less able to benefit from economies of scale, such as bulk-buying.

- Interest rates. Higher interest rates will hit profits in two ways: they will increase the cost of credit and so dissuade consumers from buying goods on credit. This will be particularly damaging for retailers of household durables, such as furniture, which are often sold on credit. They will also increase the business's costs if it is borrowing money.

- Environmental issues. Stricter laws and regulations to limit pollution and environmental damage can increase costs if a firm has to adapt its methods in order to comply with these new regulations. The firm may also incur fines if it does not comply with the legislation.

Case study: Improving profitability at Carphone Warehouse (55 marks), pages 420–1

1   Explain why postpay (pay monthly contracts) are more likely to achieve higher profits than prepay (pay-as-you-go contracts). (5)

Postpay contracts are more likely to lead to increased revenue because there is a guaranteed minimum sum paid in return for a certain level of time/texts/data. Many consumers will pay for a number of minutes that exceed their likely maximum so that no additional minutes are charged. Pay-as-you-go contracts cost less but every call is chargeable. Thus users are less likely to make so many calls (or these contracts will be purchased by people who intend to have low usage). Both contracts incur similar costs for the network and so postpay, which on average earns more income for the network, is more profitable.

2   Explain why CPW's sale and leaseback of its headquarters would improve cash flow in the short term, but might worsen profit levels in the long term. *Note: CPW = Carphone Warehouse* (6)

CPW's sale of its headquarters will bring in a large sum of cash – in 2013 it received £51 million from the sale of property in the UK. This sum of money will have a major, positive impact on its cash flow in 2013. However, because it owned the property it did not pay rent. Because the properties are now owned by another business, CPW must pay an annual rent. The new owner of the property will be aiming to make profit and therefore the annual rent will be set so that rental payments exceed the £51 million paid over a period of time. Thus, in the long-run CPW will pay more in rent than it will receive from selling its property, unless it has no use for the property in the future.

3   To what extent is the use of the marketing mix the most important method employed by CPW to improve its profit levels in 2013? (20)

- Sales revenue in Europe increased by 11.5% and the UK division increased its market share in 2013. Although the methods employed by CPW are not specified, increases of this nature are dependent on effective marketing decision-making; i.e. effective use of the marketing mix.
- CPW's customer service and employee expertise helped them to achieve 10% annual growth in the UK. Although it could be argued that this is part of the human resource function, 'people' is one of the seven Ps in the marketing mix and is one of the most important Ps for the marketing of services, such as mobile phone networks.
- CPW enhanced its status as a highly trusted brand; this would be dependent on a good product and effective promotions.
- In the text it indicates that the marketing mix has been instrumental in achieving this growth with 'the main focus being on updated smart deal promotions and price offers on specific handsets'. This combination of promotion, price and product has enabled CPW to grow by 10% in one year.
- Most of CPW's sales arise from a visit to one of its stores. In 2013, it was improving the physical environment and investing in more sophisticated IT systems to make the process of purchasing easier. Process and physical environment are two other elements that are vital in marketing of services.
- The business has also targeted postpay contracts as this 'product' may not generate more customers but does create greater profitability.
- Finally, CPW have targeted new markets in Europe because the UK market has limited scope for growth. Although this is a marketing strategy, any profitability from this approach is attributable to its use of target marketing rather than the marketing mix.

Evaluation: According to the article, virtually every decision made in 2013 assisted its growth and this led to improved levels of profit. All of these approaches were marketing activities with the vast majority centred on the marketing mix; particularly those elements of the marketing mix that have specific relevance to services, such as mobile phone networks. The marketing mix needed the support of other functional areas, such as the finance department selling assets to finance the investment and operations management improving the online systems to speed up the buying process. However, the evidence suggests that the marketing mix was the most important method employed by CPW to improve its profit levels.

4   The case study features three major developments in 2014. Evaluate the likely overall impact of these three developments on Carphone's profitability in the future. (24)

4G phone services:

- 4G services are expected to grow and lead to a significant increase in overall demand for new mobiles and tablets. This factor applies particularly to countries such as the UK, where there is great interest in mobile communication but where 4G has a very low market penetration of 1.77% of the market (compared with 72.6% penetration for 3G).

- South Korea shows the huge potential for 4G penetration, with nearly half the country converting to 4G networks within 18 months of launch. In terms of the use of technology, South Korea has similar characteristics to the UK market in most respects.

Overall impact: A sudden increase in demand in a market that had begun to stagnate, because market penetration of 3G phones was so high.

EE threats:

- This was a major threat to CPW because they had already lost '3'.
- EE has already ended its agreement with Phones4U and therefore cancelling its agreement with CPW is quite likely.
- Vodafone was setting up stores so that it might no longer need to use CPW and Phones4U to reach large numbers of potential customers.

Overall impact: subsequent to the publication of this article Phones4U went into liquidation because it lost these contracts. CPW's merger with Dixons (see below) shows that CPW was aware of this danger and had already planned an alternative strategy to provide it with different opportunities use its skills and reputation.

Dixons-CPW merger:

- This merger combined CPW's expertise with mobile phones with Dixons Retail Group's understanding of other technical items such as computers and fridges. The merged skills of the two businesses would enable it to take advantage of the 'Internet of Things'.
- Marketing experts, such as Mintel, anticipate that everyday objects will increasingly have digital identity so that every day items, such as toothbrushes and fridges, can cooperate in a 'smart' way.
- The smartphone is expected to become the keystone of this new world, and so CPW's expertise in telephone design was an ideal complement to Dixons' understanding of household goods.

Overall impact: Individually, both of these firms were vulnerable to changes in technology. Combined, they have the complementary skills to enable them to take full advantage of the development of smart technology-based everyday appliances.

Evaluation: EE's threat to CPW was likely to be significant, given that this threat led to the demise of CPW's main competitor, Phones4U. However, the other two developments are both positive influences. 4G technology is likely to lead to customers wanting expert advice when considering a new mobile device, preferably of an objective nature. CPW is ideally set to provide this service because customers are less likely to trust the advice of a store that is only selling phones for use on one network, such as '3'. The merger with Dixons has opportunities for 'synergy', with the combined skills of two businesses being worth more than the two sets of individual skills, because they complement each other so well.

20 Setting HR objectives

Practice exercise 1 (35 marks), page 434

1 Which of the following activities is not part of the HR function in an organisation? (1)
   a Recruitment and selection
   b Appraisal
   c Quality assurance
   d Fringe benefits
   e Training and development.

   The answer is c.

2 Explain why HR objectives should be related to corporate objectives. (5)

   HR objectives, like other functional objectives, will be determined by, and will contribute to, the achievement of the overall corporate objectives of a business.

3 Identify two HR objectives and explain how they are likely to contribute to overall corporate objectives. (6)
   - Employee engagement/involvement and good employer/employee relations – improves productivity, reduces labour turnover and absenteeism and hence labour costs.
   - Talent development and training – ensures that an organisation has the capabilities to achieve its objectives.
   - Diversity – ensures that a wider range of skills and ideas contribute to meeting corporate objectives.
   - Alignment of values – ensures that the values of the organisation are communicated and understood by employees, so that they understand and work towards achieving corporate objectives.
   - Number, skills and locations of employees – ensures that these are matched to requirements in order to allow other functional, and overall corporate objectives, to be achieved.
   - Maximising labour productivity and minimising labour costs – will ensure the efficient operation of a business.

4 Identify two internal factors and explain how they might influence the HR objectives of an organisation. (6)

   - Financial constraints – may affect HR objectives relating to the provision of staff training and development.
   - Trade unions and the relationship between employers and employees – may influence HR objectives concerned with the introduction of change, such as flexible working practices.
   - Organisational structure – may affect HR objectives related to motivation and communication.
   - Business performance – if an unprofitable area needs to close, may affect HR objectives related to the number, skills and locations of employees.

5 Identify two external factors and explain how they might influence the HR objectives of an organisation. (6)
   - Political factors – for example, a change in government can lead to significant change in the attitude to trade unions and the amount of power they are able to wield in the workplace.
   - Economic factors – for example, changes in the market and the economy may lead to changes in the demand for a firm's products and services, which are likely to cause changes in the number of employees.
   - Social factors – for example, a greater focus on work–life balance is leading to more flexible working patterns.
   - Technological factors – for example, a need to ensure that staff are well trained in the use of IT systems.

6 Distinguish between 'hard' and 'soft' HRM strategies. (6)
   - 'Hard' HRM strategies treat employees as a resource to be monitored and used in as efficient a way as possible so that the organisation achieves its overall aims. They include issues such as workforce planning to ensure that labour supply matches demand.
   - 'Soft' HRM strategies treat employees as valuable assets to be developed so that the firm and the individual reach their maximum potential.

7 What are the relative strengths of the soft HRM strategy compared to the hard HRM strategy? (5)

Employees today expect to be involved in, and to contribute to, decision making, and hence will prefer a soft approach. This is particularly the case for employees who are more educated and skilled. This is likely to: encourage more motivated workers; reduce labour costs (because of reduced labour turnover and absenteeism); increase productivity; and improve customer service.

Case study: The HR function in a business (25 marks), page 435

1 Analyse how the HR objective related to labour turnover and absenteeism is likely to contribute to the achievement of overall company objectives. (9)

- The overall aim of the insurance company is to provide customers with quality advice and service at competitive prices.

- Reducing labour turnover will ensure that employees stay with the firm for longer and therefore develop their knowledge and expertise. This should enable them to provide customers with better quality service.

- Reducing labour turnover and absenteeism will reduce business costs and may help the business in its objective to provide competitive prices.

2 Based on the information provided, do you believe that the company uses a soft HRM strategy? Justify your response. (16)

Answers might include the following.

- A 'soft' HRM strategy treats employees as valuable assets to be developed so that the firm and the individual reach their maximum potential.

- The alternative is a 'hard' HRM strategy that treats employees as a resource to be monitored and used in as efficient a way as possible so that the organisation achieves its overall aims. It looks at issues such as workforce planning to ensure that labour supply matches demand.

Evaluation: The case study indicates elements of a hard HRM approach in relation to the clear monitoring of HRM data about the workforce. However, it is more likely that the company employs a soft HR strategy, with employees viewed as a valuable asset, a major source of competitive advantage and of vital importance in achieving the strategic objectives of the organisation. This is supported by the fact that the business encourages high levels of employee participation in decision making.

Case study: Halfords Group plc (60 marks), pages 435–6

1 Identify and explain two areas, not mentioned in the case study, for which Halfords might set HR objectives. (8)

Halfords might set HR objectives linked to:

- the number, skills and locations of employees to ensure that they match the needs of the business and allow it to achieve its corporate objectives

- maximising labour productivity and minimising labour costs (for example, due to absenteeism) to ensure that the business overall is as efficient as possible

- alignment of values to ensure that employees understand the company's values and objectives and contribute fully to them.

2 Why might Halfords' HR objectives have been constrained by its financial objectives? (5)

Halfords' financial objectives will have been determined by specific corporate objectives. For example, a broad corporate objective to improve sales and profitability may result in a financial objective to cut costs across all departments or just in the HR department. This may conflict with an HR objective to improve training. It will be up to the HR department to consider how this conflict should be resolved.

3 Select two areas for which Halfords has HR objectives and, on the basis of the information in the case study, and your imagination, produce a SMART objective for each. (6)

SMART objectives might include:

- reduce the number of people leaving within three months of starting their employment with Halfords to less than 10% of the workforce by 2016

- increase the proportion of female employees overall by 30%, and specifically in Halfords autocentre by 30%, within the next two years

- ensure that 80% of all employees who have successfully completed the Gear 1 training programme go on to successfully complete the Gear 2 training programme by 2016.

4 Analyse why SMART objectives are more helpful to an organisation than objectives that are not SMART. (9)

- Being specific, measurable and timed enables a business to assess the extent to which objectives have been achieved and to ensure that staff are clear about what it is they are trying to do and have a clear sense of direction.
- Being realistic means objectives are more likely to motivate staff and provide them with a realistic level of challenge.
- Being agreed by the whole workforce means objectives are much more likely to be achieved than if they were simply imposed by managers.

5 Discuss the reasons why Halfords and other companies will ensure that their HR objectives are linked to, and influenced by, their overall corporate objectives. (16)

Answers might include the following.

- HR objectives, like other functional objectives, are part of the hierarchy of objectives; this hierarchical process encourages a logical and coordinated approach to planning activities and is more likely to enable an organisation to achieve its goals.
- HR objectives are set in order to coordinate the activities of, give a sense of direction to, and guide the actions of, the HR division; they should contribute directly to the overall corporate objectives.

Examples how some of Halfords HR objectives might contribute to overall corporate objectives:

- employee engagement/involvement – improves productivity
- reducing labour turnover – reduces labour costs
- training – ensures that the company has the capabilities to achieve its objectives
- diversity – ensures that a wider range of skills and ideas contribute to meeting corporate objectives.

Evaluation: Without a clear link between HR objectives and overall corporate objectives, activities would be uncoordinated. For example, the right number of employees, with the right skills and in the right places might not be available. Lack of appropriate training might mean productivity falls. Lack of good engagement and motivation might mean labour turnover and absenteeism increase and as a result labour costs rise. Such uncoordinated developments might limit the ability of Halfords to achieve its overall aim of sales of £1 billion by the end of 2016.

6 Discuss the extent to which internal and external factors are likely to influence Halfords' HR objectives and its ability to achieve these objectives. (16)

Answers might include the following.

Internal factors include:

- financial constraints, which may prevent the business meeting its training objective and ensuring that staff can meet customer needs effectively
- the relationship between employers and employees, which may influence how well the business involves its employees in company decisions and how motivated they feel
- the overall performance of the business, which may influence resources available to implement other initiatives, such as engaging and motivating employees more effectively.

External factors include:

- economic factors, which may reduce demand for the company's products, particularly the leisure-based ones, and thus reduce the resources available to achieve its training plans
- social factors, such as the desire to lead a more healthy life, which might increase demand for leisure-based products and hence facilitate the success of HR objectives
- legislation, including equal opportunities legislation, which may influence the recruitment and selection of employees.

Evaluation: A range of internal and external factors are likely to influence Halfords' ability to achieve its HR objectives, and for this reason it needs to monitor its progress in meeting objectives and adapt its actions and its objectives as appropriate.

21 Analysing HR performance

Practice exercise 1 (75 marks), page 448

1 Which of the following is not an example of human resource data? (1)

  a Labour productivity

  b Employee costs as a percentage of turnover

  c The rate of inflation

  d Labour turnover

  e Labour costs per unit

  f Retention rates.

The answer is c.

2 Define the term 'labour turnover' and explain two problems that high rates of labour turnover might cause a firm. (9)

Labour turnover is the proportion of employees leaving a business over a period. It is measured by the formula:

$$\frac{\text{number of employees leaving a business over a given period}}{\text{average number employed over a given period}} \times 100$$

Problems that high rates of labour turnover might cause a firm include:

- high recruitment and selection costs to replace staff who leave
- high induction and training costs to ensure that new employees quickly become familiar with the practices of the firm and learn the necessary skills to carry out their job effectively
- a possible fall in productivity due to the disruption caused by skilled staff leaving and new untrained staff joining the firm.

3 Distinguish between labour turnover and retention rates. (6)

- Labour turnover is the proportion of employees leaving a business over a period of time – usually a year.
- The retention rate is the proportion of employees with a specified length of service – normally one or more years – as a proportion of the total workforce.

Thus if labour turnover falls, the overall retention rate will usually increase and vice versa.

4 In a firm, 190 workers were employed at the start of the year, 178 workers were employed at the end of the year, and during the year 24 workers left. Calculate the rate of labour turnover for the year. (3)

Average number employed over the year
= (190 + 178)/2 = 368/2 = 184
Rate of labour turnover for the year
= (24/184) × 100 = 13.04%

5 A firm employs a total of 6,300 workers, 2,700 of who have been with the firm for more than one year. Calculate the retention rate. (3)

Retention rate = (2,700/6,300) x 100 = 42.86%

6 Using worked examples, explain the terms 'labour productivity' and 'labour costs per unit'. (8)

'Labour productivity' is the output per worker in a given time period.

It is measured by the formula: output per period/number of employees per period.

For example, if 35,000 units are produced by 70 people in a given month:
Labour productivity = 35,000/70 = 500 units per worker

'Labour costs per unit' is the average labour costs involved in producing one unit of output in a given time period.

It is measured by the formula: total labour costs/total units of output.

For example, if output is, as in the above example, 35,000 per month, and 70 people are employed to produce the goods at a cost of £1,000 per employee per month, total labour costs are £70,000 (£1,000 x 70).
Labour costs per unit = £70,000/35,000 = £2 per unit

7 Outline two ways in which a firm might increase its labour productivity and reduce its labour costs per unit. (6)

- Recruiting suitably skilled and trained employees.
- Providing training to enhance skills and attitudes of existing employees.

- Providing remuneration and non-financial benefits that improve motivation and effort.
- Improving working practices.
- Improving technology.

8 In a firm, output in a particular month is 60,000 units, 75 workers are employed and labour costs are £1,000 per worker per month. Calculate labour productivity and labour costs per unit. (6)
Labour productivity = 60,000/75 = 800 units per worker.
Total labour costs are £75,000 (£1,000 x 75)
Labour costs per unit = £75,000/60,000 = £1.25 per unit

9 Explain why employee costs as a percentage of turnover might be a valuable element of human resource data for a firm. (5)
- Employee costs as a percentage of turnover is the percentage of turnover needed to cover employee or labour costs.
- Employee costs as a percentage of turnover is related to the nature of a business and how labour intensive or automated it is.
- By comparing it to the industry benchmark, employee costs as a percentage of turnover is one of the most common quantitative measures to determine if a business had the right number of employees.
- If the figure is too high, this is likely to be reflected in low profit margins, prices that are too high, low labour productivity or because employees are paid above the industry average.

10 If sales turnover in a firm is £1,800,000 per annum and the firm employs 15 workers at a cost of £12,000 per worker per annum, what are employee costs as a percentage of turnover? (3)

The formula for employee costs as a percentage of turnover is:
$$\frac{\text{employee costs}}{\text{sales turnover}} \times 100$$
Employee costs are £180,000 (£12,000 x 15 workers)
Employee costs as a percentage of turnover
$$= \frac{180,000}{1,800,000} \times 100 = 10\%$$

11 In a firm, the average daily absentee rate is 15% and the total workforce is 300. What is the average number of workers who are absent on any one day? (3)

$$\text{Rate of absenteeism} = \frac{\text{number of staff absent on 1 day}}{\text{total number of staff}} \times 100$$

If the number of staff absent on any one day is x, the above formula gives:
$(x/300) \times 100 = 15\%$
Therefore the number of staff absent on any one day is 45 (x/3 = 15, which is x = 15 x 3)

12 Explain two consequences for a firm of a high rate of absenteeism. (6)
- It is costly for a firm to cover for those staff who are absent, especially if deadlines are looming and other employees need to be paid overtime or additional staff need to berecruited.
- Work may not be completed, which can delay production and affect sales.
- New or less skilled staff may have to be employed, which may reduce productivity and quality, and have an adverse impact on sales and profitability.

13 Assess the extent to which labour productivity and labour costs per unit are more or less important to the success of a business than labour turnover and retention rates. (16)

Answers might include the following.
- Explanations of what each term means and how each is measured.
- Identification of typical causes of low labour productivity/high labour costs per unit and of high labour turnover/low retention rates – mostly these are very similar and include: ineffective leadership and management and poor communication; low wages and salaries and poor working conditions; poor selection procedures; boring and unchallenging work; low morale and motivation.
- Ways of increasing labour productivity/reducing labour costs per unit and of improving labour turnover/retention rates include: better recruitment and selection processes; better training provision; appropriate remuneration, benefits and working conditions; improved working practices; improved technology.

Evaluation: Problems with labour turnover and retention rates will be reflected in labour productivity and labour costs per unit. Most businesses want to improve their labour productivity and reduce their labour costs per unit. As a result, both sets of measures of HR performance are as important to the success of a business as each other.

Practice exercise 2 (25 marks), page 448

1 Analyse why labour turnover in the hotel, catering and leisure sector tends to be higher than in most other sectors. (9)

Labour turnover is the proportion of employees leaving a business over a period of time.

Possible reasons why labour turnover in the hotel, catering and leisure sector tends to be higher than in most other sectors include:

- Internal causes: low wages in comparison with other jobs requiring similar levels of skill; boring and unchallenging jobs that usually lack career opportunities; long hours and poor working conditions.

- External causes: many of the staff recruited are students, who will therefore view the job as temporary; a substantial number of the jobs in this sector are seasonal and hence will only attract people looking for seasonal work.

- Higher than average labour turnover is usually an indication that the workforce is less content than in other industries where turnover is at or below average. However, the hotel, catering and leisure sector is different from other sectors in that much of its work is seasonal and many of the staff employed in this sector are young students and those looking for temporary employment. For these reasons, it is not surprising that labour turnover tends to be higher in the hotel, catering and leisure sector than in most other sectors.

2 Discuss why a hotel or restaurant might want to reduce its labour turnover and increase its retention rates, and how it might do this successfully. (16)

Answers might include the following:

- Improving wages – or if this is unlikely because they are at the industry average and further increases only add to business costs – improve benefits and working conditions.

- Increasing job satisfaction, making jobs more challenging and providing more promotional opportunities.

- Providing better recruitment and selection processes and better training – trying to recruit more mature people who are looking for permanent jobs rather than young students.

Evaluation: It is important to reduce labour turnover and increase retention in order to reduce labour costs and allow a business to be more competitive. There are a range of strategies that a hotel or restaurant could introduce to try to reduce its labour turnover and increase retention, but given the nature of the hotel, catering and leisure sector, where business is seasonal and firms typically employ students and seasonal workers, labour turnover is naturally higher than in most other sectors. For an individual hotel or restaurant, it is therefore more important to ensure that its own rate of labour turnover is not above the industry average and that it monitors this figure on a regular basis to ensure that it is not experiencing any particular problems.

Case study: Using human resource data (50 marks), page 449

1 Using the data provided, calculate the following measures of workforce effectiveness for each of the three years:

a Labour turnover (6)

$$\frac{\text{Number of people leaving a business over a given period}}{\text{average number employed over a given period}} \times 100$$

2012: (10/100) × 100 = 10%
2013: (15/98) × 100 = 15.3%
2014: (20/96) × 100 = 20.8%

b Retention rates (6)

$$\frac{\text{Number of employees with 1 or more years' service}}{\text{overall workforce numbers}} \times 100$$

2012: (50/100) x 100 = 50%
2013: (40/98) x 100 = 40.8%
2014: (40/96) x 100 = 41.7%

c Labour productivity (6)

Output per period/number of employees per period
2012: 67,000/100 = 670 units per employee per year
2013: 68,000/98 = 694 units per employee per year
2014: 69,000/96 = 719 units per employee per year

d Labour costs per unit (6)

Total labour costs/total units of output.

Average labour costs were £15,000 p.a. for each of the three years, making total labour costs:

£1,500,000 in 2012; £1,470,000 in 2013; £1,440,000 in 2014
2012: £1,500,000/67,000 = £22.39 per unit
2013: £1,470,000/68,000 = £21.62 per unit
2014: £1,440,000/69,000 = £20.87 per unit

e Employee costs as a percentage of turnover (6)

$$\frac{\text{Employee costs}}{\text{Sales turnover}} \times 100$$

Employee costs are the same as the figure for total labour costs calculated in 1(d)

2012: (1,500,000/6,700,000) x 100 = 22.4%

2013: (1,470,000/8,160,000) x 100 = 18.0%

2014: (1,440,000/8,660,000) x 100 = 16.6%

2   Using your calculations from question 1 and the data in Tables 21.1 and 21.2, discuss the issues, including causes and effects, which these human resource data indicators raise for the human resource management decision making and planning in this business.   (20)

Answers might include the following.

- Labour turnover has increased each year and in 2014 it was double the 2012 figure. This should be a real concern for the firm. In each of the three years, a large proportion of employees leaving the firm are from the production department. It would be useful to investigate why this is the case. Also worrying is that the number of employees leaving from the administration department increased from 0 in 2012 to 8 in 2013 and then 9 in 2014. This also requires investigation.

- Retention rates have fallen over the three years, which reflects the increasing labour turnover and means that a smaller proportion of employees have a year's experience with the firm or longer.

- Labour productivity has increased by a small amount each year, from 670 units in 2012 to 719 units in 2014.

- In line with the increases in productivity over the three years, labour costs per unit have fallen, as have employee costs as a percentage of sales turnover.

- The number of days lost due to absence has increased considerably so that in 2014 almost 50% more days were lost due to absences than in 2012. Absences in the departments vary considerably, falling progressively in the marketing and administration departments but rising significantly in the production department between 2013 and 2014 and in finance between 2012 and 2014. It will be important to explore the causes of these variations between departments and the changes over time.

Evaluation: The concerns raised for HRM policies relate to labour turnover and absenteeism. The firm will need to keep these two issues under review and to investigate reasons for the increases. In relation to labour turnover, the focus should be on the production and administration departments. Issues to consider are the level of motivation of staff, the effectiveness of the training they receive, working conditions and reward systems, the level of challenge and responsibility staff have and the quality of leadership in these areas. In the administration department, the data suggest that 80% of staff are in the 16–29 age range, but the office manager, appointed two years ago, is the 53-year-old sister of the managing director. An inappropriate management style and poor communication might be the problems here. Absenteeism in the production and finance departments need to be investigated to find out why there has been such a substantial increase over the period.

22 Making HR decisions: improving organisational design and managing the human resource flow

Practice exercise 1 (30 marks), page 454

1 Explain the term 'job design'. (4)

'Job design' is the process of deciding on the content of a job in terms of its duties and responsibilities, on the methods to be used in carrying out the job, in terms of techniques, systems and procedures, and on the relationships that should exist between the job holder and their superiors, subordinates and colleagues.

2 Explain one example of an organisational influence on job design. (3)

- Purpose and objectives of the organisation.
- Nature, range and volume of tasks to be performed.
- Ergonomics.
- The way work is organised, e.g. remote or home working.
- Quality standards.
- Speed and timeliness of task completion required.

3 Explain one example of an external influence on job design. (3)

- Technological developments.
- The general level of education and its influence on skills.
- Social changes, for example, in the nature of customer demand, e.g. 24/7 services.

4 Explain one example of an influence on job design that is employee related. (3)

- Employees' health, well-being and safety.
- Their need for fair reward and recognition.
- Their need for job satisfaction.
- Their need for good work–life balance.
- Their skills and capabilities.

5 Which one of the following is not one of the job characteristics in Hackman and Oldham's model? (1)

a Skill variety
b Task identity
c Significance tests
d Autonomy
e Feedback.

The answer is c.

6 Give two examples of what might be involved in designing or redesigning jobs. (4)

- Varying patterns of work in order to broaden skill variety and make work more meaningful.
- Reorganising work so that groups of employees focus on the production of a whole product in order to improve task identity and make work more meaningful.
- Ensuring that employees understand the value of their work in contributing to the achievement of organisational objectives and thus task significance.
- Delegating tasks to their lowest possible level in order to provide opportunities for greater autonomy and responsibility.
- Providing appropriate feedback to enable employees to improve their work.

7 Explain the three psychological states that Hackman and Oldham suggest are important to achieve high levels of motivation and engagement. (12)

- Meaningfulness of work, which is based upon the following job characteristics: skill variety, i.e. being able to use an appropriate variety of skills and talent; task identity, i.e. being able to identify with the work as part of a whole; task significance, i.e. being able to identify the task as contributing to other employees and to the organisation's objectives.

- Responsibility for work outcomes, which means an individual is given sufficient freedom of action in their job to be successful at it or to fail; they have responsibility and autonomy about how to carry out their job.

- Knowledge of work outcomes, which means employees receive feedback about how effective they are at their job and are able to use this feedback to review how they have done and how they might improve in the future.

Case study: Michelle's stressful job (25 marks), page 455

1 Explain three influences on job design. (9)

Influences on job design include: organisational influences, external influences and employee-related influences. See answers to practice exercise 1, questions 2, 3 and 4 on page 117.

2 Does Michelle's job indicate the features of good job design according to Hackman and Oldham's model? Justify your view. (16)

Answers might include the following.

- An explanation of the five job characteristics of good job design identified by Hackman and Oldham's model: skill variety, task identity, task significance, autonomy, feedback.

- An explanation of Hackman and Oldham's three psychological states: meaningfulness of work, responsibility for work outcomes, knowledge of work outcomes.

- A description of the characteristics of Michelle's job: a variety of different tasks – perhaps too many; Michelle works on her

own – and appears isolated; she knows how important her job is for the smooth running of the organisation and is often told this by others.

Evaluation: Michelle's job has many of the features of Hickman and Oldham's model of good job design. However, there is a major problem. While there is a great deal of skill variety, Michelle's level of stress, her absences and the fact that she is looking for a new job, suggest that the variety of skills and tasks is too much to cope with. It is likely that her formal job description does not reflect what she actually does – for example the informal demands colleagues put on her to guide visitors to the lifts, etc. From an HRM point of view, a review of her actual activities compared to her job description would be a useful exercise to

ensure that if she leaves and is replaced, her replacement does not experience the same levels of stress.

Practice exercise 2 (40 marks), page 459

1 Explain the term organisational design. (4)

Organisational design is the process of shaping an organisation's structure so that it meets the organisation's purpose and helps to deliver its objectives.

2 How does organisational design differ from organisational structure? (5)

- Organisational design is a strategy that defines how a company unifies its departments and individuals in order to achieve company objectives. These are management choices that form an organisational culture.

- Organisational structure represents the formal lines of authority and power and the relationship between different people and functions in an organisation. The structure is a statement of the current state of affairs, not the ideals or intentions of the organisation. Organisational structures are usually presented in the form of organisation charts.

Despite these differences, organisational design and organisational structure are closely related

and changes to one often result in changes to the other.

3 What does an organisation chart illustrate? (3)

An organisation chart shows the lines of authority and the layers of hierarchy in an organisation. In doing so, it shows the relationship between line managers and their subordinates, and the channels of communication.

4 What is meant by the chain of command? (4)

The chain of command is the reporting system shown in an organisation chart from the top of the hierarchy down to the bottom of the hierarchy. Instructions are passed from top to bottom along the chain of command.

5 Explain the terms 'hierarchy' and 'span' and the relationship between them. (6)

- 'Hierarchy' is the vertical division of authority and accountability in an organisation; levels of hierarchy are the number of levels between the shop floor and the chief executive in an organisation.

- 'Span', or span of control, is the number of subordinates that a manager is required to supervise directly.

The relationship between 'hierarchy' and 'span' is that, in an organisation of a given size, the more layers (or levels) of hierarchy, the smaller the span of control is likely to be, and vice versa.

6 Explain two implications for a business of having a flat organisational structure with a wide span of control. (6)

- Individual managers need to delegate more effectively, as they have more subordinates reporting to them directly.

- As a result of extra delegation, responsibility is passed to lower levels of the hierarchy, potentially improving motivation but also increasing an individual's workload.

- There will be fewer layers of hierarchy and therefore vertical communication should improve and decisions should be made, and implemented, more quickly.

- A reduction in overhead costs and better communication may mean greater efficiency.

- There will be fewer opportunities for promotion, although each promotion will place a manager closer to the top of the hierarchy than would occur in a taller structure.

7 Explain two implications for a business of having a tall organisational structure with a narrow span of control. (6)

- Individual managers have less need to delegate, so workloads should be managed more easily.

- Less delegation may mean less stress but could lead to low morale and less commitment.

- Tighter control of decisions and subordinates is possible if managers are responsible for just a few workers.

- Narrow spans of control will mean more layers of hierarchy and therefore communication may take longer, slowing down decisions.

- The chances of messages becoming distorted are greater.

- There will be more managers, adding to overhead costs.

- There will be more opportunities for promotion, although it will require more promotions before a manager reaches the top of the hierarchy than would be the case in a flatter structure.

8 Explain two factors that might influence the structure of an organisation. (6)

- The size of an organisation. The larger an organisation is, the more likely it might be to have wider spans of control in order to reduce the length of the chain of command.

- The nature of the organisation. Does it need tight control (and thus narrow spans of control), or can work be delegated more readily?

- The culture of the organisation. The personal preferences of managers may decide whether a business is tightly controlled from the top, or decentralised.

- The skills of the workforce. A highly skilled workforce is more likely to fit with an organisation that delegates responsibility.

Case study: High Class Furnishings (40 marks), pages 459–60

1 Explain the usefulness of an organisation chart to High Class Furnishings. (6)

An organisation chart is useful because it helps High Class Furnishings' employees and other stakeholders understand the relationship between people and functions in the company. It allows them to see: the design of the company, including the chain of command; how different departments fit together; who is answerable to whom; the span of control at each level and in each department; the levels of hierarchy in the company.

2 What are the spans of control of supervisor C in the Uttoxeter factory and of supervisor B in the Rugeley factory? (2)

Span of control of Supervisor C (Uttoxeter factory): 12

Span of control of Supervisor B (Rugeley factory): 4

3 Is there an ideal span of control? Evaluate your answer in relation to the spans of control of the directors and of the production supervisors at High Class Furnishings. (16)

Answers might include the following.

- Some theorists suggest that a narrow span of control is best because it allows close control and monitoring of subordinates. This is also vital if geographical and communication difficulties make contact problematic.

- Narrow spans are also needed if a manager is responsible for subordinates with widely differing roles and duties, as this makes the manager's job more demanding.

- A wide span of control encourages delegation and passes responsibility to subordinates, which may be good for motivation.
- Wide spans are also suited to skilled workers who can take responsibility for their own decisions.

Evaluation: The directors of High Class Furnishings have very low spans of control (only one or two subordinates). This is probably due to the complex nature of the subordinates' jobs and the difficulties in communicating. However, it is hard to justify such low spans of control without having more information about their actual responsibilities. The production supervisors have wider spans (12 at Uttoxeter) because the shop-floor workers are each carrying out similar duties in close proximity to each other.

4 Discuss the production director's view that a change in structure might 'adversely affect the current clear lines of accountability and responsibility'. (16)

Answers might include the following.

- The existing structure is based on functional management with two separate production plants. The organisation chart shows clearly the lines of accountability and responsibility.

Both product ranges have been successful, so any changes to the structure that take away these clear lines of responsibility may weaken the efficiency of the organisation. The current centralised structure creates consistency across the company.

- However, there have been difficulties in coordinating the activities of all departments. This usually means poor communication between departments, which is a common weakness of functional structures. The proposed changes would allow more decentralisation and greater responsibility, which might result in greater efficiency. In addition, a structure with divisions based on product ranges might encourage more innovation and development within each range.

Evaluation: A change in structure seems necessary because there is clear evidence that current weaknesses are threatening the company's future. A structure based on product ranges might enable the business to innovate and increase the variety of products it provides – thus satisfying customer demand more effectively. The concern raised by the production director should not be ignored when planning and implementing a new structure.

Practice exercise 3 (30 marks), page 463

1 Explain the term 'delegation' and why it is important to the success of an organisation. (5)

Delegation is the process of passing authority down the hierarchy from a manager to a subordinate. It is important to the success of an organisation because it allows activities to be carried out, and decisions to be made, at the appropriate level.

2 Distinguish between the terms 'responsibility', 'authority' and 'accountability'. (9)

- Responsibility means being accountable for one's actions. For example, an individual who is responsible for a department will be required to justify the performance of the department against set targets.
- Authority is the ability or power to carry out a task, often measured in terms of control over resources.
- Accountability is the extent to which a named individual is held responsible for the success or failure of a particular policy, project or piece of work.

3 Explain one advantage and one limitation of delegating responsibility in a business. (8)

Advantages of delegating responsibility might include:

- freeing up management time to focus on strategically more important tasks
- motivating employees by giving them more responsibility and trusting them
- subordinates having better local knowledge and therefore making better decisions
- improved flexibility and quicker decision making and response times
- staff development advantages as more staff gain management experience.

Limitations to the delegation of responsibility might include:

- the size of the firm – often too little delegation in small firms
- customer expectations – customers may wish to deal with managers regardless of whether responsibilities have been delegated further down the hierarchy
- the need for confidentiality – may limit the extent of delegation
- the quality of staff – staff may not have the skills to carry out delegated responsibilities

- attitudes and the approach of management – an authoritarian manager may be less likely to delegate
- crisis situations – in emergency or crisis situations where decisions need to be made quickly, delegation may be less appropriate and less effective.

4 Explain two factors that are likely to make delegation more effective. (8)

- Mutual trust between the supervisor and the subordinate to whom work is delegated.
- Careful selection of the person who is being delegated to, in order to ensure they have the skills and capability to undertake the tasks.
- Clear explanations and instructions so that the subordinate understands what is required and can complete tasks efficiently.
- Delegation of relevant authority so that the individual has control over sufficient resources to complete the task effectively.

Case study: Peter's problems (30 marks), pages 463–4

1 Explain why Sam might want Peter to delegate more tasks to her. (5)

- Sam possesses skills that are under-utilised, particularly in figure work. This is also one of Peter's weaknesses, so Sam believes that she can improve the firm's efficiency.
- Sam does not enjoy the time spent travelling; this is largely done to suit Peter's preferred style of working. By delegating the analytical work to Sam, Peter could create roles that would suit both of them.
- Sam is keen to take on more responsibility and this will increase her motivation.

2 Managers rely heavily on effective delegation. Analyse this statement in the context of the above case study. (9)

The statement that managers rely heavily on effective delegation would be valid in the case of a democratic manager with good organisational skills. However, the evidence in the case suggests that Peter might be an autocratic manager. He is reluctant to delegate responsibility to Sam, even though Sam possesses skills that would enable Peter's sales department to operate more efficiently. Indeed, Sam seems to undertake roles that support Peter, even though this arguably means that the two of them spend too much time out of the office. Peter does not practice effective delegation. Instead he just passes a task to Sam, but without the training and information necessary to complete it. Significantly, there is no delegation of authority, an essential feature of delegation. This is a major weakness as, without the necessary authority, Sam was unable to gain the information needed to complete the report.

3 To what extent was Peter's failure to delegate authority the main cause of the difficulties that Sam faced in completing the report? (16)

Answers might include the following. The main causes of Sam's difficulties in completing the report were:

- Sam's lack of training in report writing
- Sam's lack of experience in taking responsibility during her time as Peter's subordinate, and her limited understanding of Peter's role
- the short notice given by Peter and the lack of help offered – a maximum briefing of 20 minutes and his rough notes suggest inadequate preparation
- the circumstances in which Sam is distracted by the thought of cancelling her other appointments
- Peter's failure to delegate authority, which meant that Sam was unable to access half of the information needed to compile the report
- the difficulty in contacting Peter once the report was under way, so that Sam was unable to get clarification, including Peter's failure to keep his promise to meet on the Monday morning.

Evaluation: Peter's failure to delegate authority was a critical cause of Sam's difficulties, as it made it impossible for Sam to complete the report. However, other factors (all of which are directly attributable to Peter's leadership style) also contributed. Therefore, even with delegated authority, it is probable that Sam would have faced difficulties in completing the report.

Practice exercise 4 (55 marks), page 472

1 Distinguish between centralised organisational structures and decentralised organisational structures. (6)

- In a centralised organisational structure decision-making power rests firmly at the top of the organisation with relatively little delegation to local or lower levels.

- In a decentralised organisational structure decision-making power is delegated more readily to lower or local levels.

2 Explain one advantage and one disadvantage of a centralised organisational structure. (6)

- Some of the advantages of a centralised organisational structure include: consistent policies; quicker decision making; identical retail units so consumers know what to expect; tight financial control and efficient use of resources; emphasis on the corporate view; useful in times of crisis.

- Some of the disadvantages of a centralised organisational structure include: local branch managers may have better local knowledge, which is not used; lack of involvement in decision making may adversely affect local branch managers' motivation; inflexible and inappropriate decisions may result; the decision making process may take too long.

3 Explain one advantage and one disadvantage of a decentralised organisational structure. (6)

- Some of the advantages of a decentralised organisational structure include: empowers local managers, encouraging them to be more innovative and improves their job satisfaction; better local knowledge may mean better decisions and improved sales; reduces the volume of day-to-day communication needed between the centre and local branches; more time for senior managers to focus on corporate strategy; more flexible and more responsive to customer needs.

- Some of the disadvantages of a decentralised organisational structure include: customers may not like the reduction in the uniformity of branches; local managers may not see the 'big picture' and thus miss opportunities or trends only apparent from a central perspective; senior managers at the centre may not be well informed about what is going on in all areas of the business.

4 Which of the following is not a form of organisational structure? (1)
a Matrix
b Functional
c Fractional
d Product line
e Customer/market

The answer is c.

5 Distinguish between a functional management structure and a matrix management structure. (6)

- Functional management is the traditional structure consisting of different departments responsible for specific functions (marketing, production, finance, HR). It can also describe organisations that are structured around geographical or product divisions.

- Matrix management is a flexible management structure in which tasks are managed in a way that cuts across traditional boundaries. It tends to feature project teams that work alongside functional management.

6 Explain three influences on organisational design and structure. (9)

- Business objectives – ensuring that the choice of organisational design and structure is aligned appropriately with business objectives and purpose.

- The size of the organisation — the larger an organisation, the more complex its structure and design is likely to be.

- Nature of the organisation – whether in the manufacturing or service sector, national or multinational, single product or multi-product.

- Culture and attitudes of senior management – whether autocratic and controlling or democratic and participative.

- Skills and experience of the workforce — a highly skilled workforce is more likely to fit with an organisation that delegates responsibility.

- External environmental changes such as technology and its impact on organisational design and working practices.

7 Identify and explain one influence on delegation in an organisation. (4)

- The level of mutual trust between the supervisor and the subordinate to whom work is delegated.

- The ability and skills of the person to whom tasks are to be delegated.

- The clarity of explanations and instructions given to the person delegated to carry out the tasks.

- The extent to which authority is delegated.

8 Identify and explain two influences that determine whether an organisation adopts a centralised or decentralised approach. (8)

These are similar points to those provided in answer to question 6 above.

9 Analyse why job and organisational design might change and why such change might be of value to an organisation. (9)

To implement business strategies a company requires appropriate job and organisational design. As a company grows and develops, for example, by extending its product lines and areas of activities, job and organisational design will need to change to accommodate this. For example:

- Many start-up businesses begin with a 'spider web' structure where a group of individuals work towards the vision of the founding entrepreneur. Over time such businesses develop unintendedly tall hierarchies that separate senior and junior members of the staff. Before this begins to occur, job and organisational design need to change.

- Larger companies with established HR processes and a strategy for innovation tend to change their job and organisational design in order to provide greater individual autonomy for employees and to speed up decision making.

Thus in order to be successful, all organisations need to be responsive to changes taking place in both their external and internal environments and ensure that their job and organisational design are appropriate.

Case study: Ragbags (34 marks), pages 472–4

1 Analyse why a more thoughtful approach to organisational design might have helped the organisation as it grew in size. (9)

The case study suggests that the structure and design of the organisation evolved as it grew. As a result:

- there are elements of decentralisation that have not been well thought out – e.g. the extent to which production managers can use their discretion; the fact that administrative supervisors appear to lack authority and responsibility;

- directors are not aware of the problems brewing at the various sites because they are too focused on central issues.

This indicates that insufficient thought has been given to the type of organisational structure and organisational design that would be most appropriate for the business as it grew from a single site to a multi-site business. If a more thoughtful approach to these issues had been introduced, it is likely that there would not be the level of dissatisfaction among staff – and the danger that this may in the future affect sales and profits.

2 In moving from a single-site producer to a multisite producer, analyse the issues the company should have been aware of in order to ensure that a more decentralised approach would be a success. (9)

- Production managers at the different sites will have better 'local' knowledge and can ensure that appropriate decisions are made. By empowering them this can improve motivation and encourage them to be more innovative. However, it is important that there are clear guidelines about the level of discretion they can use to ensure that differences in working conditions and practices do not cause tension between sites.

- Good communication between sites, and a more proactive role for directors in relation to this, could ensure that where differences had been introduced that were successful, these could be shared with all sites.

- A lack of involvement in decision making for administrative supervisors may adversely affect their motivation. A successful decentralised system should reduce the volume of day-to-day communication between the centre and local sites – but the case study suggests that this is the opposite since the appointment of the business manager.

- Decentralisation should enable senior managers to focus more on corporate strategy, but it is also important that they are clear about what is going on in the decentralised sites. The case study indicates that directors at the centre are not well informed about what is going on in all areas of the business and hence are not taking prompt and effective action.

3 Discuss the influences that might impact on the organisational design of a company like Ragbags. In doing so, consider the influences on job design, delegation, centralisation and decentralisation. (16)

Answers might include the following.

Influences on organisational design of a company like Ragbags include:

- business objectives – a decentralised approach appears to fit best with business objectives and purpose

- the size of the organisation — Ragbags has grown into a more complex organisation and its size and nature suggest a decentralised structure is more appropriate

- nature of the organisation – in this case, a multi-site manufacturing business, which suggests a decentralised structure is more appropriate
- culture and attitudes of senior management – the case study suggests the company's leadership style was originally paternalistic but with open communication; it is difficult to identify the current leadership style but it is clear that communication is no longer effective
- external environmental changes such as technology and its impact on organisational design and working practices – directors judge that new technology is helping communication – but they are clearly unaware of the emerging problems.

Explanation of relevant advantages of a decentralised organisational structure for Ragbags – and the problems that are emerging – see answer provided to question 2 above for examples of points to raise in relation to this.

Job design is not as appropriate as it might be for administrative supervisors and for production managers. It would appear that administrative supervisors are not given sufficient responsibility for their work outcomes because of the tight control by the business manager, which is actually increasing the volume of communication between the centre and local sites. Delegation to production managers may have positive advantages but insufficient guidance is given about the extent of discretion individuals can exercise over their decision making.

Evaluation: As a company like Ragbags grows and develops, organisational design needs to change to accommodate this. It appears from the case study that organisational structure and design at Ragbags has simply evolved over time rather than being thoroughly considered. The emerging problems are the result of this lack of formal review of the nature of the organisation. The fact that the business currently has high sales and excellent profitability is probably why directors are not aware of the problems. Future growth and profitability may not be guaranteed if, as the case study suggests, many staff eventually leave. The fact that the MD has now been alerted to the issues by the production manager may now lead to appropriate changes being made to the organisational design.

Practice exercise 5 (50 marks), page 480

1 Explain the three elements of the human resource flow. (6)

Human resource flow is the flow of employees through an organisation. It includes:

- the inflow – when they are recruited, which includes recruitment, selection and induction processes
- the internal flow – what happens to them within the organisation, which includes evaluation of performance/appraisal, promotion and demotion, transfer, redeployment, training and development
- the outflow – when they eventually leave the organisation, which could be voluntarily or by dismissal, redundancy or retirement.

2 What is a human resource plan? (3)

A human resource plan is also known as a workforce plan. It is the process that links the human resource needs of an organisation to its strategic plan to ensure that staffing is sufficient, qualified and competent enough to achieve the organisation's objectives.

3 Identify four stages involved in human resource planning. (4)

Stages involved in human resource planning include:

- converting corporate objectives into HR objectives
- forecasting future demand for labour
- assessing the current workforce
- identifying areas of shortfall or oversupply between the current workforce and that needed in the future
- reviewing the internal and external supply of labour in relation to future requirements
- developing strategies to fill gaps or reduce the oversupply of labour.

4 Explain two factors that might influence the internal supply of labour in a firm. (6)

- Training programmes that improve skills.
- Transfers and redeployment opportunities.
- Promotional and secondment opportunities.
- Changing work patterns such as flexible working.
- Retirement.

5 Explain one local factor that might influence the external supply of labour to a firm. (3)

- Travel to work patterns, including distance to travel, cost and availability of public transport, the extent of congestion and availability and cost of parking.

- Availability of housing and amenities.
- Local cost of living.

6 Explain two national factors that might influence the external supply of labour to a firm. (6)

- More people over 60 available for work as a result of changes to pensions and retirement dates.
- Fewer younger people available for work as all must stay in education or training until they are 18 and a large proportion choose to go on to university.
- Immigration – for example, the migration of workers from other countries, such as the countries of Eastern Europe, may increase the supply of workers.
- Insufficient people with particular skills and qualifications available.

7 Explain two methods that a firm might use to overcome a potential shortage of labour. (8)

- Outsourcing – where a firm uses sources outside the business to undertake functions that used to be done internally by a section of the business itself. Thus if there is a shortage of admin or production staff, the firm might outsource this function to another firm or country.
- Retraining existing employees will help to ensure that there are appropriately qualified staff within a firm. Good training provision will also attract more external candidates.
- Offering better terms and conditions of employment are likely to attract more or better applicants, particularly if conditions are better than those being offered by competitors.

8 Briefly explain two internal and two external influences on human resource plans. (8)

Internal influences include:

- If the organisation's corporate objectives change, this is likely to lead to changes in the human resource plans.
- An organisation's marketing and production plans, in order to ensure that sufficient workers with the right skills are available.
- The financial position of the organisation and the budget available for recruitment and training will determine whether the organisation is able to fund the human resource plan.

External influences include:

- An increase in competition may cause demand to fall, thus leaving the firm with an oversupply of employees – the human resource plan may be affected and redundancy notices issued.
- Human resource plans may be affected by changes in legislation (e.g. in terms of meeting stringent health and safety requirements).
- Economic conditions and government policy may affect demand and thus workforce requirements.

9 Explain two possible long-term consequences for a firm that does not have a human resource plan. (6)

- A firm may have problems recruiting and selecting appropriately skilled individuals.
- Staff may be inadequately trained for new processes being introduced.
- There may be morale problems if existing workers are expected to cover staff shortages, which could lead to higher labour turnover and absence rates.
- A firm may simply react to events rather than being prepared for them and as a result make hasty and poor quality decisions.

Case study: Workforce planning in the mining industry (40 marks), pages 480–1

1 Consider how a business in the mining industry might benefit from producing a human resource (or workforce) plan. (6)

A human resource plan may enable it to:

- avoid a labour shortage
- have a sufficient and appropriately skilled workforce to allow it to meet its objectives
- cover the outflow of skilled workers due to retire by attracting, recruiting and retaining skilled workers
- 'capture' the knowledge of those experienced employees who are about to retire.

2 Explain how a company's corporate objectives are likely to influence its HR objectives and its human resource plans. (8)

A company's corporate objectives will determine its HR objectives, which in turn will influence its human resource plans. The case study suggests that mining companies have had to cut their capital spending and their labour costs with the aim of streamlining operations and improving efficiency. This is likely to lead to HR objectives linked to ensuring that staffing meets operational needs as economically and efficiently as possible. Human resource plans will need to reflect these objectives by covering the type of issues identified in the answer to question 1 above.

3 Identify two factors that are likely to influence the supply of labour to the mining industry. (2)
  - Internal factors such as labour turnover, retirement, training, transfers, redeployment and promotions.
  - External factors, such as the size of the local population, migration, education, proportion of people entering the workforce, amount of unemployment – all of which determine the availability of appropriately skilled workers prepared to consider employment in the mining industry.

4 Explain two ways in which businesses in the mining industry, or an industry you are familiar with, might fill the gaps between its demand for labour and the supply of labour. (8)

  Businesses could:
  - reduce their demand for labour by, for example, automating production or outsourcing production
  - try to improve the supply of labour by making it more attractive to work for them by, for example, improving pay and conditions or by improving the training offered to potential applicants.

5 Discuss the major internal and external influences that are likely to require a business in the mining industry, or a business of your choice, to review its human resource plans to ensure it can meet its objectives. (16)

  Answers might include the following.

  Internal influences on human resource plans might include:
  - organisational objectives a mining business is likely to focus upon streamlining operations and increasing efficiency, which in turn will mean HR objectives linked to ensuring that its workforce meets operational needs as effectively and efficiently as possible
  - internal labour supply, which is determined strongly by the number of people expected to retire
  - financial position, which is currently challenging and will determine whether businesses are able to fund the requirements of the human resource plan and thus meet objectives.

  External influences on human resource plans might include:
  - changing economic conditions, which have led mining businesses to cut costs and streamline their operations
  - changing labour market conditions and demographic trends – the pool of skilled workers is smaller and more companies are competing for the same skills; this is made more difficult because of the number of employees due to retire from mining companies
  - legal issues about ensuring high standards of health and safety.

  Evaluation: Both external and internal factors are likely to have had a significant impact on the human resource plans of mining companies. A global labour shortage of mining engineers together with expectations that approximately 20% of workers will be retiring in the next few years are the key issues. This is compounded by the need to cut costs and streamline operations to meet the difficult economic conditions. Human resource plans will need to reflect these objectives and in particular will need to enable a mining company to: avoid a labour shortage; have a sufficient and appropriately skilled workforce to allow it to meet its objectives; cover the outflow of skilled workers due to retire by attracting, recruiting and retaining skilled workers; 'capture' the knowledge of those experienced employees who are about to retire.

Practice exercise 6 (35 marks), page 486

1 Identify the main stages in the recruitment and selection process. (6)
  - Identifying the vacancy.
  - Writing the job description.
  - Writing the person specification.
  - Deciding whether to recruit internally or externally.
  - Devising advertisements and placing them in the media.
  - Candidates returning applications.
  - Short-listing the candidates.
  - Conducting interviews and tests.
  - Making the selection.

2 Explain one advantage of recruiting an internal candidate for a job and one advantage of recruiting an external candidate for a job. (6)

  Advantages of recruiting an internal candidate might include:
  - the skills and qualities of candidates are already known, so there is less risk of error

- a shorter induction period
- the recruitment process is cheaper and quicker
- motivates the workforce to know internal promotional opportunities are available.

Advantages of recruiting an external candidate might include:

- wider choice of applicants
- brings in fresh ideas
- helps the business to find out how other organisations operate
- may prevent jealousies and internal conflicts arising when one internal candidate is chosen for promotion ahead of others.

3 Distinguish between a job description and a person specification. (6)

- A job description tells candidates what is expected in the job and helps a firm to identify the qualities needed in the individual to be selected for the job. It consists of the job title, the main purpose of the job, who the job holder is answerable to, the main duties and tasks contained in the job, and any authority the job holder has.
- A person specification provides details of the ideal candidate by listing the essential and desirable characteristics of that person. It is used to identify the criteria that should be used in short-listing and then in selecting the best candidate from those who apply for the position.

4 Identify and explain two methods of selecting the best individual for a job other than by interview. (6)

- Aptitude and attainment tests, which measure how well an applicant deals with a simulated business situation, or a candidate's level of skill in tasks that are relevant to the job.

- Psychometric tests, which assess the personality and character of an applicant in order to measure his/her suitability for the role.
- Assessment centres, where a group of candidates undergo in-depth assessment. This tends to include the features of the earlier techniques, but also group and teamwork.

5 Identify and explain two factors that will influence the method of recruitment and selection used. (6)

- The seniority of the job – the more senior the job, the more thorough the process is likely to be.
- The size of the organisation – whether a large multinational or a small shop
- The resources available to fund recruitment and selection processes.
- The cost of particular methods – this factor is linked to the importance or seniority of the job and the resources available.
- The supply of labour and number of applicants – a limited number of candidates may lead to a simpler process, although the savings in cost may enable more detailed approaches to be used.
- Whether recruitment is internal or external – internal recruitment is usually a simpler, cheaper and quicker process; the culture of an organisation may dictate whether promotional opportunities go to internal or external candidates.

6 Explain the importance of effective recruitment and selection to an organisation. (5)

Effective recruitment should help the efficiency and productivity of an organisation by making sure that the best candidates are appointed. In turn, this should lead to greater motivation, lower levels of absenteeism and lower labour turnover, which reduces labour costs and future recruitment and selection costs.

Case study: Ernst & Young and its use of social media in recruitment (35 marks), pages 486–7

1 Analyse the benefits of Ernst and Young's social media approach to attracting and recruiting new staff compared to more traditional methods. (9)

- EY customise and constantly update their social media options so that people interested in jobs can access the most appropriate information, whether they are students, recent graduates, experienced workers or executives. Its sites enable individuals to raise questions and get answers, find out what it is like to work at EY and what might be expected of them if they got a job at EY.

- It focuses on Facebook to reach students and recent graduates because it believes this is the best place to target potential young professionals. The case study indicates that it had 85,000 'likes', suggesting this approach is successful at attracting people in the first instance.
- The key benefits of EY's social media approach is that it attracts potential applicants to review the site and also makes sure that only the right people actually go on to apply for positions. This is because it provides good information about what it is like to work at EY and what

might be expected of a person if they got a job with EY. This is a useful approach because in a sense the information it provides acts as an initial self-selection process – people can get an idea of whether they would fit into the organisation and whether they might have a chance of getting selected.

2 Having attracted people to consider applying to the company, explain the additional processes that will be involved before the company will be able to select the right candidates. (10)

   - Identifying the vacancy.
   - Writing the job description.
   - Writing the person specification.
   - Devising advertisements and placing them in the media.
   - Candidates returning applications.
   - Short-listing the candidates.
   - Conducting interviews and tests.
   - Making the selection.

3 Discuss the issues that Ernst & Young or other companies might face in deciding whether to recruit middle and senior managers from within the company or from outside. (16)

   Answers might include the following.

   - Internal recruitment will mean that the talents of those staff who rise to senior management are well known and established over many years. Shorter induction periods will be possible, reducing costs. EY is likely to be aware of the potential of its existing staff and so will be able to react quickly to projected shortages. Internal promotion may be very motivating for the existing workforce.
   - External recruits may bring in fresh ideas and help EY to find out how other organisations operate. Jealousies and internal conflict may arise when one internal candidate is chosen ahead of others, and this can be avoided with external recruitment.

   Evaluation: There are advantages and disadvantages of recruiting middle and senior managers from within a company like EY or from outside. Talent is crucial to profit, which suggests that firms like EY should select their middle and senior managers from as wide a range of people as possible – internally and externally. Overall, for a company in the professional services and accounting sector, it may depend on the importance and specialist nature of a particular role and the extent to which the role requires substantial internal company knowledge or fresh thinking from a different perspective. For jobs with high salaries a key factor is the risk of employing the wrong person – particularly if that person's skills and talents are unknown compared to someone who may have proven themselves within the business already.

Practice exercise 7 (20 marks), page 490

1 What is the difference between 'on-the-job training' and 'off-the-job training'? (4)

   - 'On-the-job training' is where an employee learns a job by seeing how it is carried out by an experienced employees; also known as 'sitting by Nellie'. It is usually cheaper than off-the-job training because existing resources can be used. The training takes place in a realistic working environment and is focused completely on the company's methods.
   - 'Off-the-job' training involves all forms of employee education apart from that at the immediate workplace. The environment where training takes place is likely to have fewer distractions than on-the-job training. A broader range of skills will probably be developed, increasing worker adaptability. Specialist trainers and facilities are used.

2 Explain two advantages of internal training. (8)

   Internal training ensures that training is tailored to the specific needs of the organisation; it is usually cheaper than external training.

3 Explain two advantages of external training. (8)

   External training gives employees the opportunity to meet people from other organisations, allowing for an interchange of ideas and a broadening of understanding; it can make employees feel valued and increase motivation; training is usually provided by specialist organisations, which should ensure high quality.

Case study: Recruitment and training at McDonald's (25 marks), pages 490–1

1 Explain why McDonald's offers induction training to all its employees. (5)

   - Workers settle more quickly and therefore reach maximum efficiency sooner.

- Staff motivation may improve if a feeling of belonging is generated.
- Labour turnover may be reduced.
- Employees understand the overall aims and culture of the organisation more readily.

2 Do you believe that McDonald's training programme is suited to the needs of both the company and its employees? Justify your view. (20)

Answers might include the following.

The benefits of any training should include the following:

- helping new employees reach the level of performance expected of experienced workers – this is particularly the case in relation to crew members who are expected to meet performance standards of new recruits in a few days
- ensuring that employees have the necessary skills, knowledge, attributes and qualifications for the job, both at present and in the future – this applies to both crew and manager training
- developing a knowledgeable and committed workforce, with increased motivation and job satisfaction – this could apply to workers and managers
- increasing efficiency and productivity, enabling a business to produce high quality products and services, which may in turn lead to improved profits
- identifying employees' potential and thus increasing employees' job prospects and chances of promotion, which may improve

motivation – this is likely to apply in particular to managers.

The training programme for crew members (i.e. the general workforce) is such as to ensure that workers meet standards and expectations in all areas of their work. For this group of employees, most training is on-the-job and needs to be completed in the shortest time scale possible in order to ensure that new workers are performing as well as experienced workers in as short a time as possible.

The training programme for managers is quite different. It includes both on-the-job and off-the-job training and is focused on developing the skills needed to manage a shift and to lead a restaurant. In addition, it involves a period of secondment in a regional office to develop and learn new skills, see a different side of the business and how roles contribute to the company's goals. For this group of employees, training is focused on their ability to contribute as soon as possible in their role as leaders but also on their ability to contribute in the future.

Evaluation: McDonald's training programme appears to be suited to the needs of both the company and its employees. The company invests a huge amount of money in training and development each year because it believes its success is built on the quality, service and cleanliness it provides customers and that the well-trained crew and managers are the first step to achieving this. Its differentiated training programmes for crew and managers ensure that this is the case.

Practice exercise 8 (30 marks), page 495

1 Explain the term redeployment. (3)

Redeployment is the process of moving existing employees to a different job or different location within the same organisation.

2 Explain two advantages to a business of providing redeployment opportunities for its staff. (6)

- Maintaining job security for employees whose current jobs are at risk.
- Improving the morale of employees.
- Retaining valuable skills, knowledge and experience.
- Reducing the cost and time associated with recruitment and selection and also the time needed for induction and training of staff new to the organisation.

3 Explain the term redundancy. (3)

Redundancy is when an employer dismisses an employee because their job no longer exists.

4 Identify two reasons why redundancy might occur. (6)

Redundancy might occur because a business is: changing what it does; doing things in a different way, for example, becoming more automated; changing its locations; closing down

5 Identify three alternatives to making employees redundant. (3)

Alternatives to making employees redundant might include: natural wastage and recruitment freezes; stopping or reducing overtime; asking people to volunteer for early retirement; retraining or redeployment; pay freezes; short-time working; pay cuts in return for taking time off work; 'alternatives to redundancy' (ATR) schemes

6 Which of the following is unlikely to be one of the criteria for choosing which employees will be made redundant? (1)

a   Length of service

b   Attendance records

c   How far away from the firm they live

d   Disciplinary records

e   Skills and qualifications.

The answer is c.

7 Explain the negative effects the announcement of redundancies can have on a firm. (8)

- Adverse effects on the morale, motivation and productivity of remaining employees, which is likely to lower productivity and workers' commitment to a firm.
- Depending on the publicity it receives locally or nationally, redundancy can also damage the reputation of a firm and result in lower sales.
- Costs may increase – including the costs of redundancy pay, and costs associated with the indirect effects of making people redundant, including higher labour turnover and lost output as a result of the lower moral of the remaining workforce.

Case study: Cadbury job cuts (40 marks), pages 495–6

1 Explain two alternative actions Cadbury might have introduced rather than making a large number of its employees redundant. (8)

Answers could include: natural wastage and recruitment freezes; stopping or reducing overtime; asking people to volunteer for early retirement; retraining or redeployment; pay freezes; short-time working; pay cuts in return for taking time off work; 'alternatives to redundancy' (ATR) schemes.

2 Assess the potential negative effects on a business such as Cadbury of carrying out a programme of redundancies and how it might minimise these negative effects. (16)

Answers might include the following. Explanations of potential negative effects are identified in the answer to question 7 of practice exercise 8 above. Cadbury might minimise these negative effects by:

- Adopting the suggestion of the trade union to ensure that redundancies were voluntary rather than compulsory. If a voluntary redundancy package was offered to willing volunteers this might avoid the need for compulsory redundancies and the associated negative effects on the motivation and morale of the remaining workforce.
- Ensuring that information about the reasons for redundancies is clearly made known to stakeholders. This might reduce the potentially negative publicity that the company is likely to receive about redundancies and the subsequent impact on its reputation.
- Providing workers who are to be made redundant with support in finding new jobs or in transferring to other jobs within Cadbury. This would reduce the negative impact on the morale of the workforce and on its reputation with stakeholders.

- Ensuring that consultation with the trade unions is open and transparent. This will minimise the threat of any form of industrial action by union members.

Evaluation: The action of making people redundant is always going to have a negative impact on workers and therefore on an organisation. However, a business such as Cadbury can take steps to minimise the negative impact by introducing the actions identified above. Such actions are unlikely to reduce the immediate costs associated with redundancies but they may reduce the more indirect and longer term costs, particularly those related to loss of reputation and reduction in morale and motivation of remaining workers.

3 Evaluate why investment, such as that planned at Cadbury, might lead to redundancy in the short term but more employment in the long term. (16)

Answers might include the following.

- Explanation of what redundancy is and what it involves.
- Explanation of the investment planned at Cadbury.

Evaluation: The case study does not state how many of the 960 Bourneville workers will be made redundant. However, the fact that production costs are currently twice as much as many of its competitors is a powerful reason to go ahead with the updating process. Making the current production process more efficient may mean the business is more competitive in the longer term. This is likely to ensure that, despite the need to make redundancies in the short term, in the longer term there may be greater security of jobs within the company.

23 Making HR decisions: improving motivation and engagement

Practice exercise 1 (70 marks), page 504

1 Explain the terms motivation and engagement. (6)
  - Motivation is the desire and energy to be continually interested and committed to a job, role or subject, or to make an effort to attain a particular goal.
  - Engagement means feeling positive about doing a good job, thinking hard about the job and how to do it better, and actively taking opportunities to discuss work-related improvements with others at work.

2 Explain two benefits to an organisation of having motivated and engaged employees. (8)

  Benefits might include: improved productivity; reduced costs; improved reputation; improved likelihood of meeting company objectives; improved work ethic; competitive advantage.

3 Briefly explain the views of F. W. Taylor and the scientific management school of thought. (6)
  - Managers need to organise and closely supervise workers in order to ensure that they make sufficient effort.
  - Businesses should adopt a scientific, efficiency-centred approach to work that should maximise productivity.
  - Businesses should use extreme division of labour and payment by piecework.

4 Outline the main problems with these views in relation to motivating employees. (6)
  - Money is considered the only factor that provides motivation.
  - Payment has to be clearly linked to efficiency.
  - The recommended production methods – extreme division of labour – lead to boring, repetitive jobs.
  - The potential importance of the job itself is overlooked.

5 Briefly explain the views of Elton Mayo and the human relations school of management. (4)
  - Recognition by managers and a sense of belonging to a group are more important in motivating workers than money and working conditions.
  - Firms should recognise the importance of groups (formal and informal) within the working environment.
  - Managers need to communicate with both formal and informal groups in order to make sure that their goals are in keeping with the firm's aims.

6 Identify and explain each of the levels of Maslow's hierarchy of human needs. (10)
  - Physiological needs – the basic requirements of life, such as food and shelter.
  - Safety needs – security and freedom from danger.
  - Social needs – the desire for friendship and belonging.
  - Esteem needs – self-respect and the respect of others.
  - Self-actualisation – fulfilling one's potential through achievement.

7 Explain the relevance of Maslow's hierarchy of human needs in a work context. (6)

  A higher-level need can only become a motivator in the workplace if lower-level needs are satisfied. Therefore managers need to understand the needs of their workers in order to find the most appropriate methods of motivation.

8 Which of the following is not one of Herzberg's motivators? (1)

   a Sense of achievement

   b Responsibility

   c Company policy

   d Recognition for effort.

The answer is c.

9 Which of the following is not one of Herzberg's hygiene or maintenance factors? (1)

   a Pay

   b Supervision

   c Promotion opportunities

   d Working conditions.

The answer is c.

10 Distinguish between the effect of Herzberg's motivators and that of his hygiene or maintenance factors on the motivation of employees. (6)

- Herzberg's motivators, if present, will inspire workers to improve their efficiency and productivity.

- Herzberg's maintenance or hygiene factors prevent dissatisfaction but do not, in themselves, cause motivation, although they provide the foundation for motivators to operate successfully.

11 Assess how valuable the various theories of motivation considered in this chapter are to organisations today. (16)

Answers might include the following.

Explanations of each theory:

- F. W. Taylor and scientific management – extreme division of labour, payment by piecework, tight management control.

- Maslow's hierarchy of human needs – physiological, safety, social, esteem, self-actualisation – and how the different levels are linked.

- Herzberg – motivators vs hygiene or maintenance factors and the difference between 'movement' and motivation.

- Elton Mayo and the human relations school (not a requirement in the AQA specification) – the importance of the group or team as a motivating factor.

Discussion of the value of each theory:

- Taylor – had considerable influence on mass production processes introduced at the Ford Motor Company; influence on the workforce was less successful; extreme division of labour meant jobs became more boring and repetitive and workers were deskilled, leading to low morale and poor industrial relations.

- Maslow – intuitively appealing in the sense that if people have insufficient income to enjoy adequate food, clothing and shelter, they are unlikely to be overly influenced by whether, for example, a job provides a good social atmosphere. However, once people satisfy their physiological and safety needs, it is questionable whether, for all individuals, social needs come before esteem needs.

- Herzberg – many of his ideas have been borne out in practice, for example, that wage increases and changes to working conditions are rarely sufficient to produce a highly motivated workforce but that if wages and working conditions are perceived to be inadequate this can create immense dissatisfaction, with negative consequences for firms.

- Mayo – important developments resulted from his work such as the introduction of social facilities at work and an increase in the quantity and quality of communication and consultation between managers and workers.

Evaluation: Taylor's theory is not particularly valuable to organisations in the UK today because the focus is now much more on improving skills, enriching jobs and engaging and motivating employees. Maslow's theory could still be relevant to organisations in the UK today but only if managers are able to identify the particular needs of different individuals and can establish whether the next level of Maslow's hierarchy will motivate them sufficiently. Herzberg's theory is still highly relevant to organisations in the UK today and particularly that attention to hygiene factors, although minimising dissatisfaction does not generally motivate workers over the longer term. Mayo's ideas are also still highly relevant today as evident in the extent to which organisations need to give close attention to the welfare of employees and to the quality and extent of communication and consultations between managers and workers.

Case study: Herzberg, Maslow and teachers (25 marks), pages 504–5

1 This passage shows how theories can always be challenged. Identify and explain other problems with the theories of Herzberg and Maslow, using examples from real organisations wherever possible. (9)

Herzberg:

- The theory is likely to be more relevant to skilled jobs than to unskilled roles; in the latter there is often less scope for job enrichment, and understanding issues such as company policy is less likely.

- Basing a theory on answers to questions, rather than real-life experience, lacks rigour. When faced with an actual situation, workers may react differently from the way in which they answer hypothetical questions.

- Even in the original answers, the distinction between motivators and hygiene factors was not as clear-cut as Herzberg's theory suggests. Some motivators caused dissatisfaction to some workers, while some hygiene factors were a source of motivation to some workers.

Maslow:

- The idea that a worker will not be motivated by a higher level need in the hierarchy unless a lower level need in the hierarchy has been met is debatable. The transition between levels may be blurred.

- It is very difficult for a manager to know which level of the hierarchy is applicable to an individual employee; thus it might be of limited practical use in an organisation with many employees.

- Workers' needs may change and, as shown in the teacher survey, the hierarchy may not follow the sequence outlined by Maslow.

2 Discuss how the 'esteem needs of teachers' in schools could be met more effectively by their senior managers. (16)

Answers might include the following.

- Training, which would improve teachers' skills and possibly their belief in their capabilities.

- Promotion or improvements in status.

- Greater responsibility.

- Positive feedback in the form of praise from headteachers or senior leaders.

- Achieving targets and helping students achieve success.

Evaluation: Meeting the 'esteem needs of teachers' requires that their achievements are recognised both within school and beyond. The above measures might contribute to this, but in addition the respect that pupils, parents, and society as a whole hold for the profession of teachers is an important factor in meeting their esteem needs.

Case study: ARM Ltd (20 marks), pages 505–6

1 Assess how well the ideas of each of the motivation theorists you have studied are being applied at ARM Ltd. (20)

Answers might include the following.

Explanations of each theory:

- F. W. Taylor and scientific management – extreme division of labour, payment by piecework, tight management control.

- Maslow's hierarchy of human needs – physiological, safety, social, esteem, self-actualisation – and how the different levels are linked.

- Herzberg – motivators vs hygiene or maintenance factors and the difference between 'movement' and motivation.

- Elton Mayo and the human relations school (not a requirement in the AQA specification) – the importance of the group or team as a motivating factor.

Application of the various theories to information about ARM Ltd such as:

- Maslow: 'opportunities to fulfil higher order needs through challenging and interesting work'.

- Herzberg: motivators – ' employees ... take responsibility for their own jobs and are constantly involved in improvement and change'; 'does not rely on pay as a motivator'; hygiene factors – 'good working conditions, a safe and supportive working environment and competitive pay'.

- Mayo: 'involving them in decisions about the future direction the business might take and the products it might focus on'; 'teamwork ... provides ... opportunities to share knowledge and ideas and contribute to innovation'; 'open and honest communication'.

Evaluation: Other than Taylor, the ideas of each of the motivation theorists studied are being applied to a greater or lesser extent at ARM Ltd. The case study provides clear evidence that Maslow's lower level needs are fully satisfied and the company aims to satisfy employees' higher level needs. Similarly there is clear evidence that Herzberg's hygiene factors are met well and that the company focuses on motivators. Mayo's ideas about teamwork, communication and consultation are clearly evident in the case study. Given the skills and specialist expertise of its employees and what the company expects of them, Taylor's ideas about extreme division of labour, piecework and tight management control would be wholly inappropriate.

Practice exercise 2 (40 marks), page 515

1 Explain the meaning of 'piece rate' (piecework). (4)

In a 'piece rate' system a worker is paid according to the number of items (pieces) they produce.

2 Identify and explain two problems a business might encounter as a result of using piece rates to pay its employees. (6)

- Workers may concentrate on quantity rather than quality. This will cost the business money in terms of waste and a loss of customer goodwill and, ultimately, a loss of sales.
- According to Herzberg this type of reward creates 'movement', a temporary change in what the worker does, rather than a fundamental change in motivation.
- Output may increase at times that suit the workforce (e.g. before Christmas) rather than when the business needs the extra output.
- Workers may be reluctant to undertake vital activities, such as on-the-job training of new employees because such actions will reduce their output.

3 Explain how commission is used as a financial method of motivation. (4)

Commission is used as a financial method of motivation because, like piece rates, it acts as an incentive or reward for the quantity or value of work achieved. It is a sum of money paid to an employee upon completion of a task, which usually involves selling a certain amount of goods or services. Commission may be paid as a percentage of sales made or as a flat rate based on sales volume. It may be paid in addition to salary or instead of salary.

4 Explain basic rate or time rate schemes and, in doing so, distinguish between wage and salary schemes. (6)

- Basic rate or time rate schemes are payment systems based on time worked rather than on effort or output.
- A salary scheme is a basic rate payment system based on an annual salary which is usually paid in monthly installments.
- A wage scheme is a basic rate payment system based on an hourly rate that is usually paid weekly.

5 Explain the term 'performance-related pay'. (4)

Performance-related pay is a system that rewards individual employees based on an assessment of their individual performance, usually measured against pre-agreed objectives or targets. Such a system generally takes the form of a bonus or increase in salary awarded for above-average employee performance.

6 Briefly explain two advantages and two disadvantages to a business of using performance-related pay. (8)

Advantages of performance-related pay (PRP) might include:

- The direct link between effort and pay might encourage workers to improve their level of effort.
- Individuals' targets can be linked to corporate objectives, thus encouraging everyone to 'pull' in the same direction.
- Less supervision may be needed if staff are committed to achieving their targets, which may reduce costs.
- The potential sense of achievement may improve motivation and reduce absenteeism and staff turnover.

Disadvantages of performance related pay (PRP) might include:

- It can cause conflict if workers believe that the system is being used unfairly, with some workers being given easier targets.
- PRP still faces the difficulty of measuring output, a major problem if reward is based on a measure of achievement.
- Because, in most jobs, PRP represents only a small percentage of total income, it may only have a limited effect on motivation.

7 Identify two other financial methods of motivation. (2)

Other financial methods of motivation include: profit sharing; share ownership and share options; fringe benefits (which have implicit financial benefits).

8 Taking one of the methods identified in question 7, explain one advantage and one disadvantage in using this method to motivate employees. (6)

Advantages of profit sharing might include:

- It can help to unite a business, as everyone shares in the success of the business.
- It may encourage staff to seek out and suggest methods that will improve the profitability of the business.

Disadvantages of profit sharing might include:

- Because in most jobs it represents only a small percentage of income, it will probably have only a limited effect on motivation.
- It may be seen as unfair if some workers are known to make little effort but share the rewards.

Practice exercise 3 (65 marks), page 523

1 Explain two problems for a business that might result from a low level of motivation among its employees. (6)

Low productivity; high labour turnover; high levels of absenteeism.

2 Explain the terms 'job enlargement', 'job rotation' and 'job enrichment'. (6)

- Job enlargement means increasing the scope of a job – either its range or its diversity. It includes job rotation and job enrichment.
- Job rotation gives a worker more tasks, but with the same level of responsibility (horizontal extension).
- Job enrichment involves giving the worker more responsibility (vertical extension).

3 Explain one advantage and one disadvantage to a business of introducing a system of job rotation. (6)

Advantages of job rotation might include:

- It may relieve boredom by providing a constantly changing range of tasks.
- It can help to create a multi-skilled workforce, which provides greater flexibility for a business in times of staff absence or changing patterns of demand.

Disadvantages of job rotation might include:

- The reduction in specialisation may lead to lower efficiency, as workers no longer use their main skills as often.
- It will involve greater levels of training and therefore increase the costs associated with training.

4 Explain two advantages to a business of introducing job enrichment. (6)

- It will enable workers to take on more responsibility and, according to Herzberg, this will increase motivation and productivity.
- It prepares people for promotion, enabling a business to cover managerial absences and to plan its future workforce more efficiently.
- It allows workers to use their skills more fully and may result in increased output.

5 Explain two problems that a business might encounter as a result of introducing job enrichment. (6)

- Some workers might not want to take on greater responsibility, as this could cause them stress or make them feel that they are not on top of the job.

- Job enrichment can be used to pass workloads down the hierarchy, so workers may mistrust the motives behind it.
- It is possible that a job cannot be enriched; some tasks are routine and difficult to modify in order to give greater responsibility.

6 Explain how job enrichment is linked to the motivation theories with which you are familiar. (6)

- Maslow: esteem needs can be satisfied by the greater status achieved through taking on a role with greater responsibility.
- Herzberg: recognition is one of the motivating factors that will encourage greater efforts from employees.
- Mayo: greater responsibility may be a way of showing recognition to a worker.

7 Explain the term 'empowerment'. (3)

Empowerment means giving employees the means by which they can exercise power over their working lives.

8 How might empowering its employees benefit a business? (4)

Empowering its employees might benefit a business because empowerment motivates workers, which may mean productivity increases and efficiency improves. If empowerment is accompanied by delegation, it can also reduce costs by removing layers of management.

9 Explain two benefits of teamworking to a business. (6)

- Through the sharing of ideas, a team of workers will be able to identify solutions to problems that would have been beyond the capabilities of the same group working in isolation as individuals. This is known as synergy.
- Teamworking assists motivation, according to motivation theories.
- Teamworking encourages multi-skilling within the group, leading to a more flexible, adaptable group.

10 Discuss the most suitable approach to motivate employees in a business where most of the workforce are unskilled, young and rarely remain with the business for longer than six months and where the tasks they are employed to do are simple and require little training. (16)

Answers might include the following.

- The identification and explanation of relevant financial methods of motivating employees, for example, piece rates, commission, time rates, performance related pay, fringe benefits.

- The identification and explanation of non-financial methods of motivating employees, for example, job rotation and job enrichment.

Evaluation: Given the nature of the jobs and the workforce – unskilled, young, rarely remain for longer than six months, simple tasks and little training required – (and assuming the objective is not to increase retention rates) the key motivating factor is likely to be some form of piece rate or commission – i.e. some form of payment by results. However it will be important to ensure that the job is broken down sufficiently to ensure employees meet quality standards.

Note: answers could take another perspective – suggesting approaches that aim to improve motivation and thus retention rates by redesigning jobs to make them more challenging and at the same time improve training and the skills of employees.

Case study: TGI Friday's (40 marks), pages 523–4

1 Identify and explain two approaches to motivation that appear to be successful at TGI Friday's. (8)
- Instant rewards, in the form of gifts such as iTunes vouchers, for jobs well done.
- 'Medals of honour', i.e. badges earned for various achievements.
- 'Friday's Legends', i.e. peer-nominated 'unsung heroes' who are treated to days out.
- Performance bonuses for managers.

2 To what extent do the motivation methods used at TGI Friday's suggest that financial incentives are less important than non-financial incentives and how might the effectiveness of the methods used be assessed? (16)

Answers might include the following.
- Little information is provided about financial incentives at TGI Friday's other than bonuses for managers and the gifts for good performance (e.g. iTunes vouchers and days out), which have an implicit monetary value. However, the case study notes that employees are happy with their wages. Tips may be a significant proportion of an employees' income at a restaurant like TGI Friday's, which hosts a lot of group parties.

Non-financial incentives at TGI Friday's include:
- a strong focus on recognising achievement, including on-the-spot recognition and reward systems (in the form of gifts such as iTunes vouchers), personal recognition for jobs well done via the 'medals of honour' badges and peer nomination of 'unsung heroes'
- managers are said to be 'excellent role models' who make staff feel motivated and encourage a strong sense of family in work teams
- internal promotional prospects – the examples in the case study suggest that people can start at the bottom and work their way up to management roles.

Evaluation: The case study suggests that financial incentives are less important than non-financial incentives at TGI Friday's. The company clearly focuses more on recognising and rewarding achievement. Some rewards are in the form of gifts and days out, which have an implicit financial value. However, this is not the case with the badges or 'medals of honour', which indicate a non-financial motivator based solely on public recognition of a job well done. The effectiveness of TGI's motivational techniques (whether financial or non-financial) can be assessed by the quality of its staff, including rates of labour turnover and absenteeism, customer satisfaction with the service received and the performance of the business. The case study indicates that the business is successful, has a 'solid financial foundation' and is planning to open 20 new restaurants over the next three years. The MD states that its success is due to 'happy and well-engaged people' who 'do a great job'. In addition the company was one of 'The Sunday Times 100 Best Companies to Work For' in 2013. All of which suggests that the methods used are effective.

3 Discuss how the effectiveness of methods used to motivate staff at TGI Friday's might be assessed. (16)

Answers might include the following.

Explanations of the financial and non-financial methods used to motivate staff at TGI Friday's (as noted in the answer to question 2 above).

A successful business will select methods of motivation (whether financial or non-financial) that match the needs of its employees and the nature of their jobs, enable employees to perform at the highest level and contribute as fully as possible to meeting business objectives.

The methods selected will be influenced by a number of factors. These might include:
- organisational design, including characteristics such as levels of hierarchy and spans of control; lines of accountability; delegation and empowerment
- the nature of the job and the nature of employees

- the clarity and purpose of business objectives
- the quality of communication and organisational culture
- the size of the organisation and time scales involved
- the state of the economy and the performance of the organisation.

TGI Friday's is staffed by young people and their clientele is mainly young people and families. Because staff are young, mainly part-time, and often students, motivational methods need to focus on meeting their needs for a 'fun'

place to work and where their enthusiasm will attract customers.

Evaluation: The effectiveness of TGI's motivational techniques (whether financial or non-financial) can be assessed by the quality of its staff, including rates of labour turnover and absenteeism, customer satisfaction with the service they receive and the performance of the business. The case study indicates that the business is successful; see the evaluation to question 2 above for factors contributing to its success.

Case study: Richer Sounds (50 marks), page 525

1 Explain one type of financial incentive used by Richer Sounds to motivate its workforce. (4)

- Sales people rated 'excellent' by customers receive a bonus; those rated 'poor' are penalised.
- A suggestion scheme that provides a cash bonus for each idea.
- Store managers with the independence to set their own reward systems for their staff.
- A range of fringe benefits, with implicit financial benefits, including trips abroad and access to holiday homes.

2 Identify two non-financial incentives used by Richer Sounds to motivate its workforce and explain one of them. (5)

- 'Results and performance of stores and of individuals' are regularly measured and examined so that everyone is aware of how they are doing and that their efforts are noticed.
- Staff are 'encouraged to take on new responsibilities and promotion from within is the norm'.

3 Analyse possible advantages and disadvantages of giving managers the independence to set up their own reward scheme. (9)

Advantages might include:

- It is likely to motivate managers by giving them more autonomy in how to run their branch.
- It may mean that individual staff are more motivated if they feel that their efforts are likely to be acknowledged and rewarded.

Disadvantages might include:

- It may distract them from other vital managerial roles and diminish the level of efficiency of the branch.
- The responsibility may not match the strengths of the manager.

- The reward systems may not be objective or consistent, creating a sense of unfairness within and between branches.

4 Financial incentives at Richer Sounds are an important, but not the only, element of the reward system. Evaluate the extent to which it appears that financial incentives are the most effective way for Richer Sounds to motivate its staff. (16)

Answers might include the following.

- Explanation of the financial incentives used by Richer Sounds (see answer to question 1 above).
- Explanation of the non-financial incentives used by Richer sounds (see answer to question 2 above).

Evaluation: Financial incentives at Richer Sounds are an important element of the reward system, but they do not appear to be the most effective ways for the company to motivate its staff. Financial incentives are an important form of recognition for work done well. They satisfy Maslow's safety and security needs and, according to Herzberg, help prevent work dissatisfaction. They therefore provide a strong foundation upon which to build employee commitment and engagement with the non-financial approaches that are used.

5 Discuss whether it is easier to motivate workers with financial incentives in the short term rather than in the longer term. Use the context of Richer Sounds or any other business you are familiar with. (16)

Answers might include the following.

- According to Herzberg, financial incentives create movement rather than motivation. This means that incentive systems based on financial reward do not change the attitude of the worker, but simply provide a temporary change in effort and commitment.
- 'A reward once given becomes a right.' If a worker regards a payment as a reward, he or

she will be motivated to work hard in response to the offer of a reward. However, once the worker perceives the payment as a right, it ceases to motivate. Usually, workers will see such payments as a motivator, an incentive to work harder in the short term. However, subsequently the worker will regard the payment as having been earned. Additional payments will therefore be needed to generate an increase in effort in the future.

Evaluation: The logical conclusion to these views is that money can only motivate in the short term. Other methods, based on non-financial incentives, are required to sustain motivation in the longer term. Motivators such as recognition can be constantly reinforced through rewarding new achievements, on a regular basis.

Case study: Honda (25 marks), page 526

1 Analyse how 'a powerful team spirit and sense of empowerment' might benefit Honda UK. (9)

- Teamworking encourages multi-skilling within groups, leading to a more flexible, adaptable group.
- Through the sharing of ideas, a team of workers will be able to identify solutions to problems that would have been beyond the capabilities of the same people working in isolation as individuals.
- Teamworking assists motivation, according to various motivation theories.
- Empowerment motivates workers (thus increasing their efficiency) by giving them greater responsibility.
- Empowerment creates a culture in which workers are encouraged to be innovative rather than following procedures. Consequently, staff are more likely to introduce new ideas to improve the company.
- It reduces the need for close supervision, freeing managers for more strategic roles.

2 Using your knowledge of motivation, discuss how effective Honda's approach to its staff is likely to be in producing a successful company. (16)

Answers might include the following.

- Honda attaches considerable importance to teamwork and the development of a strong team spirit.
- Workers' skills are recognised and they are given high levels of responsibility.
- Workers are empowered to take responsibility.
- Teamwork meets social needs and empowerment develops workers' feelings of esteem.
- A benefits package based on profit-related pay and incentive schemes based on involvement in improvement processes and attendance are provided.

Evaluation: There is a strong focus on positive motivators and empowering workers. The result is a rate of staff turnover that is half the industry average. 'Your growth is the key to Honda's growth' reflects the company's recognition that its success is closely linked to the motivation and skills of its staff.

24 Making HR decisions: improving employer–employee relations

Practice exercise 1 (80 marks), page 537

1 Explain the term 'employee representation'. (4)

Employee representation means informing, consulting and involving employees in the decision-making process. It may take many forms, including trade unions, works councils and other employee groups. It is essential in order to maintain good employer–employee relations and, for organisations over a certain size, it is also a legal requirement.

2 Explain one advantage and one disadvantage of employee representation for a business. (6)

- Advantages of employee representation: if employees feel involved, they are likely to be more motivated, which may result in lower labour turnover, less absenteeism and increased productivity.
- Disadvantages of employee representation: as more people, with different perspectives, become involved, the decision-making process becomes slower and it becomes more difficult to reach a consensus.

3 What is a trade union? (3)

A trade union is a pressure group that represents the interests of people at work.

4 Explain three main functions that trade unions carry out on behalf of their members. (9)

- Negotiation/collective bargaining – union representatives discuss with management and negotiate settlements on behalf of their members.
- Representation – a union represents individual union members when they have problems at work.
- Advising – unions provide information and advice on a range of issues, including conditions of service, such as holiday entitlement and maternity leave.

5 Explain two benefits of trade unions for employers. (8)

- Trade unions provide a valuable communication link between senior management and the workforce.
- If managers take employees' concerns more seriously because of the presence of a trade union, this may improve worker morale and have a positive influence on productivity.
- Management can avoid time-consuming negotiation with individual employees.
- When trade unions are consulted at an early stage of the decision-making process concerning difficult situations, such as relocation or downsizing and redundancy, employer–employee relations may be better.

6 What is a works council? (3)

A works council involves committees of management and workforce representatives meeting to discuss issues such as training and working practices. Its role is to look ahead at company plans and to provide an opportunity to consult, and gain ideas from, the shop floor.

7 Under what circumstances must a business set up a European works council? (3)

Under EU legislation, the European Works Council Directive requires that large companies (with at least 1,000 employees) operating in two or more EU countries must set up European Works Councils (EWCs). The directive aims to 'improve the right to information and to consultation of employees'.

8 Explain two influences on the level of employee involvement in decision making in a business. (8)

- Organisation size – in large organisations employee involvement is likely to involve more formal procedures.

- External environment – government policy and legislation influence the role of trade unions and European Works Councils; the state of the economy might influence the nature of the relationship between employers and employees.
- Style of leadership – a more democratic leadership style is likely to encourage more employee involvement.
- Quality of communication – good communication systems are likely to encourage more employee involvement.
- Organisational culture – this is linked to leadership style and communication, for example whether all decisions are made by a small group of individuals at the top or by a more participative approach that empowers employees.

9 Explain three benefits to a firm of good communication with its employees. (9)
- Employees know exactly what they are required to do.
- Change is likely to be easier to introduce if employees are kept well informed, understand the reasons why, and have the opportunity to raise concerns.
- A firm will have more successful coordination and control, ensuring that different departments work together effectively to achieve the firm's aims and objectives.

10 Explain two problems that a firm might encounter if it has poor communication with its employees. (6)
- Poor morale and motivation of the workforce, which could result in increased absenteeism, and labour turnover, increased labour costs and reduced productivity.
- If people are not clear about their roles and responsibilities or about the aims and objectives of the firm, they are likely to be less efficient in their work, with negative effects on productivity.

11 Explain how the number of intermediaries can affect the quality of communication. (4)

Intermediaries are individuals or groups within official communication channels through whom messages must be passed in order to reach the intended receivers. The greater the number of intermediaries, the longer the chain of command and the less effective the communication system is likely to be. Messages are likely to take longer to reach the intended receiver and may become distorted or may not even be delivered.

12 Identify and explain three approaches to making and improving employer and employee communication and relations. (9)
- Recognising the other side's objectives and needs, which usually results in compromise.
- Appropriate leadership and culture – workers are more likely to trust and have confidence in leaders who encourage employee involvement.
- Structural issues including intermediaries and hierarchies – flatter hierarchies and fewer intermediaries are likely to encourage better employer–employee communication and relations.
- Communication and large organisations – effective delegation, decentralisation and open communications systems are likely to improve communication and relations between employers and employees.

13 Identify and explain two examples of the value of good employer–employee relations to a business. (8)

Good employer–employee relations:
- enhance business performance and competitiveness
- make it easier to introduce and implement change
- improve worker motivation and commitment to meeting business objectives
- can improve decision making.

Case study: Ragbags (25 marks), page 537

1 Examine the main communication problems facing Ragbags as it has grown from a single-site producer to a multi-site producer. (9)
- Originally the founder of the business knew all the employees and had an 'open-door policy' for all staff to raise issues and make suggestions. However, today the MD and senior management have no idea about the discontent among the workforce because they are not in touch.
- Growth led to a more complex organisational structure and more layers of hierarchy.

Problems arose, such as the directors not being seen at certain sites for months at a time and the lack of lateral communication between staff at the different sites.
- The new business manager's approach to communication is to rely more on emails and procedures rather than face-to-face communication. The possible problems of this are information overload, lack of feedback and a failure to spot misunderstandings.

The above are classic problems for a business which grows larger and fails to take account of the consequences of increasingly formal communication systems on the effectiveness of that communication and on employees' motivation.

2   Joe Watts recognises that Ragbags needs to manage and improve its employer–employee communications and relations. Discuss why this is important to the business and how it might be achieved. (16)

Answers might include the following.

Discussion of the value of good employer–employee communications and relations to Ragbags, for example, in terms of:

- enhancing business performance and competitiveness
- making it easier to introduce and implement change
- improving worker motivation and commitment to meeting business objectives
- improving decision making.

Discussion of how Ragbags can manage and improve its employer–employee communication and relations, for example, by:

- recognising the needs of workers, production managers and administrative supervisors

- providing appropriate leadership and culture that employees can trust and have confidence in
- addressing any structural issues in terms of intermediaries and hierarchies
- communication – for example, ensuring that delegation is effectively organised so that managers are clear about the discretion they have, that there is more frequent and open communication with directors and with the business manager, and more opportunities for communication with people at other sites
- creating works councils to provide employees with a means of being consulted and to ensure that senior management are aware of the general morale of the employees.

Evaluation: A major problem is that senior managers are unaware that employees are unhappy with the state of communication within the firm. Although ICT systems may be effective, the business needs to consider the impact of its systems on its employees. Without effective communication, motivation can decline quickly, with adverse consequences for productivity and efficiency. Rapid improvements (such as those identified above) are needed to prevent employer-employee relations worsening further.

Case study: Thames Water (40 marks), page 538

1   Explain two methods of employee representation in place at Thames Water. (6)

- Employees are represented by three recognised trade unions (GMB, Unison and Unite) that are involved in joint working with management.
- A 'workplace listening' initiative provides opportunities at monthly team meetings for employees to discuss any issues they feel are preventing them from doing their job effectively.

2   Employees at Thames Water belong to one of three trade unions. Explain two possible benefits to employees of belonging to a trade union. (6)

- Negotiation/collective bargaining. Individual employees have little power to influence decisions and are in a very weak position compared with a large employer. By joining together with other workers in a trade union, there is more chance of influencing their terms and conditions of work.
- Representation. A union will represent an individual union member when they have problems at work.

- Advising. Unions provide information and advice on a range of issues, including conditions of service, such as holiday entitlement and maternity leave.

3   What does the case study suggest are the benefits of employee representation to:
a   employees of Thames Water (6)

- Improved terms and conditions – for example, the annual pay negotiations were completed much more quickly and employees had more say over the shift system and hours they worked.
- Motivation is likely to improve because of employees' involvement in decision making and less antagonistic relations with management.

b   Thames Water itself? (6)

- By improving motivation, employee representation may result in lower labour turnover.
- Involving employees in discussions about working practices enabled the company to change its shift system, and to reduce the

time taken in negotiating over pay, which led to cost savings and less antagonistic relations with employers and trade unions – all of which saves time and effort.

Both of the above benefits may, in turn, lead to increased productivity.

4   To what extent has the partnership approach between the trade unions and Thames Water effectively avoided or resolved potential industrial disputes and improved employee involvement in decision making?   (16)

Answers might include the following.

- Theories of motivation suggest that employees are happier if they feel involved, if they have a part to play in the organisation they work for and if their views are valued by management. This has happened at Thames Water as a result of its partnership approach. More involvement of employees can improve motivation, which in turn may result in lower labour turnover. It may also lead to more innovation and effective problem solving. All of this might lead to increased productivity.

- At Thames Water, the partnership approach involved unions and employees working together with an open-minded management to generate positive change and growth for the business. Pay negotiations were much shorter and more productive because the union and the management had all the important information, as a result of their day-to-day shared approach to decision making. The new shift system saved a substantial amount of money as well as giving employees more control over their working hours.

- A partnership approach is not without problems. Involving more people in decision making may slow the whole process down, although this may not be a bad thing if it causes firms to review situations from different perspectives and therefore make more informed decisions. The approach can be costly in terms of the actual and opportunity cost of the time that workers and management are involved in meetings.

Evaluation: The partnership approach appears to have been very successful for Thames Water, bringing benefits to both the organisation and its employees. By reducing antagonism and conflict, potential industrial disputes are likely to be avoided and improved employee involvement in decisions making benefits employees and employers.